GERMAN EXPRESSIONISM

In the same series

GERMAN EXPRESSIONISM
Series edited by J.M. Ritchie

PLAYS VOLUME ONE

Georg Kaiser

Translated from the German by
B.J. Kenworthy, Rex Last, J.M. Ritchie

JOHN CALDER · LONDON
RIVERRUN PRESS · NEW YORK

This edition published in Great Britain in 1985 by
John Calder (Publishers) Ltd
18 Brewer Street, London W1R 4AS

and in the USA in 1985 by
Riverrun Press Inc
1170 Broadway, New York, NY 10001

Originally published in English in 1971 by Calder & Boyars Ltd, London

The following plays were first published by Gustav Kiepenheuer, Potsdam in 1916
and 1920 respectively:

Von Morgens Bis Mitternachts (From Morning to Midnight)
Gas Zweiter Teil (Gas II)

The following plays were first published by S. Fischer, Berlin in 1914, 1917 and
1918 respectively:

Die Bürger von Calais (The Burghers of Calais)
Die Koralle (The Coral)
Gas (Gas I)

ISBN 0 7145 0242 1

Printed and bound in Italy by Stabilimento Poligrafico Cappelli

CONTENTS

INTRODUCTION

From Morning to Midnight, Kaiser's thirtieth play, was written in 1912 about one year before the *Burghers of Calais*. Both plays were performed for the first time in 1917 and together with *Gas*, which was performed about one year later, they made Kaiser internationally famous. The careful craftsman Kaiser had by this time developed the new Expressionist techniques to a high pitch of perfection. *From Morning to Midnight*, for example, presents a carefully balanced structure after the pattern of Strindberg's *The Way to Damascus*. It is clearly divided into two parts shared between the little town of W. and the big city of B. Significantly the two towns are not named. It is a characteristic of the Expressionist play that the action is not naturalistically restricted to any one particular place (e.g. W.=Weimar, B.=Berlin), at any one particular time. As in a Kafka story, the action is intended to be transferable, if not universal. The Cashier in his flight from W. to B. thereby becomes a kind of modern Everyman caught up in the dilemmas of contemporary life. The play then proceeds in a quick sequence of revue-type scenes similar to the Moritat technique later exploited by Brecht in his *Threepenny Opera*. A further pointer to Brecht is the move from play to 'parable' for the apparently so modern and revolutionary techniques of *From Morning to Midnight* are also broadly based on the medieval and 16th century German tradition of the Mystery Play on which Brecht was also to draw. Exploiting the Expressionist reaction against individual psychological motivation, Kaiser never makes any attempt to create 'rounded' characters of flesh and blood. Psychological naturalism was felt to be just as limiting and restrictive as the conditioning factors of milieu, race, creed, etc. Man was not the slave of such factors, he was always free to choose, always free to make his own decisions, always capable of rebirth. This was to be the theme of the whole play, as indeed of all Kaiser's plays. His aim at all times, he claimed, was to present the VISION of the regeneration of man. The Vision as

7

he saw it meant the avoidance of all circumstantial detail from real life, in order to penetrate immediately to the heart of the matter and reveal all the potential inherent in man. So the Cashier is shown at the beginning as a crushed captive of the capitalist system. But there is no condemnation of 'social conditions': instead the opening scene shows how the slightest incident (in this case, the arrival of an exotic Italian woman and the subsequent stirrings of the flesh) are sufficient to open even such an automaton's eyes. From being a bank clerk dealing every day with money without thought for its significance, he suddenly sets out to test its power. This sudden 'New Beginning' (*Aufbruch*) and the 'Quest for Life' are favourite Expressionist situations, as too is the refusal to accept anything less than absolute values. Money is to be weighed in the balance. Can it live up to its promises, can it guarantee the full life, or provide the answers to absolute demands? The result as Walter Huder puts it is a Pyrrhic victory for both parties. The cashier unmasks money and dies in the process, but money will never again be able to cover its brutal nakedness after such an unmasking.

The Burghers of Calais has never been translated into English before, though in Germany at least it has always been considered the greatest of Kaiser's many works and the 'classic' of Expressionist drama. The most likely reason why no complete English version of *The Burghers of Calais* has ever been published is to be found in the incredible difficulty of the text. In it Georg Kaiser stretched the resources of the German language to their utmost, exploiting all the linguistic techniques of the Expressionist Telegram style and more. The play ranges from one extreme of vast expansiveness to another of extreme concentration, from stylized gesture and mime to unnaturally long monologues. But even the latter, of which there are many, are built up from small speech units of extreme precision. Definite and indefinite articles are eliminated, subjunctives avoided, rhetorical questions, alliterations and exclamations heaped one on top of the other. The level of address constantly reaches an incredible height as the proliferating punctuation indicates, yet at the same time the vocabulary is utterly basic. The result is a combination of Nietzschean Zarathustra-pathos and the simplicity of the Luther Bible. As in

8

From Morning to Midnight, though the play is non-Christian, Christian parallels are constantly being invoked, culminating in the final tableau before the steps of the cathedral. At no time is there any suggestion that this is the normal everyday speech of real people in an historical setting. The language is deliberately stylized, not in the direction of 'poetic' drama, but in that of mannered Expressionist diction. There is simply nothing like this in English.

In the same way as the language of the play is strikingly non-naturalistic, so too the structure of the play is a deliberate departure, despite its apparently traditional three-act form. The stage directions at the beginning of the play would seem by their very length to indicate a wealth of localizing detail. In fact the opposite is the case. Despite the 'Gothic' setting so beloved of the Expressionists and despite the choice of a famous incident from the Hundred Years' War in the 14th century, the work does not rely on historical accuracy. Instead of conjuring up a picture of a past age every aspect of the play conspires to free it from one particular frame of reference, and make it relevant for any time. Instead of historically accurate clothing or geographically precise details, it revels in all the purely theatrical possibilities of geometric stage-design, choreographic crowd scenes, stylized colour sequences, special lighting and sound-effects, exaggerated gestures, mimes and movements. The total effect is that of a pageant, a series of tableaux or set pieces, but one in which the static quality of such a form is counterbalanced not only by the sheer theatricality of the staging, but also by the dynamic presentation of the dialectic. As always Kaiser makes the clash of speech and counter-speech, argument and counter-argument dramatically gripping. Since plot has been virtually eliminated or at least reduced to a basic situation, the heart of the matter is the decision that has to be taken. Hence only the leading figures in the conflict, like Eustache de Saint-Pierre and Duguesclins, need be named, the rest are designated simply as Third, Fourth, Fifth Councillor, Father, Mother, Nurse, Daughter, English Officer etc.

It is clear that Kaiser was not attempting anything like the traditional historical drama when in 1913 he turned from the famous Rodin group of figures to Froissart's Chronicle for the theme of this work. His aim was to write a visionary play and the dedication he gave it—*ad aeternam memoriam*—indicates not so much a desire to perpetuate the *names* of the individuals concerned as to reveal the symbolic significance of their act for all ages. Important too in this connection is the date of the play's conception, expressing *before* the outbreak of the Great World War the message of peace and conciliation and a readiness for self-sacrifice in the cause of constructive communal achievement, rather than the traditional blind militarism. All in all, therefore, the play is completely Expressionistic in its themes : the idea that a new start has to be made; the readiness for sacrifice; the longing for salvation; the idea of a brotherhood of man; the vision of a rebirth of mankind; the manifestation of an aggressive pacifism. Man, it is argued, is conditioned no more by history and tradition than he is by milieu, race or psychological make-up. He is at all times free to make a break with the past, free to abandon antiquated ideas of honour and heroism which lead only to open aggression. He can turn to new paths. Hence this, too, is a play of ideas along the lines of a Platonic dialogue in which a case is argued out publicly by the main protagonists before the people. But of far greater importance than any of the many ideas expressed through the play is the process of purification which it exemplifies. The decision to accept the extreme demands of the King of England and to face death is not enough in itself. Each of the six must come to realize *why* he is prepared to do so and must arrive at the point where he makes this sacrifice for the right reasons. This is why the simple situation is complicated by the extra man, the choosing of lots, the walk to the square. These are not extraneous elements or unnecessary repetitions, they demonstrate that the choice is not something done in the heat of the moment to 'get it over with' : the choice must be constantly repeated. The old way was characterized by simple responses to clear-cut situations. Now there can be no such certainty.

While in *The Burghers of Calais* some at least of the main protagonists were named and historically identifiable, the anti-naturalism of Kaiser's *Gas* trilogy is obvious from the start of *The Coral*. Now all have become generalizations : father, son and daughter; or are differentiated only by colour; The Gentleman in Grey (=Socialist), The Man in Blue (=Worker), The Lady in Black (=Widow), The Yellow Stoker, The Coloured Man-servant etc. In *Gas II*, the final phase of the trilogy, mankind is divided into two kinds: Blue Figures and Yellow Figures. The setting for most of the action is geometrical, depersonalized and arranged according to colour sequences. Act I of *The Coral* is set in an oval room furnished only with two armchairs in white elephant-hide. Through this room pass people in various colours. In Act II the millionaire and his guests, all dressed in tropical white, sit in white lacquered cane chairs in marked contrast to the son from the black stoke-hold of the collier, the Yellow Stoker and the Coloured Man-servant. Act III is set in a square room whose back wall is all glass. The side walls, consisting of floor-to-ceiling sepia-coloured photographs, must have looked unbelievably 'modern' in 1917, and also the Kafkaesque, unnaturally sterile blue quadrilateral of the last act interrogation room with its many doors and iron bars, metal table and inhuman arc-light.

Whatever interpretation is given to this play it is certainly not a social drama in the normal sense of one dealing with the fate of the masses or class-hatred. As Diebold put it: instead of Marx and the social problem we are given Schopenhauer and life as will and illusion. Accepted ideas are deliberately turned upside down and ultimate insight reserved for the individual:

> 'But the most profound truth is not proclaimed by you and thousands like you—only the single individual ever discovers it. And then it is so overwhelming that it becomes powerless in its effect.'

These words, among the last spoken by the millionaire to the chaplain with 'solemn tranquillity', are taken up again as the motto for the second play of the trilogy, *Gas*. Here the technological advance of society with its successive waves of expansion and collapse has moved even further. In the same way socialization with its specialization of skills, profit-sharing, etc., has reached an unprecedented pitch. Once again Kaiser is concerned not with a naturalistic picture of modern life, but with fundamental questions: what is it all for? what does this mean in terms of the quality of human life? how can a rebirth of mankind be

11

brought about and what are the forces resisting such change? As in *The Coral* the characters are unnamed though the colours are significant. Where the millionaire has been aware of the 'horror' of poverty and the capitalistic system, the millionaire's son, who has identified himself with the workers, must be made to see the 'white terror' reached when technology arrives at its ultimate limits. There is no flaw in the mathematical formula and yet the gas inevitably explodes. While the millionaire's son sees the white terror and the vast devastation caused by it as 'what was needed to give us the impetus,—violently—to hurl us forwards by a thousand years' this insight is reserved for him alone and he meets immovable resistance to change in everyone from the clerk and the engineers to the workers, men, women and children. Like the cashier in *From Morning to Midnight* the millionaire's son feels that he has been buried under layer upon layer and this blast has freed him for the first time; he knows that the present path is a blind alley and that it means only destruction. He alone asks the vital questions. Work is done for the sake of work. Where does it lead? Man has been reduced to a part, to a function, instead of fulfilling his full potential. This is why he refuses to rebuild the works and gropes towards a new solution, however, wrong-headed it may appear. The garden-city he offers is in fact to be a fountainhead from which the new message will go forth into the world : mankind must rediscover man. This is his insight. Resistance to it is inevitable, not least from the representatives of business and government who need the vital source of technological power for a war that is in the offing. The clerk must push his pen, the worker must work, the engineer must build his engines, the officer is incapable of abandoning his uniform and the 'black lords over labour' see things only in terms of immediate need. These 'gentlemen in black', so reminiscent of the swarm of anonymous stewards in black dinner jackets at the sports palace in *From Morning to Midnight* appear in Act IV, whose concrete hangar lit by the incandescence of arc-lamps and filled with a frenzied mob, also recalls the hectic atmosphere and setting of the six-day cycle race, in which audience and participants are caught up in a meaningless and frenzied pursuit of money. It is against the background of these massed workers that

12

the millionaire's son and the engineer argue out their case, just as Eustache de Saint-Pierre and Duguesclins do in *The Burghers of Calais*. The irony of the situation here is that the workers are aware of the dehumanizing effect of their advanced technology, yet they prove incapable of renouncing its implications or of resisting the engineer's appeals. 'You are heroes—you are the rulers—not peasants.' Where Eustache de Saint-Pierre apparently triumphs in his demand for the New Man, the millionaire's son fails to persuade them that they have reached the end of one road, the path of progressive technology which can mean only the destruction of humanity. The engineer is reinstated, the works are rebuilt and compulsorily taken over in the national interest. It is left to the daughter to promise to give birth to the New Man the millionaire's son has envisaged—the New Man whose birth has proved incompatible otherwise with the demands of the technological civilization.

In *Gas II* the destruction of humanity predicted in *Gas I* now seems imminent. Apart from the millionaire-worker and the chief engineer all characters are reduced to Blue Figures, Yellow Figures and workers. The world is completely denaturalized into concrete hangars, electronic panels and radar screens. The war is global and the balance of terror a simple calculation. The yellow hordes are superior in numbers but inferior in technical resources; therefore the annihilation of both sides is inevitable, 'not a single soul escaping the destruction'. Again the situation is akin to the siege of Calais in global terms, with the chief engineer the parallel of Duguesclins, prepared to drive his half of mankind 'into the tunnel with no way out' while the youthful millionaire-worker is the Eustache de Saint-Pierre figure still protecting his grandfather's legacy and pleading the cause of humanity. Again the workers seem on the point of self-awareness, profit-sharing techniques are no longer sufficient to make them slaves to the work process and whip them on to the maximum production of energy. They cease work and the industrial miracle grinds to a halt. The millionaire-worker has his brief moment of triumph when he addresses the assembled workers, persuades them to open the dome to the outside world and send out the message of humanity. But the world does not answer and the triumph is short-lived for with the strike the balance of power has been upset and the yellow hordes are able to conquer the world. With the engineer (who changes sides as easily as Duguesclins does in *The Burghers of Calais*) in charge of technology, the Yellow Figures take over, production continues, this time, however, with the workers reduced to subsistence level. The stage is now set for the final twilight of mankind when the chief engineer offers the 'automata' release from serfdom by the ultimate technological triumph—a poison gas capable of annihilating the tyrant. 'Now there is triumph in a thin glass membrane that shatters and at once eats away the flesh, leaving bleached brittle bones!' The final discussion between the chief engineer and the millionaire-worker on whether to use this ultimate weapon or not is argued out in public. The millionaire-worker has only a mystic appeal akin to the vision of the millionaire in *The Coral* that the end is the beginning: 'Widen your vision for the new that intermingles with the primal.' The kingdom is not of this world, he claims, mankind has to be the kingdom. But this still proves an unattainable ideal. Like Eustache de Saint-Pierre he asks the people to return to the work, not to thoughts of military greatness. But his appeal, like all appeals of his family before him, has been in vain: man is not ready to change, and he himself drops the bomb and unleashes the final orgy of total destruction.

Georg Kaiser's three plays, written fifty years ago, were to prove a prophetic vision of the balance of nuclear terror in the world today.

J. M. Ritchie

14

RECOMMENDED READING

H. F. Garten: *Modern German Drama* (London, 1959)

Walter Gropius ed.: *The Theatre of the Bauhaus* (Wesleyan University Press, 1961)

M. Hamburger & C. Middleton eds.: *Modern German Poetry 1910-1960* (London, 1963)

Claude Hill & Ralph Ley: *The Drama of German Expressionism* A German-English Bibliography (University of North Carolina Press, 1960)

B. J. Kenworthy: *Georg Kaiser* (Oxford, 1957)

B. J. Kenworthy, ed.: *Die Koralle, Gas-Erster Teil, Gas-Fweiter Terl*, A Trilogy by Georg Kaiser (London, 1968)

Egbert Krispyn: *Style and Society in German Literary Expressionism* (University of Florida, 1964)

Hector Maclean: Expressionism in *Periods of German Literature* ed. J. M. Ritchie (London, 1966)

Paul Raabe: *The Era of German Expressionism* in preparation (Calder and Boyars)

J. M. Ritchie: German Theatre between the Wars and the Genteel Tradition, *Modern Drama*, Feb. 1965
The Expressionist Revival, *Seminar*, Spring, 1966

J. M. Ritchie (ed.): *Vision and Aftermath*, four Expressionist War plays (Calder and Boyars, 1969)

J. M. Ritchie (ed.): *Seven Expressionist Plays*, Kokoschka to Barlach (Calder and Boyars, 1968)

R. H. Samuel & R. Hinton Thomas: *Expressionism in German Life, Literature and The Theatre*, 1910-1924 (Cambridge, 1939)

Walter H. Sokel: *The Writer in Extremis: Expressionism in 20th Century German Literature* (Stanford, California, 1959)
An Anthology of German Expressionist Drama, a prelude to the absurd (Doubleday Anchor, A365)

August Strindberg: *Eight Expressionist Plays* (Bantam Classics, QC 261)

FROM MORNING TO MIDNIGHT

Play in Two Parts

Translated by J. M. Ritchie

Characters

CASHIER
MOTHER
WIFE
FIRST and SECOND DAUGHTER
MANAGER
ASSISTANT
COMMISSIONAIRE
FIRST and SECOND GENTLEMAN (Fat Man, Other Man)
MESSENGER BOY
MAID SERVANT
LADY
SON
WAITER in Hotel
JEWISH RACING STEWARDS
ONE TWO THREE FOUR FEMALE MASKS
GENTLEMEN in Evening Dress
WAITER
SALVATION ARMY SOLDIERS and OFFICERS
PUBLIC AT A SALVATION ARMY MEETING (Clerks, Prostitutes)
WORKERS, etc
POLICEMAN

The little town of W. and the big city of B.

PART I

Interior of small bank. Left, cashier's counter and door marked 'Manager'. In the centre, door marked 'To the Strong Room'. Exit (right), behind the barrier. Beside it a cane sofa and table with water-jug and glass. Behind the grille, cashier and at the desk, assistant, writing. The fat gentleman seated on the cane sofa snorts. Somebody goes off right. Messenger boy at the counter stares after him.

CASHIER *raps on the counter.* MESSENGER BOY *quickly places his chit in the* CASHIER'S *waiting hand.* CASHIER *writes, takes money from under the counter counts it out into his hand, then onto the counter.* MESSENGER BOY *moves to one side with money and sweeps it into a linen bag.*

FAT MAN: (*stands up.*) Now it's the turn of us heavyweights. (*Pulls a bulging leather wallet out of his inside coat pocket.*)

(*Enter a* LADY. *Expensive fur. Rustle of silk.* FAT MAN *stops short.*)

LADY: (*has difficulty opening the barrier, smiles involuntarily in the* FAT MAN'S *direction.*) At last!

(FAT MAN *pulls a face.* CASHIER *raps impatiently.* LADY *makes a questioning gesture to the* FAT MAN.)

FAT MAN: (*stepping back.*) Always last, we heavyweights.

(LADY *with a slight bow steps up to the counter.* CASHIER *raps.*)

LADY: (*opens her handbag, takes out an envelope and places it in the* CASHIER'S *hand.*) Three thousand, please.

(CASHIER *looks at it from all sides, pushes it back.*)

LADY: (*understands.*) Sorry. (*She extracts the folded letter and pushes it across.*)

(CASHIER *as before.*)

LADY: (*unfolds the letter.*) Three thousand, please.

(CASHIER *skims over the paper and places it in front of the* CLERK. CLERK *stands up and goes through the door marked 'Manager'.*)

FAT MAN: (*getting down in the cane sofa again.*) I'll take longer. We heavyweights always take longer.

(CASHIER *busy counting money.*)

LADY: In notes, please.

(CASHIER *does not look up.*)

MANAGER: (*youngish, rotund—comes out left with the letter.*) Who is—(*Struck dumb at the sight of the* LADY.)

(ASSISTANT *writing again at his desk.*)

FAT MAN: (*loudly.*) Good morning.

MANAGER: (*with a brief glance in his direction.*) Everything all right?

FAT MAN: (*patting his paunch.*) Rolling along nicely, thanks.

MANAGER: (*laughs briefly. To the* LADY.) You wish to draw some money?

LADY: Three thousand.

MANAGER: Yes, three—three thousand. I should be delighted to let you have it—

LADY: Is there something wrong with the letter?

MANAGER: (*saccharine-sweet, self-important.*) Nothing wrong with the letter. Up to twelve thousand. (*Spelling it out.*) B-A-N-C-O-.

LADY: My bank in Florence assured me—

MANAGER: Your bank in Florence has written a perfectly valid letter.

LADY: Then I fail to under—

MANAGER: You had this letter made out in Florence—

LADY: I did.

MANAGER: Twelve thousand and payable at the towns—

LADY: —at which I break my journey.

MANAGER: You had to give the bank in Florence several specimen signatures–

LADY: –which have been sent to the banks listed in the letter, to identify me.

MANAGER: We have not received any letter of advice with your signature.

(FAT MAN *coughs, winks at the* MANAGER.)

LADY: Does that mean I have to wait till–

MANAGER: We have to have something to go on.

(MAN *wrapped up in winter coat with fur hat and woollen scarf comes in, takes up position at the counter. He darts furious looks at the* LADY.)

LADY: I wasn't prepared for this–

MANAGER: (*with a brash laugh.*) We were even less prepared, in fact not at all!

LADY: I do need the money urgently!

(FAT MAN *on the sofa laughs loudly.*)

MANAGER: Which of us doesn't?

(FAT MAN *on the sofa neighs with laughter.*)

MANAGER: (*as if addressing an audience.*) Me, for instance. (*To the* MAN *at the counter.*) You've probably more time than I have. You can see I'm still talking to this lady. Now come, madam, what did you imagine? Did you expect me to pay out–on your–

(FAT MAN *on the sofa titters.*)

LADY: (*quickly.*) I'm at the 'Elephant'.

(FAT MAN *on the sofa hoots.*)

MANAGER: Delighted to have your address, madam. · I'm a regular at the 'Elephant'.

LADY: Can't the hotel manager vouch for me?

(FAT MAN *on the sofa having a wonderful time.*)

21

LADY: My luggage is at the hotel.

MANAGER: Do you want me to inspect the contents of your trunks and cases?

LADY: I'm in a most unfortunate position!

MANAGER: Then we're in the same boat. You can't–I can't. That's the position. (*He gives her back her letter.*)

LADY: What do you advise?

MANAGER: Our little township is a pleasant place–the 'Elephant' a famous hotel–there are nice surroundings–there are nice people–and time soon passes–a day here, a night there–take it as it comes.

LADY: A few days here wouldn't matter.

MANAGER: The company at the 'Elephant' will be delighted to help make your stay pleasant.

LADY: But I simply must have the three thousand today!

MANAGER: (*to the* FAT MAN *on the sofa.*) Anybody here prepared to put up three thousand for a lady from abroad?

LADY: I couldn't possibly accept that. I shall be in my room at the 'Elephant'. May I ask you to inform me by telephone as soon as the verification comes through from Florence?

MANAGER: I shall telephone personally if madam wishes!

LADY: Whichever way is quickest. (*She pushes the letter into the envelope and puts it in her bag.*) I shall call in again this afternoon.

MANAGER: At your service.

(LADY *departs with curt good-bye.*)

(MAN *at the counter moves up and bangs a crumpled paper onto the counter.*)

(MANAGER *ignoring this, looks at the* FAT MAN *on the sofa in merriment.*)

(FAT MAN *on the sofa sniffs.*)

MANAGER: All the fragrance of Italy–out of a perfume bottle.

(FAT MAN *on the sofa fans himself with his hand.*)

MANAGER: Brings on the heat, doesn't it?

FAT MAN: (*pours himself a glass of water.*) Three thousand is a bit steep. (*Drinks.*) Three hundred is more like it.

MANAGER: Perhaps you could bring the price down–at the 'Elephant', in her room?

FAT MAN: That's not for heavyweights like us.

MANAGER: Our waistlines protect our morality–they keep us out of trouble.

(MAN *at the counter bangs his fist on the counter for the second time.*)

MANAGER: (*unperturbed.*) What's the matter with you? (*Smoothes out the paper and hands it to the* CASHIER.)

(MESSENGER BOY *has been staring at the* LADY, *then the speakers–misses the barrier and collides with the* FAT MAN *on the sofa.*)

FAT MAN: (*takes his money-bag away from him.*) Yes, my lad, making eyes at pretty girls can be a costly business–now you've lost your money-bag.

(MESSENGER BOY *gives an embarrassed laugh.*)

FAT MAN: Now what are you going to do when you get home?

(MESSENGER BOY *laughs.*)

FAT MAN: (*returns his bag.*) Let that be a lesson to you. All your life. You are not the first whose eyes ran away with him– and then all the rest of him.

(MESSENGER BOY *exits.*)

(CASHIER *has been counting out coins.*)

MANAGER: And to think people entrust money to a young rascal like that.

FAT MAN: Stupidity brings its own punishment.

MANAGER: A wonder his boss can't see it. Chap like that absconds the first chance he gets. Born embezzler. (*To the* MAN *at the counter.*) Is there something wrong?

(MAN *examines every coin.*)

MANAGER: That's a 25 pfennig piece–45 pfennig all in all. All you had coming, wasn't it?

(MAN *pocketing it with great care.*)

FAT MAN: You want to be careful and keep such a vast amount in the strong room.–Now it's time for the heavyweights to unload.

(MAN *at counter off right.*)

MANAGER: Well, what have you brought us?

FAT MAN: (*places the leather bag on the counter and brings out his wallet.*) You with your chic clientèle. Can I still trust you? (*Shakes hands.*)

MANAGER: Anyway, pretty faces can't influence us where business is concerned.

FAT MAN: (*counting out his money.*) How old was she? What's your guess?

MANAGER: Haven't seen her without make-up. Yet.

FAT MAN: What's she after here?

MANAGER: We'll find out tonight at the 'Elephant'.

FAT MAN: Who might be interested?

MANAGER: Any of us in the long run.

FAT MAN: Whatever does she need the three thousand for here?

MANAGER: She must need it pretty badly.

FAT MAN: I wish her the best of luck.

MANAGER: In what?

FAT MAN: In getting hold of her three thousand.

MANAGER: From me?

FAT MAN: Who from is beside the point.

MANAGER: I wonder when the notification from the bank in Florence will come.

FAT MAN: If at all!

MANAGER: If at all–that has me even more intrigued!

FAT MAN: We could whip the hat round to help her out of her difficulties.

MANAGER: Something like that is probably what she has in mind.

FAT MAN: You're telling me.

MANAGER: (*laughs.*) Have you won the lottery?

24

FAT MAN : (to CASHIER.) Take this off me. (To MANAGER.) What does it matter whether we invest our money outside or let it accumulate interest with you–open an account for the Building Society.

MANAGER : (sharply to the ASSISTANT.) Account for the Building Society.

FAT MAN : There's more to come.

MANAGER : Keep it rolling in, gentlemen. We can use it, just now.

FAT MAN : Fity–sixty thousand–fifty thou. in notes–ten thou. in gold.

(CASHIER counts it.)

MANAGER : (after a pause.) Everything all right otherwise?

FAT MAN : (to CASHIER.) Yes; that note is patched.

MANAGER : We'll accept it, of course. Soon get rid of it. Reserve it for our customer from Florence. She had beauty patches herself.

FAT MAN : But there's a thousand in this one.

MANAGER : Collector's piece.

FAT MAN : (uncontrollable laughter.) Collector's piece–that's good !

MANAGER : (in tears.) Collector's piece–Gives him the CASHIER'S receipt.) Your receipt. (Choking.) Sixty–thou.—

FAT MAN : (takes it and reads it: ditto.) Sixty–thou.—

MANAGER : Collector–

FAT MAN : Coll–(They shake hands.)

MANAGER : See you to-night.

FAT MAN : (nods.) Collector– (Buttons up his coat, departs shaking his head.)

(MANAGER stands there, wipes away tears from behind pince-nez. Exits left into his room.)

(CASHIER bundles up the notes he has just received, stacks the coins in rolls.)

MANAGER : (comes back in.) That lady from Florence–supposedly from Florence–ever had a vision like that appear at your counter before? Furs–perfume. Still linger on, romance fills the air !—That is the full treatment. Italy, the very word has a dazzling effect–fabulous. Riviera–Mentone–Bordighera–Nice–Monte Carlo! But, where oranges grow, crooks thrive too. There is not a square yard of ground free of fraud down there. That's where the raids are planned. The gang scatters in all directions. Slip away to the smaller towns–off the main highways. Then visions in silks and fur. Women! They are the modern sirens, singing their song of the blue south–o *bella Napoli*! One captivating glance and they'll take the very suit off your back, you're stripped naked, stripped to your bare skin! (*He drums on the* CASHIER'S *back with his pencil.*) I don't doubt for an instant that the Bank in Florence which issued the letter knows as much about it–as the man in the moon. The whole thing is a swindle, long prepared. And the perpetrators are not in Florence at all, but in Monte Carlo! That's the place that immediately springs to mind. Can count on it. We have seen before us one of those beings who thrive in the jungle of the gambling den. And I wager we never see her again. The first attempt was a failure. She won't risk a second one! I maybe like a joke–but I still keep my eyes peeled. We bankers!–I should really have tipped off our Police Chief–But what happens now is not my business. After all the bank is expected to observe a discreet silence. (*At his door.*) Watch the out-of-town papers: when you read that a woman swindler has been arrested you'll see what I'm talking about. Then you'll have to admit that I was right. That's the last we'll ever see of our lady friend from Florence. (*Exit.*)

(CASHIER *seals rolls.*)

PORTER: (*enters from right with letters, gives them to the* CLERK.) One registered letter. I keep the receipt.

(CLERK *stamps the chit, gives it to the* PORTER.)

(PORTER *re-arranges glass and water carafe. Exit.*)

(CLERK *carries letters into* MANAGER'S *office–comes back.*)

LADY: (*returns; walks up to the counter quickly.*) Oh. Excuse me.

(CASHIER *sticks out his hand, palm up.*)

26

LADY: (*louder.*) Excuse me.

(CASHIER *raps on counter.*)

LADY: I don't want to trouble the MANAGER again.

(CASHIER *raps.*)

LADY: (*smiling in despair.*) Listen, please, wouldn't it be possible if we did it this way–I leave the bank the letter for the whole amount and you advance me three thousand? (CASHIER *raps impatiently.*) I should even be prepared to deposit my diamonds as security. Any jeweller in the town will give a valuation on them. (*She pulls off a glove and fumbles with the bracelet.*)

(MAID SERVANT *enters quickly from right, sits down on the cane sofa, turns everything out of her shopping basket, looking for something.*)

(LADY *has turned round slightly startled: her hand comes to rest on the hand of the* CASHIER *for support.*)

(CASHIER *bends over the hand he holds in his. Slowly his bespectacled eyes travel up her wrist.*)

(MAID SERVANT *finds the cheque with a sigh of relief.*)

(LADY *nods in her direction.*)

(MAID SERVANT *puts things back in basket.*)

(LADY *turning to the* CASHIER *suddenly meets his gaze.*)

(CASHIER *smiles.*)

LADY: (*rescues her hand.*) I wouldn't want to make the bank do anything irregular. (*She puts on the bracelet, has difficulty with the catch. Holding her arm out to the* CASHIER.) Would you be so kind–I can't manage with just one hand.

(CASHIER *bushy beard bristles; eye-glasses sink into glowing caverns of wide-open eyes.*)

LADY: (*to* MAID SERVANT.) Will you help me?

(MAID SERVANT *does so.*)

LADY: Now the safety catch. (*Utters a faint cry.*) Oh, you are sticking it into my bare flesh. That's it. Many thanks. (*Waves to the* CASHIER. *Exit.*)

(MAID SERVANT *at the counter, lays her cheque down.*)

(CASHIER *seizes it in fluttering hands. Gropes around under the counter for a long time. Then pays out.*)

MAID SERVANT: (*looks at all the money; then at the* CASHIER.) I don't have all that coming.

(CASHIER *writing.*)

(ASSISTANT *beginning to take notice.*)

MAID SERVANT: (*to* ASSISTANT.) That's too much!

(ASSISTANT *looks at* CASHIER.)

(CASHIER *takes back some.*)

MAID SERVANT: Still too much!

(CASHIER *writes.*)

(MAID SERVANT *shakes her head, puts money in her basket. Off.*)

CASHIER: (*his voice struggling through hoarse croaking.*) Fetch –glass–water!

(ASSISTANT *goes from the counter to the table.*)

CASHIER: That's stale. Fresh–from the tap.

(ASSISTANT *goes with glass into the Strong Room.*)

(CASHIER *quickly to electric bell–presses.*)

(COMMISSIONAIRE *enters.*)

CASHIER: Fetch fresh water.
COMMISSIONAIRE: I'm not allowed to leave the outside door.
CASHIER: For me. That's slime. I want fresh drinking water.

(COMMISSIONAIRE *into the Strong Room with the water carafe.*

28

(CASHIER *with quick movements stuffs the notes and coins he has just sorted into his pockets. Then he takes his coat from the hook, throws it over his arm. Then his hat. He comes round the counter—and exits right.*)

MANAGER: (*enters left, deeply engrossed in a letter.*) The confirmation from Florence has come!

(ASSISTANT *with the glass of water from the Strong Room.*)

(COMMISSIONAIRE *with the carafe of water from the Strong Room.*)

MANAGER: What the devil does this mean?

Writing room in a hotel. Glass door at the back. Writing table and telephone left. Sofa right, with table and journals, etc.

(LADY *writing.*)

(SON *enters with coat and hat on—under his arm large flat object wrapped in a dust-sheet.*)

LADY: (*surprised.*) You've got it?
SON: The wine-merchant is sitting in the lounge downstairs. The funny old codger suspects me of wanting to run off with it.
LADY: Why, this morning he was glad to get rid of it.
SON: Now he smells something fishy.
LADY: You must have aroused his suspicion in some way.
SON: I did show I was rather pleased.
LADY: That would open a blind man's eyes.
SON: And believe me, they *shall* open their eyes. But keep calm, Mama, the price is the same as this morning.
LADY: Is the wine-merchant waiting?
SON: Let him wait.
LADY: I'm afraid I must tell you—
SON: (*kisses her.*) Silence. Solemn silence. Don't look till I tell you to. (*Flings off hat and coat, sets the picture up on a chair and lifts the dust-sheet.*)
LADY: Not yet?

SON: (*very quietly.*) Mama.

(LADY *turns round in her chair.*)

SON: (*comes to her, puts his arm round her shoulders.*) Well?

LADY: It certainly does not belong in a wine-bar.

SON: Well, it was turned face to the wall. The wine-merchant had stuck his own photograph on the back.

LADY: Did you buy that too?

SON (*laughs.*) What do you think of it?

LADY: I find it–very naive.

SON: Marvellous, isn't it? Fantastic for a Cranach.

LADY: Do you really rate it so highly–as a picture?

SON: As a picture? Of course! But also for the remarkable presentation. Unique for Cranach–and for the treatment of the subject unique in the whole history of art. Where will you find the like? In the Palazzo–the Uffizi–the Vatican? Even the Louvre can't match this. Without a doubt we have here the first and only erotic presentation of the first human couple. The apple is still there lying on the grass–out of the indescribably green foliage leers the serpent–we see that the scene takes place in Paradise itself and not after the banishment. This is the Fall itself!–Unique! Cranach painted dozens of Adam and Eves–stiff–with the branch of the tree in the middle–and always the two separate. It is written: they knew each other. Here for the first time the glorious proclamation of the birth of true humanity trumpets forth: they *loved* each other. Here a German and Northerner reveals himself as a master of the erotic of truly southern, completely southern vigour! (*Gazing at the picture.*) And yet, at the same time how great the discipline in such ecstasy. This line of the male arm cutting across the female hip, the horizontal line of her thighs underneath and the diagonal line of his. It never wearies the eye for a moment. It creates love in the beholder–the flesh tone naturally helps a great deal. Don't you find the same?

LADY: You are naive, like your picture.

SON: What do you mean?

LADY: I beg of you hide the picture in your hotel room.

SON: It will really only take effect on me once I have it at home.

Florence and this Cranach. I shall have to postpone finishing my book for a long time. This kind of thing has to be digested, and then recreated out of one's own flesh and blood, otherwise the art historian betrays his trust. At the moment I feel completely overwhelmed–fancy finding this picture on the first stage of the trip.

LADY: You were pretty sure it was here.

SON: But one is still blinded by the reality. Isn't it enough to drive one out of one's mind? Mama, I must be born lucky.

LADY: You are reaping the benefits of your intensive research.

SON: And what about your help? Your kindness?

LADY: My happiness lies in yours.

SON: You are infinitely patient with me. I drag you from your lovely, quiet life in Fiesole. You are Italian, I drag you through Germany in the middle of winter. You sleep in trains–second and third-class hotels–get involved with all sorts of people–

LADY: I've certainly had my fill of that today.

SON: I promise to hurry. I am impatient myself to get my treasure to safety. We leave at three. Will you give me the three thousand?

LADY: I have not got it.

SON: The man who owns the picture is here now.

LADY: The bank could not let me have it. The notification from Florence must have been delayed.

SON: I agreed to pay cash.

LADY: Then you must give him back the picture until the bank can let me have the money.

SON: Can't that be speeded up?

LADY: I have just made out a telegram. I'll have it sent off. We left so quickly–

(WAITER knocks.)

LADY: Yes.

WAITER: A gentleman from the bank wishes to speak to madam.

LADY: (to SON.) They've sent the money straight to the hotel (To WAITER.) Ask him to come right up.

(WAITER exits.)

31

SON : Call me when you have the money, will you? I don't want to let our man out of the hotel.

LADY : I'll phone you immediately.

SON : I'll be in the lounge downstairs. (*Exit.*)

(LADY *closes her writing-case.*)

(WAITER *and* CASHIER *appear behind the glass door.* CASHIER *passes the* WAITER *and opens the door;* WAITER *turns and goes.*)

(CASHIER *still with coat over arm, enters.*)

(LADY *points to a chair and sits on the sofa.*)

(CASHIER *his coat beside him on the chair.*)

LADY : Has the bank–?

(CASHIER *sees picture.*)

LADY : This picture is closely connected with my visit to the bank.

CASHIER : Is it you?

LADY : Do you see a likeness?

CASHIER : (*smiling.*) Yes, in the wrist!

LADY : Are you a connoisseur?

CASHIER : I'd like to–become more of one!

LADY : Are you interested in pictures like these?

CASHIER : I'm in the picture!

LADY : Do you know of the existence of more such pictures in this town? You would be doing me a great favour. Why, that is even more important to me–well, as important as the money!

CASHIER : I've got money.

LADY : In the end the sum I had my letter of credit made out for won't be enough.

CASHIER : (*pulls out the notes and rolls of coin.*) This is enough.

LADY : I can only draw up to twelve thousand.

CASHIER : Sixty thousand.

LADY : How is that possible?

CASHIER : That's my business.

LADY : What do I have to do?

CASHIER : We have to take a trip.

LADY: Where to?

CASHIER: Across the border. Pack your case–if you have one. You leave from the Central Station–I walk to the next stop and board the train there. We'll spend the first night at–time-table? (*He finds it on the table.*)

LADY: Have you brought more than three thousand from the bank?

CASHIER: (*busy.*) Put sixty thousand in my pocket. Fifty thousand in notes–ten thousand in gold.

LADY: Of that, I'm entitled to–?

CASHIER: (*breaks open a roll, counts them professionally into his hand and then onto the table.*) Take it. Put it away immediately. We may be observed. The door has glass panels. Five hundred in gold.

LADY: Five hundred?

CASHIER: More later. When we're safe. Here we mustn't let anybody see. Let's go. Put it away. This is not the moment for tenderness. The wheel of time turns, crushing any arm stuck in the spokes to stop it. (*He leaps up.*)

LADY: I need three thousand.

CASHIER: If the police find it on you, you'll be put behind bars!

LADY: What have the police got to do with it?

CASHIER: Your presence was observed by the whole bank today. Suspicion attaches to you, the link between us is clear.

LADY: I entered the bank–

CASHIER: Coolly.

LADY: I asked for–

CASHIER: You at-tempted–

LADY: I tried–

CASHIER: –to defraud the bank by presenting a forged letter.

LADY: (*taking the letter from her handbag.*) This letter isn't genuine?

CASHIER: As genuine as your diamonds.

LADY: I offered my valuables as security. Why should my precious stones be imitations?

CASHIER: Women of your type only dazzle.

LADY: What type am I then? Dark hair–dark complexion. A southerner, from Tuscany.

33

CASHIER: From Monte Carlo!

LADY: (*smiles.*) No, from Florence!

CASHIER: (*suddenly his eye falls on coat and hat of the* SON.) Am I too late?

LADY: Too late?

CASHIER: Where is he? I'll make a deal with him. He'll listen. I have the wherewithal. How much should I offer him? How high do you reckon the compensation? How much should I stuff into his pocket? I'll go as high as fifteen thousand–is he asleep? Still sprawling in bed? Where's your room? Twenty thousand–five thousand extra for immediate withdrawal. (*He seizes hat and coat from the chair.*) I'll take him his things.

LADY: (*baffled.*) The gentleman is sitting in the lounge.

CASHIER: That is too dangerous. Too many people downstairs. Ask him up. I'll checkmate him. Ring the bell. Tell the waiter to hurry. Twenty thousand–in notes! (*He counts them out.*)

LADY: Can my son vouch for me?

CASHIER: (*staggers back stunned.*) Your—son?

LADY: I'm travelling with him. I'm accompanying him on a study-trip from Florence to Germany. My son is collecting material for his book on art history.

CASHIER: (*stares at her.*) Son?

LADY: Is that so appalling?

CASHIER: (*confused.*) This—picture.

LADY: Is his great find. Three thousand is enough to buy it. That's the three thousand I need so badly. A big wine-merchant –whom you are sure to know when you hear his name–is prepared to part with it at that price.

CASHIER: —furs—silk—shimmered and rustled—the air was heavy with exotic perfumes!

LADY: It's winter. I don't dress out of the ordinary, by my standards.

CASHIER: The forged letter.

LADY: I've just been making out a telegram to my bank.

CASHIER: Your wrist–all naked–I was supposed to put the bracelet on.

LADY: Everyone is clumsy with the left hand.

CASHIER: (*dully.*) I have—embezzled—

LADY: (*amused.*) Are you and the police satisfied now? My son is well known in academic circles.

CASHIER: Now—right at this moment, they'll be missing me. I asked for a drink of water, once to get rid of the assistant—and again to remove the porter from the door. The notes and coins have disappeared. I have embezzled!—I mustn't be seen on the streets—in the market-place. Must not go to the railway station. The police are on the alert. Sixty thousand!—I must go across country–through the snow, before the general alarm is given.

LADY: (*horrified.*) Be quiet!

CASHIER: I pocketed all the money—you pervaded the bank—you shimmered and rustled—you rested your bare hand in mine—I felt the warmth of your body—the caress of your breath—

LADY: I am a lady!

CASHIER: (*doggedly.*) Now you simply must—! !

LADY: (*controlling herself.*) Are you married? (*He makes a sweeping gesture.*) I think that matters a great deal. If indeed I'm not to take the whole business as a joke. You have let yourself be carried away. Committed an ill-considered act. You must repair the damage. Go back to your counter and intimate that suddenly you weren't feeling quite yourself. You still have all the money on you?

CASHIER: I took money from the–

LADY: (*abruptly.*) Then I can take no further interest.

CASHIER: I robbed the bank–

LADY: You are becoming a nuisance, sir.

CASHIER: Now you must–

LADY: What I must do is–

CASHIER: Don't you see, now you must do it! !

LADY: Ridiculous.

CASHIER: I have robbed, stolen. I have sacrificed my life–I have destroyed my existence–I have burned my boats–I am a thief –a criminal—(*Flinging the words across the table at her.*) Now you must. You simply must! ! !

LADY: I'll call my son, perhaps—

CASHIER: (*suddenly changed, alert.*) Call somebody? Sound the alarm? Splendid!–Stupid. Clumsy. They won't catch me. I won't walk into the trap. I've got my wits about me, ladies and gentlemen. Your wits are always a long way behind–I'm invariably miles ahead of you. Don't move. Sit still till I–(*Stuffs the money in his pockets, pulls the hat over his face, clutches the coat to his chest.*) Till I–(*Alertly and silently off through glass door.*)

(LADY *remains standing, somewhat bewildered.*)

SON: (*enters.*) The man from the bank just left the hotel. You are all tense, Mama. Is the money–

LADY: The interview was rather a strain. Money matters, my boy. You know they always tend to upset me.

SON: Have difficulties arisen which might delay payment?

LADY: Perhaps I'd better tell you–

SON: Do I have to return the picture?

LADY: It's not the picture I'm thinking about.

SON: But that's all we're really interested in.

LADY: I think I ought to notify the police immediately.

SON: About what?

LADY: Send the telegram. At all costs I must have a confirmation from my bank.

SON: Is your letter of credit not enough?

LADY: No, not quite. Go to the Post Office yourself. I don't want to send the porter with an unsealed telegram form.

SON: And when will the money get here? (*The telephone bell rings shrilly.*)

LADY: They're ringing me already. (*Speaking into the phone.*) Who? Oh, the Bank Manager? It has arrived! I'm to call for it myself. Gladly. Don't mention it. I am not angry at all. Florence is a long way away. Yes, the Italian Postal Services. What? Why? Why? Yes, why? Oh, I see, via Berlin–that is a long way round.–Not in the least. Thank you. In ten minutes. Goodbye. (*To* SON.) Everything's fixed; my telegram is no longer needed. (*She tears up the telegram form.*) You have your picture. Your wine-merchant can come along with us and be paid his money at the bank. Pack up your treasure. From the

36

bank we drive straight to the station. (*Telephones, while son drapes picture.*) The bill, please. Rooms 14 and 16. Immediately. Please.

Snow-covered field, tree with maze of low-hanging branches. Sun casting blue shadows.

CASHIER : (*comes in backwards. With his hands he is shovelling snow over his tracks. Standing up.*) What a wonderful piece of work a man is. How smoothly the mechanism works. Suddenly potentials are uncovered and briskly activated. How do these hands of mine know what to do? Where did they ever shovel snow before? Now they displace such masses of snow that the flakes fly. Moreover, my tracks across the snow-field are effectively obliterated. An impenetrable incognito is achieved! (*Peels off his soaked cuffs.*) Dampness and frost are conducive to chills. In no time, fever breaks out and influences decisions. Control over actions is lost, land in bed, and you're finished! (*He takes cuff-links out, flings the cuffs away.*) Retired from active service. Lie there. You'll be missed in the wash. The lamentations will wail through the kitchen : a pair of cuffs is missing. A calamity in the washtubs. End of the world! (*He picks up the cuffs again and stuffs them into his coat pockets.*) Amazing, my wits are working again. With infallible precision. I take infinite pains to cover my footsteps in the snow and betray myself with two bits of laundry flung away foolishly. Mostly it's a mere trifle–a slip –a piece of carelessneses, which betrays the criminal. Hopla! (*He hunts out a comfortable seat in the fork of a tree.*) I'm really curious. A tremendous feeling of tenseness is building up in me. I have reason to think I'm on the brink of momentous discoveries. Experiences gained in flight will be invaluable. This morning, still a faithful employee. Considerable fortunes were entrusted to me, the Building Society deposited gigantic sums. By midday an out-and-out scoundrel. Cunning as they come. The details of escape were executed with technical perfection. The job done and away, sensational achievement–and the day

still only half gone. (*He props his chin on the back of his fist.*)
I am prepared to welcome each and every eventuality with
open arms. I possess infallible signs that there's an answer for
all demands made upon me. I'm on the march–there's no turning back. I'm marching–so no beating about the bush, out with
the trumps–I have staked sixty thousand on a single card–
that calls for a trump. I play too high to lose. No nonsense.
Cards on the table. Show your hand and hey presto! Got it?
(*He laughs a croaking laugh.*) Now it's your turn, lovely lady.
That's your cue, silken lady. Give it to me, shimmering lady,
why you're letting the show down. Stupid bitch. How did you
get into the act? Fulfil your natural obligations, bear children
–and don't bother the prompter!–Beg your pardon, you have a
son. You are completely absolved. I withdraw my insinuations.
Farewell and give my best wishes to the manager. His sheep's
eyes will smear you with revolting slime, but don't you worry
about that. The man has been done out of sixty thousand.
Terrible loss to bear. The Building Society will have to cover
him. I release you from all your obligations towards me, dismissed, you can go.–Take my thanks with you on your way–
on the train.–What? No occasion to thank you? I think I have
excellent cause to! Not worth mentioning? You are joking, I
owe you everything!–How so?–I owe you my life!–For
heaven's sake!–Me exaggerate? I was a robot, your rustling
electrified me, shook me free. I leapt after you and landed in
the focus of fantastic events. And with this load in my breast
pocket I pay cash for all favours. (*With a nonchalant gesture.*)
Now fade, you are already outbid and with your limited
means–you mustn't forget your son, must you?–can expect
no more! (*He pulls the bundle of notes out of his pocket and
slaps it on the palm of his hand.*) I pay cash! The amount is
in ready cash–payment precedes supply. Come on, now, what's
offering. (*He looks into the field.*) Snow. Snow. Sunlight.
Silence. (*He shakes his head and puts the money away.*) Pay
for blue snow with this money–that would be a disgraceful
piece of profiteering. No deal. I withdraw my offer. The deal
is no good. (*Flinging out his arms.*) I must pay!—I have the
money in cash! !—Where are goods worth total investment?!

38

Sixty thousand--and the buyer to boot, body and soul?—
(*Screaming.*) You must deliver the goods--you must give a fair
deal--value for value ! ! ! ! (*Sun obscured by clouds. He climbs
down from the fork.*) The earth is in labour--spring storms.
It's coming. It's coming. I knew I did not call out in vain.
The demand was urgent. Chaos is affronted--does not want to
look small, alongside my colossal deed of this morning. I knew
it, in such cases one must persevere ! Attack hard--rip the cloak
off the body and then you see something !--To whom do I
raise my hat so politely? (*His hat is whipped off. The hurricane has lashed the snow from the branches. Remnants stick
in the crown and form a human face with grinning jaws. A
skeleton hand holds the hat.*) Have you been sitting behind
me all the time eavesdropping? Are you an agent of the
police? Not in the usual narrow sense. All-embracing ! Exis-
tential Police?--Are you the definitive answer to my probing?
Do you who stand there looking so threadbare want to suggest
the final truth--that you're bankrupt?--That is rather feeble.
Very feeble. In fact nothing !--I reject the information as being
incomplete. Thanks for the help. Shut your rag and bone shop.
I am not just anybody who can be bamboozled !--It's true the
proceedings would be enormously simple. Your answer removes
further complications. But I prefer complications. So fare you
well--if you *can* in your condition !--I still have various things
to settle. When one is on the march, one can't call on everyone.
No matter how pressing the invitation. I can see I have a whole
lot of calls to make before nightfall. You can't possibly be the
first. More likely the last. And even then only as a last resort--
it would hardly be a pleasure. But as I say--as a last resort--
well, that's worth considering. Ring me again about midnight.
Ask the exchange for my current number !--I'll be on the move
all the time ! Excuse me for being so formal. We are really
much closer. Our relationship is intimate. I even believe you
are inside me. So disentangle yourself from the branches
penetrating you from all sides and slip right inside me. In my
ambiguous position I don't like to leave traces. First of all give
me my hat. (*He takes the hat from the branch which the storm
bends towards him--bows.*) I see we have reached some sort of

understanding. That is a beginning which inspires confidence and provides the necessary support in the whirl of the great events to come. I know how to appreciate that fully. My profound respects—(*Roll of thunder. A final gust of wind sweeps the shape from the tree. Sun breaks through. It is bright as at the beginning.*) I said right away it was just a passing apparition! (*Pulls his hat down over his face, turns up his coat collar and trots off through the cloud of snow.*)

PART TWO

Living room at CASHIER'S *house. Window with withered geraniums. Two doors at the back, door right. Table and chairs. Piano.* MOTHER *sitting at the window.* FIRST DAUGHTER *embroidering at table.* SECOND DAUGHTER *practising the Overture to Tannhäuser.* WIFE *comes and goes through the back door right.*

MOTHER: What are you playing now?

FIRST DAUGHTER: Why, it's the Overture to 'Tannhäuser'.

MOTHER: 'In a Monastery Garden' is a pretty piece too.

FIRST DAUGHTER: That's not what she got from the library this week.

WIFE: (*enters.*) Time I fried the chops.

FIRST DAUGHTER: Not nearly time yet, mother.

WIFE: No, it's not time I fried the chops yet. (*Exit.*)

MOTHER: What are you embroidering now?

FIRST DAUGHTER: I'm doing the scalloping.

WIFE: (*comes to* MOTHER.) We're having chops today.

MOTHER: Are you going to fry them now?

WIFE: It's not time yet. It's not even noon.

FIRST DAUGHTER: It's not nearly noon.

MOTHER: When he comes it's noon.

WIFE: Yes. (*Exit.*)

SECOND DAUGHTER: (*pricking up ears, listening.*) Father?

FIRST DAUGHTER: (*similarly.*) Father?

WIFE: (*comes.*) My husband?
MOTHER: My son?
SECOND DAUGHTER: (*opens door right.*) Father!
FIRST DAUGHTER: (*has stood up.*) Father!
WIFE: Husband!
MOTHER: Son!

(CASHIER *enters right, hangs up hat and coat.*)

WIFE: Where have you been?
CASHIER: In the cemetery.
MOTHER: Has somebody died suddenly?
CASHIER: (*pats her on the back.*) Well, you can die suddenly, but you can't be buried suddenly.
WIFE: Where have you come from?
CASHIER: From the grave. I have bored my brow through clods of earth. There's still ice clinging to me. It was quite an effort to get through. Quite an effort. I dirtied my hands a bit. You have to be nimble-fingered to extricate yourself. You lie deeply buried. Life keeps dumping loads of rubbish on you. Mountains of it are piled on top of you. Heaps of rubbish–till you're a giant rubbish tip. The dead lie the regulation six feet beneath the surface—the living are buried far, far deeper.
WIFE: You are frozen from head to foot.
CASHIER: Thawed out! Shaken by storms–springlike. It rushed and roared–I tell you it ripped the flesh off me down to the bare bones. Bones–bleached within minutes. Boneyard! At last the sun welded me together again. It was a complete rejuvenation. And here I am.
MOTHER: You've been out in the open?
CASHIER: In dreadful dungeons, mother! Arrested in bottomless pits beneath precipitously steep towers. Clanking chains deafened my ears! Darkness plucked my eyes out!
WIFE: The bank is closed. The manager has been drinking with you. Has there been a happy event in the family?
CASHIER: He has his eye on a new mistress. An Italian woman–fur–silk–from where the oranges grow. Wrists like ivory. Black hair–dark complexion. Diamonds. Genuine–all genuine. Tus-Tus- the ending sounds like Canaan. Fetch an atlas. Tus-

41

canaan. Is there such a place? Is it an island? A mountain range? A swamp? Geography can tell us everything! But he will burn his fingers–be turned down–brushed off like a speck of dirt. There he lies–our fat little manager–twitching on the carpet–with his legs in the air!

WIFE: The bank isn't closed?

CASHIER: Of course not, my dear. Prisons never close. The steady flow of clients never ends. The eternal pilgrimage knows no limits, like sheep they go bounding in–to the slaughterhouse. A seething mass. There's no escape–unless you take a bold leap over their backs.

MOTHER: Your coat is torn at the back.

CASHIER: Look at my hat. Behold a tramp!

SECOND DAUGHTER: The lining is in shreds.

CASHIER: Put your hand in my pockets–right and left!

(FIRST DAUGHTER *pulls out a cuff.*)

(SECOND DAUGHTER *ditto.*)

CASHIER: Well?

BOTH DAUGHTERS: Your cuffs.

CASHIER: Without cuff links. The links I have here. Triumph of cold-bloodedness!–Overcoat–hat–yes, you can't go leaping over their backs without ripping something here and there. They grab at you–dig their nails in! Hurdles and fences–must have order. All men are equal. But one mighty leap–don't hesitate–and you are out of the pen–out of the treadmill. One mighty leap and here I am! Behind me: nothing–and ahead? (*He looks round the room.*)

(WIFE *stares at him.*)

MOTHER: (*semi-whisper.*) He is ill.

(WIFE *with quick decision to the door, right.*)

CASHIER: (*stops her. To one of the* DAUGHTERS.) Fetch my jacket. (DAUGHTER *through door left; comes back with braided velvet jacket. He puts it on.*) My slippers. (*The other* DAUGHTER *brings them.*) My smoking cap. (DAUGHTER *comes with embroidered cap.*) My pipe.

42

MOTHER: You shouldn't smoke, if you've been—

WIFE: (*silences her quickly.*) Shall I bring you a light?

CASHIER: (*dressed in indoor clothes: makes himself comfortable at the table.*) Light her up!

WIFE: (*flutters round him solicitously for a while.*) Is it drawing?

CASHIER: (*busy with pipe.*) I shall have to send it away for a thorough clean. There are probably accumulations of unused tobacco fragments in the stem. I have noticed some kind of blockage. I have to suck harder than should be necessary.

WIFE: Shall I remove it right away?

CASHIER: No, stay where you are! (*Puffing out mighty clouds of smoke.*) It'll do. (*To* SECOND DAUGHTER.) Play.

(SECOND DAUGHTER *obeys sign from* MOTHER, *sits at piano and plays.*)

CASHIER: What piece is that?

SECOND DAUGHTER: (*breathless.*) Wagner.

CASHIER: (*nods approval. To* FIRST DAUGHTER.) Are you sewing, mending, darning?

FIRST DAUGHTER: (*sitting down rapidly.*) I'm doing the scalloping now.

CASHIER: Practical.—And you, mama?

MOTHER: (*infected by the general unease.*) I was just having forty winks.

CASHIER: Peaceful.

MOTHER: Yes, my life has become peaceful.

CASHIER: (*to* WIFE.) And you?

WIFE: I'm going to fry the chops.

CASHIER: (*nods.*) The kitchen.

WIFE: I'll fry yours now.

CASHIER: (*as before.*) The kitchen.

(WIFE *exits.*)

CASHIER: (*to* FIRST DAUGHTER.) Open the doors wide.

(FIRST DAUGHTER *pushes the doors at the back open: right, the* WIFE *busy at the stove in the kitchen; left, the bedroom with the twin beds.*)

WIFE: (*at the door.*) Do you feel hot? (*Back to the stove.*)

CASHIER: (*looking round.*) Dear old grandmother at the window. Daughters at the table, embroidering, playing Wagner. Wife busy in the kitchen. Family life–within four walls. The cosy comfort of togetherness. Mother–son–child all assembled. Familiar magic weaves its spell. The parlour with its table and hanging lamp. Piano on the right. The tiled stove. The kitchen –daily bread. Morning coffee, midday chops. Bedroom:–beds, in--out. Familiar magic. In the end–you're flat on your back–stiff and white. The table pushed against the wall there–a yellow coffin laid across it, removable mountings–some crêpe round the lamp–and the piano isn't played for a year—

(SECOND DAUGHTER *stops playing and runs sobbing into the kitchen.*)

WIFE: (*at the door, trembling.*) She is still practising her new piece.

MOTHER: Why doesn't she get out the music for 'In a Monastery Garden'?

(CASHIER *lets pipe go out. Begins to change his clothes.*)

WIFE: Are you going to the bank? Have you got to go somewhere on business?

CASHIER: To the bank–business–no.

WIFE: Where do you mean to go, then?

CASHIER: That's a difficult question, my dear. I have clambered down from wind-swept trees to find an answer. I looked in here first. That was only natural. Everything is absolutely wonderful–I do not dispute its undoubted advantages, but it does not survive the supreme test. The solution does not lie here–so I know what I have to do. The answer here is negative. (*He is fully dressed now as before.*)

WIFE: (*shattered.*) Husband, how wild you look!

CASHIER: A tramp. I told you so. Don't scold! Better a ragged wanderer on the street–than a street with no wanderers on it at all!

WIFE: But we're just going to have lunch.

CASHIER: Chops; I smell them.

MOTHER: You don't mean you're going out–before lunch–?
CASHIER: A full stomach makes a man sleepy.

(MOTHER *flails around with her arms, falls backwards.*)

FIRST DAUGHTER: Grandmama–
SECOND DAUGHTER: (*from the kitchen.*) Grandmama. (*Both fall on their knees beside her.*)

(WIFE *stands rigid.*)

CASHIER: (*walks over to arm-chair.*) Because a man leaves before lunch, she drops dead. (*He looks at the dead woman.*) Grief? Mourning? Floods of tears, sweeping all before. Are the bonds so close that when they snap fulfilment is found in intensest grief? Mother–son? (*He pulls the banknotes from his pocket and weighs them in his hand–shakes his head and pockets them again.*) No total paralysis in grief–no fulfilment so absolute that it streams from the eyes. Eyes dry–thoughts work on. I must hurry if I want to break through to valid truths! (*He puts his worn wallet on the table.*) Take note. These are my honourably earned wages. The remark may become important. Take note. (*Goes off right.*)

(WIFE *stands motionless.*)

BANK MANAGER: (*enters through door right.*) Is your husband home?–Has your husband been here?–I have to make a rather distressing announcement. He has absconded with the bank's money. We discovered his defection some hours ago. There's a matter of some sixty thousand deposited by the Building Society. I have refrained from reporting him to the police in the hope that he might think better of it. This is the most I can do. I came personally.–Your husband has not been here? (*He looks around, notices jacket, pipe, etc., all doors open.*) To all appearances–(*His eyes stop at the group by the window, nods.*) I see things have already reached an advanced stage. Well, in that case–(*He shrugs his shoulders, puts his hat on.*) There only remains the honest expression of my personal regret, of which I desire to assure you–apart from that, the consequences. (*Exit.*)

45

BOTH DAUGHTERS : (*crowd round* WIFE.) Mother–
WIFE : (*exploding.*) Stop screeching. Stop gaping at me. What do you want? Who are you? Brats–monkey-faces–what do I care about you? (*Flings herself across the table.*) My husband has left me.

(BOTH DAUGHTERS *shyly holding hands.*)

Sports Palace. Six-day cycle Race. Arc light. In the haze roughly carpentered suspended wooden ramp. The JEWISH GENTLEMEN *acting as* STEWARDS *come and go. They are all indistinguishable; little scurrying figures, in dinner jackets, dumpy top hats tilted back, binoculars on leather straps round neck. Rumbling roar of wheels over boards. Whistles, shouts, cat-calls from packed public above and below. Bands playing.*

A GENTLEMAN : (*entering.*) Is everything ready?
A GENTLEMAN : See for yourself.
A GENTLEMAN : (*through binoculars.*) The potted plants–
A GENTLEMAN : What's up with the potted plants?
A GENTLEMAN : I thought as much.
A GENTLEMAN : Well, what's the matter with the potted plants?
A GENTLEMAN : Who arranged them like that?
A GENTLEMAN : You're right.
A GENTLEMAN : Why, it's crazy.
A GENTLEMAN : Did nobody bother about how they were arranged?
A GENTLEMAN : Simply ridiculous.
A GENTLEMAN : Whoever did it must be blind.
A GENTLEMAN : Or asleep.
A GENTLEMAN : That's the only acceptable explanation.
A GENTLEMAN : What do you mean–asleep? This is only the fourth night.
A GENTLEMAN : The pots must be moved more to the side.
A GENTLEMAN : Will you see to it?
A GENTLEMAN : Right against the walls.

A GENTLEMAN: There must be a clear view of the whole track.
A GENTLEMAN: And the Royal Box.
A GENTLEMAN: I'll help you. (*All exit.*)

(A GENTLEMAN *comes in, fires a starting pistol. Exit.*)

(TWO GENTLEMEN *enter with red lacquered megaphone.*)

FIRST GENTLEMAN: How big is the prize?
SECOND GENTLEMAN: Eighty. Fifty to the first. Thirty to the second.
FIRST GENTLEMAN: Three laps. No more. We're exhausting the competitors.
OTHER GENTLEMAN: (*announces through megaphone.*) A prize of £80 is offered from the bar–to be competed for immediately, over three laps:£50 to the winner, £30 for the runner-up. (*Clapping.*)

(SEVERAL GENTLEMEN *enter, one with a red flag.*)

ONE GENTLEMAN: Start them off now.
ANOTHER GENTLEMAN: Not yet–Number seven is changing over.
A GENTLEMAN: Start.

(A GENTLEMAN *lowers the red flag. Noise reaches a crescendo. Then clapping and whistling.*)

A GENTLEMAN: The little fellows have to win sometimes.
A GENTLEMAN: It's a good thing the big boys are holding back.
A GENTLEMAN: There's still a lot of work ahead of them tonight.
A GENTLEMAN: The tension among the riders is tremendous.
A GENTLEMAN: I can imagine.
A GENTLEMAN: You wait and see. Tonight will be decisive.
A GENTLEMAN: (*shrugging his shoulders.*) The Americans are still fresh.
A GENTLEMAN: Our lads will make them show what they are made of.
A GENTLEMAN: Anyway, it would make the Royal Visit worth while.
A GENTLEMAN: (*looking through binoculars.*) The Royal Box is clear now. (*All GENTLEMEN exit except one with megaphone.*)

A GENTLEMAN: (*with a ticket.*) The result.

A GENTLEMAN: (*through megaphone.*) Prize from the bar. Fifty for number eleven, thirty for number four.

(*Victory fanfare from Band. Whistles and clapping. The stewards' ramp is empty. ONE GENTLEMAN enters with CASHIER. CASHIER in tails, evening cloak, top-hat, white gloves, pointed beard; hair carefully parted.*)

CASHIER: Tell me how this works.

GENTLEMAN: I'll introduce you.

CASHIER: My name is not important.

GENTLEMAN: You have the right to be introduced to the Board.

CASHIER: I'll remain incognito.

GENTLEMAN: You are a lover of our sport?

CASHIER: I have not the slightest idea what it's all about. What are these fellows down there doing? I see an arena and the line of colour snaking round it. Every so often one comes in and another falls out. Why?

GENTLEMAN: The riders race in pairs. While one is in–

CASHIER: The other chap is out having a good sleep?

GENTLEMAN: Being massaged.

CASHIER: And you call that a six-day cycle race?

GENTLEMAN: What do you mean?

CASHIER: You might just as well call it a six-day cycle rest. There's always one partner asleep.

A GENTLEMAN: (*enters.*) The ramp is reserved for the management.

FIRST GENTLEMAN: This gentleman offers a prize sum of one thousand pounds.

OTHER GENTLEMAN: Allow me to introduce myself.

CASHIER: On no account.

FIRST GENTLEMAN: The gentleman wishes to remain incognito.

CASHIER: Impenetrably.

FIRST GENTLEMAN: I have just been explaining some of the rules to him.

CASHIER: Yes. Don't you find it funny?

SECOND GENTLEMAN: In what way?

CASHIER: This six-day cycle rest.

SECOND GENTLEMAN: So one thousand pounds it is–over how many laps?

CASHIER: You decide.

SECOND GENTLEMAN: How much for the winner?

CASHIER: You decide.

SECOND GENTLEMAN: Eight hundred pounds and two hundred pounds. (*Through megaphone.*) Prize awarded by a gentleman who wishes to remain anonymous, over ten laps, to be run off immediately: eight hundred pounds for the winner–two hundred pounds for the runner-up. One thousand pounds in all. (*Mighty roar.*)

FIRST GENTLEMAN: Then tell me, if you regard the whole show as a mere joke, why do you award one thousand pounds in prizes?

CASHIER: Because the effect is marvellous.

FIRST GENTLEMAN: On the speed of the riders?

CASHIER: Rubbish.

A GENTLEMAN: (*coming in.*) Are you the gentleman who is putting up the thousand?

CASHIER: In gold.

GENTLEMAN: That would take too long.

CASHIER: What, to count? Watch me. (*Takes a roll out, tears it open, shakes the contents into his hand, checks the empty packet, throws it away and quickly counts the clinking gold coins into his cupped hand.*) Besides, it takes the weight off my pockets.

GENTLEMAN: Sir, I see you are an expert in these matters.

CASHIER: A mere trifle, sir. (*He hands over the sum.*) Take it.

GENTLEMAN: Received with thanks.

CASHIER: All part of the service.

A GENTLEMAN: (*enters.*) Where is the gentleman? Allow me–

CASHIER: Nothing.

A GENTLEMAN: (*with the red flag.*) I'll signal for the start.

A GENTLEMAN: This time the big stars will go flat out.

A GENTLEMAN: All the champions are in the race.

A GENTLEMAN: (*waving the flag.*) Start. (*Drops the flag. Wild howl starts up.*)

CASHIER: (*seizing two GENTLEMEN by the neck and bending*

their heads round backwards.) Now I shall answer your question. Look up!

A GENTLEMAN: What you have to follow are the changing phases of the struggle down below on the track.

CASHIER: Childish. Somebody has to be first, because he's better than the others.—The magic is revealed up there. In three tiers —one above the other—packed full with spectators there—the excitement rages. In the first tier—apparently the better class public still shows some restraint. Just stares, wide-eyed stares. One row higher you already have bodies beginning to move. And shout—that's the centre balcony!—Right up in the Gods all restraints are dropped. Fanatical screams. Total abandon. The gallery for passion!—Just look at that group. Five entwined as one. Five heads on one shoulder. One demented body sprouting five pairs of arms. One man is in the centre. He is being crushed—squeezed forward—there, see his bowler tumbling down —idly drifting down through the haze—to the centre balcony. On to a lady's bosom. She is unaware of it. There it rests. Delightful! Delightful! She'll never notice the hat, she'll go to bed with it, and wear the bowler on her bosom, year in, year out.

GENTLEMAN: The Belgian is putting his spurt on.

CASHIER: The centre balcony is starting to scream. The hat has made the connection. The lady has crushed it against the rail. Great weals appear on her bosom. Lovely lady, you have to go to the rail, and have your bosom branded. It is inevitable: it is senseless to struggle. Caught up in that tangled mass of humanity you are pressed to the wall and must reveal what you are. Give yourself, your all—without a whimper!

GENTLEMAN: You know the lady?

CASHIER: Now look: up top the five are squeezing the man in the middle over the railing—he swings free plunges—there—sails down into the first row. Where is he? Choking to death somewhere? Eliminated—buried without trace. Nobody cares. A spectator—someone who dropped in—a chance visitor, no more among thousands and thousands!

A GENTLEMAN: The German is moving up.

CASHIER: The first rows are frantic now. That fellow has made the contact. Restraint has gone by the board. Dinner-jackets quiver. Shirt fronts split. Studs pop in all directions. Beards twitch, lips snarl, dentures rattle. Top and bottom and the middle rows are one. One single howl from all levels–without distinction. All distinctions are lost. That much has been accomplished.

GENTLEMAN: (*turning round.*) The German has it. What have you got to say to that?

CASHIER: Utter rubbish.

(*Tremendous din. Clapping.*)

A GENTLEMAN: A fabulous spurt.

CASHIER: Fabulous fiddlesticks.

A GENTLEMAN: We'll get the office to check the result. (*All exeunt.*)

CASHIER: (*holding on to this* GENTLEMAN.) Have you still any doubts?

GENTLEMAN: The Germans are bound to win.

CASHIER: That's unimportant. (*Pointing upwards.*) That's where it is, there you have the compelling fact. There you have the ultimate compression of reality. Here we witness the dizzy, soaring heights of accomplishment. From the first rows right up to the Gods, fusion. Out of the seething dissolution of the individual comes the concentrated essence. Passion! All restraints–all differences melt away. Concealing coverings stripped off nakedness. Passion!–To break through here is to experience. Doors–gates fade away. Trumpets blare and walls crumble. No resisting–no modesty–no mothering–no childhood: nothing but pure passion! This is it. This is it. This is really worth while. This is worth the grab–that's your reward brought to you on a platter!

A GENTLEMAN: (*coming in.*) The Ambulance Squad is working magnificently.

CASHIER: The man who fell was ground to pulp?

A GENTLEMAN: Trampled to death.

CASHIER: There are bound to be deaths, where others live feverishly.

A GENTLEMAN: (*through megaphone.*) Result of the prize

51

awarded by the gentleman wishing to remain anonymous: eight hundred pounds won by Number Two; two hundred pounds by Number One.

(*Mad applause. Fanfare.*)

A GENTLEMAN: The teams are exhausted.

A GENTLEMAN: The tempo is visibly slackening.

A GENTLEMAN: We must get their managers to keep things quiet on the track.

CASHIER: A new prize!

A GENTLEMAN: Later, sir.

CASHIER: There must be no let-up in this situation.

A GENTLEMAN: The situation is getting dangerous for the riders.

CASHIER: Never mind about them. The public is bubbling with excitement. This must be exploited to the full. The conflagration must reach heights never before experienced. Fifty thousand pounds.

A GENTLEMAN: You mean it?

A GENTLEMAN: How much?

CASHIER: I'm wagering everything on it.

A GENTLEMAN: An incredible prize.

CASHIER: And the effect must be incredible too. Alert the Ambulance Squads on all levels.

A GENTLEMAN: We accept the offer. We'll have it contested when the Royal Box is occupied.

A GENTLEMAN: Splendid.

A GENTLEMAN: Great idea.

A GENTLEMAN: The Royal Visit will undoubtedly be worth while now.

CASHIER: What does that mean: with the Royal Box occupied?

A GENTLEMAN: We'll discuss the conditions in the office. Thirty thousand the winner; fifteen thousand second; five thousand third.

A GENTLEMAN: The field will be blown sky-high tonight.

A GENTLEMAN: This will pretty well finish the racing.

A GENTLEMAN: Anyway, the Royal Box will be occupied.

(SALVATION ARMY GIRL *appears. Laughter from spectators Whistles. Cat-calls.*)

SALVATION ARMY GIRL: (offering.) The War Cry–a shilling, sir.

CASHIER: Another time.

SALVATION ARMY GIRL: The War Cry, sir.

CASHIER: What kind of rag are you hawking there?

SALVATION ARMY GIRL: The War Cry, sir.

CASHIER: You come too late. The battle is in full swing here.

SALVATION ARMY GIRL: (with the collecting box.) A shilling, sir.

CASHIER: You want to launch a war with a shilling?

SALVATION ARMY GIRL: A shilling, sir.

CASHIER: I'm subsidizing this war to the tune of fifty thousand.

SALVATION ARMY GIRL: A shilling.

CASHIER: For a wretched little skirmish. I only subsidize top performances.

SALVATION ARMY GIRL: A shilling.

CASHIER: I only carry gold.

SALVATION ARMY GIRL: A shilling.

CASHIER: Gold–

SALVATION ARMY GIRL: A–

CASHIER: (roars at her through the megaphone.) Gold–gold –gold!

(SALVATION ARMY GIRL exit.)

(Neighing laughter from the spectators. Clapping. Many GENTLEMEN enter.)

A GENTLEMAN: Would you care to announce the prize yourself?

CASHIER: I'll remain vaguely in the background. (He gives him the megaphone.) You announce it now. Give them the final convulsion!

A GENTLEMAN: (through megaphone.) A new prize offered by the same gentleman who wishes to remain anonymous. (Cries of 'Bravo!') Total sum of fifty thousand (deafening screams)– five thousand to the third–(screaming)–fifteen thousand to the second–(screaming reaches crescendo) to the winner thirty thousand–(ecstasy.)

CASHIER: (stands apart, nodding.) This'll be it. This is the climax. Fulfilment. The howling gale of a spring hurricane.

Surging wave of humanity. Unleashed–free. Curtains raised–pretences lowered. Humanity. Free humanity. High or low–just man. No different levels, no social strata–no classes. Release from class and wage-slavery in passion sweeping to infinity. Not pure, but free! That will be the reward for my boldness. (*He pulls the bundle of notes out.*) Given gladly–account settled without hesitation.

(*Sudden dead silence. National Anthem. The* GENTLEMEN *have taken off their silk hats and stand with bowed heads.*)

A GENTLEMAN: If you'll hand me the money, we can have the race for your prize immediately.

CASHIER: What is the meaning of this?

GENTLEMAN: What, sir?

CASHIER: This sudden unexpected silence above and below?

GENTLEMAN: Not at all unexpected. His Royal Highness has entered the Royal Box.

CASHIER: His Royal Highness–the box.—

GENTLEMAN: Your considerable prize comes at a most opportune time.

CASHIER: I've no intention of throwing my money away!

GENTLEMAN: What do you mean?

CASHIER: It's too high a price to pay to subsidize grovelling lick-spittles.

GENTLEMAN: Would you be kind enough to explain.

CASHIER: The flame that was raging just a moment ago has been stamped out by His Highness's patent leather boot. You must be mad, to think I'm crazy enough to throw sixpence to these dogs. Even that would be too much. A boot where the dog takes its tail between its legs, that's the prize offered!

GENTLEMAN: The prize is announced. His Royal Highness awaits in his box. The public too is waiting, quietly and respectfully. What does this mean?

CASHIER: If you cannot grasp the meaning of my words–then you cannot fail to gain the necessary insight, if I administer an unequivocal indication of my feelings. (*He bashes the* GENTLEMAN'S *silk hat over his head onto his shoulders. Exit.*)

(National Anthem again. Silence. People on ramp bow.)

Night Club. Chambre séparée. Still dark. Muted dance rhythms from orchestra.

(WAITER opens the door, turns red light on.)

(CASHIER tails, cloak, scarf, gold-headed malacca cane.)

WAITER: All right?

CASHIER: Perfectly.

(WAITER takes cloak.)

(CASHIER at the mirror.)

WAITER: How many places, sir?

CASHIER: Twenty-four. I'm expecting my grandmother, my mother, my wife and various aunts. I'm celebrating my daughter's confirmation.

(WAITER amazed.)

CASHIER: *(to him in the mirror.)* Ass! Two! Or what do you pad these discretely lit alcoves for?

WAITER: Which brand do you prefer, sir?

CASHIER: You greasy fixer. My good friend, you can leave me to decide which bloom I'll pluck off the dance floor—bud or full-blown flower—short or slim. I shall not over-extend your inestimable services. Inestimable—or have you fixed rates?

WAITER: Which brand of champagne, sir?

CASHIER: *(clears throat.)* Er, Grand Marnier.

WAITER: That is a liqueur for after the champagne.

CASHIER: Oh—then I shall let myself be guided by you.

WAITER: Two bottles of Pommery. Dry?

CASHIER: Of course I'm dry.

WAITER: Extra dry?

CASHIER: None of your business, but I am; better make it three bottles. O.K.

WAITER: *(with the menu.)* And for dinner.

CASHIER: Pinnacles!

WAITER: Oeufs pochés Bergère? Poulet grillé? Steak de veau truffé? Parfait de foie gras en croûte? Salade coeur de laitue?

CASHIER: Pinnacles–from start to finish, nothing but pinnacles.

WAITER: Beg your pardon, sir?

CASHIER: (*tapping him on the nose.*) Pinnacles are ultimate peaks of perfection. And that's what we must have from your pots and pans. The most delicate of delicacies. The menu of menus. As garnish for great events. That's your affair, my friend, I am not the cook.

WAITER: (*lays a larger menu-card on the table.*) Ready to serve in twenty minutes. (*Arranges glasses etc.*)

(*Through the half-open door heads with silk masks appear.*)

CASHIER: (*talking into the mirror, with threatening finger.*) Wait, my little moths, I'll hold you up to the light directly. We'll discuss that when we have a seat together. (*He nods.*)

(*Giggling masks disappear.*)

(WAITER *hangs a 'Reserved' sign on the door. Exits.*)

CASHIER: (*pushes his top-hat back, takes cigarettes out of gold case and lights up.*) To-re-ador, To-re-ador–the things one comes out with! The mind is simply loaded. Everything, just everything. Toreador–Carmen–Caruso. Read the junk somewhere–it stuck. Stored up. At this very moment I could give an account of the Baghdad Railway deal. The Crown Prince of Roumania marries the Czar's second daughter. Tatiana. Right, let her marry. Happy honeymoon. The people need princes. Tat- Tat- iana– (*Exits, twirling cane.*)

(WAITER *with bottles and ice-bucket: uncorks and pours. Exits.*)

CASHIER: (*shooing in a female mask–red and yellow chequered harlequin costume fitting boyishly from top to toe and open at the bosom.*) Moth!

MASK: (*running round the table.*) Bubbly! (*Pours both glasses of champagne down her throat, falls into the sofa.*) Bubbly!

CASHIER (*refilling.*) Liquid dynamite. Load your chequered body.

MASK: Bubbly!

CASHIER: Action stations, ready to fire!

MASK: Bubbly!

CASHIER: (*putting away the bottles.*) Empty. (*Joins* MASK *on sofa.*) Ready to fire.

(MASK *leans over drunkenly.*)

CASHIER: (*shakes her limp arms.*) Wake up, Moth.

(MASK *limp.*)

CASHIER: Give yourself a shake, pretty butterfly. You have licked the prickly yellow honey. Open your butterfly wings. Descend on me. Bury me, cover me up. In certain respects I have fallen out with the world of decent security–now you fall out and cover me with your body.

MASK: (*drunkenly.*) Bubbly.

CASHIER: No, my bird of paradise. You have taken on a sufficient load. You've had enough.

MASK: Bubbly.

CASHIER: Not another bubble. Or you'll get hazy. And do me out of all your glorious possibilities.

MASK: Bubbly.

CASHIER: Or haven't you any? Any at all? Look–if I take deep soundings: what have you got?

MASK: Bubbly.

CASHIER: You've certainly got that. I gave it to you. But what can you give me?

(MASK *falls asleep.*)

CASHIER: You want to sleep it off here? Little devil. I haven't the time for jokes of that kind. (*Stands up, fills a glass, throws it in her face.*) Rise and shine. Wakey! Wakey!

MASK: (*leaps up.*) Swine!

CASHIER: You have an unusual name. Unfortunately I am not in a position to reciprocate and give you my name. Well then, now we know you belong to one of the many branches of the pig family, clear out.

MASK: I'll make you pay for this.

CASHIER: More than reasonable, considering I've paid for everything so far.

(MASK *exits*.)

(CASHIER *drinks champagne*. Exits.)

(WAITER *enters, brings caviar; takes empty bottles away*.)

(CASHIER *enters with two black Masks*.)

FIRST MASK: (*flinging the door shut*.) Reserved.
SECOND MASK: (*at the table*.) Caviar.
FIRST MASK: (*running up*.) Caviar.
CASHIER: Black like you. Eat it up. Stuff it down your throats. (*Seating himself between the two on the sofa*.) Talk Caviar. Sing Champagne. I can do without your brains. (*Fills the glasses, heaps the plates*.) You're not to speak. Not a syllable, not an exclamation. Silent as the fish, which spawned this black caviar over the Black Sea. Giggle, carry on, but don't talk. 'Cause nothing comes out of it anyway. At most you might have to get out of the sofa. I've cleared it once already.

(MASKS *look at each other giggling*.)

CASHIER: (*grabbing the first one*.) What colour are your eyes? Green–yellow? (*To the other*.) And yours? Blue–red? Charming game of eyeballs in the slits. Very promising. Must find out. I'll offer a prize for the prettiest!

(MASKS *laugh*.)

CASHIER: (*to the first*.) You are the more beautiful. You put up powerful resistance. Wait, I'll tear down the curtain and see the show!

(MASK *breaks away*.)

CASHIER: (*to the other*.) Do you have to conceal your identity? Your modesty is overwhelmingly attractive. You wandered into this dance hall by mistake. You are seeking adventure. Well, you have found the adventurer you were seeking. Off with your mask–let me see the peaches-and-cream complexion.

58

(MASK *moves away from him.*)

CASHIER: I've reached my goal. I sit trembling–my blood is pounding. This is it!–And now pay. (*Brings out wad of notes and splits it.*) Lovely mask, because you are lovely. Lovely mask, because you are lovely. (*Covering his eyes with his hands.*) One–two–three!

(MASKS *raise their masks.*)

CASHIER: (*looks, laughs.*) Cover up–cover up–cover up! (*Runs round the table.*) Horrors–horrors–horrors! Get out right now –I mean now–or–(*swings his cane.*)
FIRST MASK: Do you want us?
SECOND MASK: You want us–
CASHIER: I'll want you!!

(MASKS *off.*)

CASHIER: (*shuddering, drinks champagne.*) You hags! (*Exits.*)

(WAITER *with new bottles. Exits.*)

CASHIER: (*pushes the door open: dances in with a pierrette, whose cloak reaches down to her shoes. He leaves her standing in the middle of the floor and flings himself on the sofa.*) Dance!

(MASK *stands still.*)

CASHIER: Dance, spin. Dance, dance. Brains don't count. Beauty doesn't count. The dance is the thing–twisting–spinning. Dance! Dance! Dance!

(MASK *comes to the table.*)

CASHIER: (*waving her away.*) No pause. No let-up. Dance.

(MASK *stands still.*)

CASHIER: Why don't you skip? Do you know what dervishes are? Dancing-men. Alive while they dance. Dead when they stop. Death and dancing–erected at the turning-points of life. Between–

(*The* SALVATION ARMY GIRL *comes in.*)

CASHIER: Hallelujah!
SALVATION ARMY GIRL: The War Cry.
CASHIER: A shilling.

(*The* SALVATION ARMY GIRL *offers box.*)

CASHIER: When do you expect me to jump into your box?
SALVATION ARMY GIRL: The War Cry.
CASHIER: You really expect me to, don't you?
SALVATION ARMY GIRL: A shilling.
CASHIER: All right—when?
SALVATION ARMY GIRL: A shilling.
CASHIER: You're hanging on to my coat-tails, aren't you?

(SALVATION ARMY GIRL *shakes the box.*)

CASHIER: And I'll shake you off again!

(SALVATION ARMY GIRL *shakes.*)

CASHIER: All right! (*To* MASK.) Dance!

(SALVATION ARMY GIRL *off.*)

(MASK *comes to the sofa.*)

CASHIER: Why do you sit in the corners of the rooms, why
don't you dance in the middle of the floor? That's what drew
my attention to you. The others are all leaping about and you
stay still. Why do you wear long skirts, when all the others
show as much of their legs as school-boys?
MASK: I don't dance.
CASHIER: You don't dance like the others.
MASK: I cannot dance.
CASHIER: Not to the music—following the rhythm. That's stupid
anyway. You know other dances. You conceal something
beneath your skirts.— Your special kicks, not to be confined
within the structures of rhythms and steps. Whirling movements of far greater tempo, that's what you go in for. (*Pushing
everything off the table onto the carpet.*) There is your dance-
floor. Jump up. Boundless tumult within the narrow confines

of this table. Jump up. Leap from the carpet. Effortless. Soaring off the springs which lie coiled in your feet. Leap. Prick your heels. Arch your thighs. Let your dress swirl round your dancing limbs!

MASK: (*nestling up to him on the sofa.*) I cannot dance.

CASHIER: You are whipping me up to a state of high tension. You don't know what's at stake. You shall know. (*He shows her the notes.*) Everything!

MASK: (*slides his hand down her leg.*) I can't.

CASHIER: (*leaps up.*) A wooden leg! (*He grabs the ice-bucket and rams it on her head.*) We'll make it sprout. I'll water it!

MASK: I'll teach you—

CASHIER: Exactly what I'm here for.

MASK: Wait here. (*Exit.*)

(CASHIER *leaves a note on the table, takes cloak and stick, hurries off.* GENTLEMEN *in evening dress enter.*)

A GENTLEMAN: Where is the fellow?

A GENTLEMAN: We'll give him what for.

A GENTLEMAN: Stealing our girls—

A GENTLEMAN: Showing off with champagne and caviar—

A GENTLEMAN: Then insulting them—

A GENTLEMAN: We'll give the fellow a piece of our mind.

A GENTLEMAN: Where is he?

A GENTLEMAN: Cleared out!

A GENTLEMAN: Taken off!

A GENTLEMAN: The Gentleman smelled trouble.

A GENTLEMAN: (*discovering the note.*) Look at the size of this note!

A GENTLEMAN: Wow!

A GENTLEMAN: He's sure got some nerve.

A GENTLEMAN: Is that to pay the bill?

A GENTLEMAN: Who cares? He's done a disappearing trick. We'll make the note disappear too. (*Puts it in his pocket.*)

A GENTLEMAN: That'll be our compensation.

A GENTLEMAN: For stealing our girls.

A GENTLEMAN: Let's dump the tarts.

A GENTLEMAN: They're sozzled anyway.

A GENTLEMAN: They'll only soil our evening suits.

A GENTLEMAN: We'll go to a brothel and rent the place for three days.

ALL: Bravo! Let's go. Let's blow. Look out, here comes the waiter.

(WAITER with loaded tray; dismayed at the sight of the table.)

A GENTLEMAN: Looking for somebody?

A GENTLEMAN: Carry on serving him under the table. (Laughter.)

WAITER: (bursting out.) The champagne–the supper–the private room–nothing paid for. Five bottles of Pommery–two helpings of caviar–two special suppers–I have to cover the lot. I have a wife and children. I've been out of work for four months. I had contracted a weak lung. You won't see me ruined, gentlemen?

A GENTLEMAN: What's your lung got to do with us? We've all got a wife and family. What do you want of us? Did we slip off without paying? What are you talking about?

A GENTLEMAN: What sort of place is this anyway? Where exactly are we, here? This is a low clip-joint, for sure. You entice people into such company? We are respectable people, we pay for what we drink. Eh What? Eh?

A GENTLEMAN: (who has changed the door-key from inside to outside.) Look behind you. This is how we pay. (Gives the WAITER, who has turned round, a push in the back.)

(WAITER staggers forward, collapses on the carpet.)

(GENTLEMEN exeunt.)

WAITER: (gets up, runs to the door, finds it locked. Hammering the wood with his fists.) Let me out–you don't have to pay– I'm going to throw myself into the river.

Salvation Army Hall–seen in depth. Backed by yellow curtain with black Cross sewn on, big enough to take a man. On the platform right, Penitents' Bench–on left the brass band instruments, kettle drums, etc. Closely packed rows of benches. Hanging light bracket over everything with tangle of wires for electric light bulbs.

Entrance front. Music of Salvation Army Band. From one corner, clapping and laughter.

SALVATION ARMY GIRL *goes over and sits down beside the trouble-maker—a clerk—takes his hands and talks to him in an earnest whisper.*

VOICE : *(from the other corner.)* Closer, closer.

(SALVATION ARMY GIRL *goes to this fellow, a young* WORK-MAN.)

WORKMAN : Well, what do you want?

(SALVATION ARMY GIRL *looks at him solemnly, shaking her head. Laughter.*)

SALVATION ARMY OFFICER : *(a woman, appears on platform.)* I've a question I want to put to you.

(Some 'SSSh' for silence.)

OTHERS : *(amused.)* Speak louder. No, don't. Music. Bring on the band. Bring on the cherubs with trumpets.

VOICE : Begin.

ANOTHER VOICE : No, don't.

OFFICER : Why are you sitting down there on these benches?

ANOTHER VOICE : Why not?

SALVATION ARMY OFFICER : You've filled every single place. You're packed in, each one hard up against the next. And yet there is one bench empty.

VOICE : Nothing doing.

SALVATION ARMY OFFICER : Why do you stay down there, where you have to press and crush? Isn't it unpleasant, to sit in a crowd? Who knows his neighbour? You rub knees with him and maybe he is sick. You look into his eyes—and maybe murderous thoughts lurk behind them. I know there are many sick and sinful people in this room. The sick and the sinful come in and sit down with everybody else. Therefore I warn you ! Beware of the man sitting beside you on these benches. These benches are full of the sick and sinful.

VOICE: Oh, Mum, she's getting at me.

SALVATION ARMY OFFICER: I know it and so I advise you: steer clear of your neighbour. That is the advice we are given. Sickness and crime are so widespread in this asphalt jungle. Who is there among you who is not festering? Your skin can be white and smooth, but your eyes proclaim you. You have eyes, but not to see with–your eyes are open, only to betray you. You betray yourselves. You are no longer free of the great plague: the risk of infection is great. You have been keeping bad company too long. So if you do not wish to be like your neighbour in this asphalt jungle, step forward from these benches. This is the last warning. Repent! Repent! Come up, come up to the stool of repentance. Come to the stool of repentance. Come to the stool of repentance.

(*Salvation Army band starts up.*)

(SALVATION ARMY GIRL *brings in the* CASHIER.)

(CASHIER *excites some attention in his tails.*)

(SALVATION ARMY GIRL *shows him to a seat, sits beside him and explains things to him.*)

(CASHIER *looks round in amusement.*)

(*Bands stops. Ironical applause, loud and long.*)

SALVATION ARMY OFFICER: (*stepping forward on the platform again.*) Let our young comrade tell you how he found the path to repentance.

(YOUNG SALVATION ARMY MAN *steps forward onto the platform.*)

VOICE: You look just the type. (*Laughter.*)

YOUNG SALVATION ARMY MAN: I want to tell you of my sin. I led a life with no thought for my soul. I lived only for my body. I set it up in front of my soul, if you like, and made my body stronger and bigger. My soul was completely absorbed by it. I sought fame through my body and failed to see that this only magnified the shadow under which my soul was languishing. My besetting sin was sport. I practised and practised, never stopping to consider what I was doing or why. I was conceited about the speed of my feet on the pedals, the strength of my arms on the handlebars. When applause engulfed me I forgot everything. I redoubled my efforts and became the national sporting champion. My name was on every hoarding, every bill-board and on millions of coloured hand-outs. Then I became world champion. At last my soul cried out in protest. It lost patience. In one big race I fell. I was only slightly injured. My soul wanted me to have time for repentance. My soul gave me the strength to find a way out. I stepped forward from the benches in this room—up to the stool of repentance. Only then did my soul have peace to speak to me. And what it tells me I cannot tell you here. It is too beautiful and my words are too weak to give you a picture of it. You must come forward yourselves, and hear it within yourselves. (*He steps aside.*)

(VOICE *dirty laugh.*)

(OTHERS *shush for silence.*)

SALVATION ARMY GIRL: (*to* CASHIER.) Do you hear him?
CASHIER: Leave me alone.
SALVATION ARMY OFFICER: You have heard the testimony of our comrade. Doesn't it sound tempting? Can anyone gain anything more lovely than his soul? And it's so easy, because it is there inside all of you. You only have to give it peace. It just wants to sit quietly beside you. This bench is its favourite seat. There must be somebody among you who has sinned like our comrade. Our comrade wants to help him. He has prepared the way for him. Come now. Come to the stool of repentance. Come to the stool of repentance. Come to the stool of repentance. (*Silence reigns.*)

(*One powerful young man, his arm in a sling, stands up in one corner, crosses the room smiling embarrassedly and climbs up to the platform.*)

(VOICE *utters an obscenity.*)

65

ANOTHER VOICE: (*indignantly.*) Who was the filthy swine who said that?

(*Cause of disturbance stands up and heads for the door in shame.*)

VOICE: That's him.

(SALVATION ARMY GIRL *hurries to him and leads him back to his place.*)

VOICE: Don't handle him so gently.

SEVERAL: Hear, Hear!

PENITENT: (*on the platform, awkward at first.*) This city of asphalt has erected a stadium. I was a rider in that stadium. I am a professional cyclist. In the Six-day Cycle Race. On the second night I was rammed by another cyclist. I broke my arm. I had to scratch from the race. The race rages on—I have peace. I have time to think things out in peace. I have been racing all my life without pause for thought. I want to think everything out—everything. (*Loud.*) I want to think of my sins at the stool of repentance. (*Led there by a soldier, he sinks down on the bench. Soldier stays close beside him.*)

SALVATION ARMY OFFICER: A soul has been saved!

(*Salvation Army band plays. The soldiers scattered round the room have all leapt up and rejoice, arms upstretched. Band stops.*)

SALVATION ARMY GIRL: (*to* CASHIER.) Do you see him?

CASHIER: The Six-day Cycle Race.

SALVATION ARMY GIRL: What are you muttering?

CASHIER: My own story. My own story.

SALVATION ARMY GIRL: Are you ready?

CASHIER: Be quiet, will you?

SALVATION ARMY OFFICER: (*appearing on platform.*) Now this comrade wants to testify. (*Somebody hisses.*)

MANY: (*shout.*) Quiet!

SALVATION ARMY GIRL: (*appearing on platform.*) Whose sin is my sin? I want to tell you about myself without shame. I come from a home in which things were sordid and dissolute.

66

The man–he was not my father–was an alcoholic. My mother consorted with fine gentlemen. She gave me as much money as I wanted. He gave me more beatings than I wanted. (*Laughter.*) Nobody looked after me, least of all did I look after myself. So I became a lost woman. For I didn't know then that the wild state of affairs at home was meant to make me pay all the more attention to my soul–and devote myself entirely to it. I learned that in one night. I had a man with me and he wanted me to put the lights out in my room. I switched the lights out though it was not what I was accustomed to. Later when we were together I understood why he wanted it that way. For I felt only a man's trunk against me, his legs had been amputated. I was not meant to see that before. He had wooden legs, which he had secretly removed. At that point, horror seized me and never let me go. My body I now detested–only my soul could I love. Now I only love my soul. It is so perfect it's the loveliest thing I know. I know too much about my soul to be able to tell you everything. If you ask your soul, it will tell you everything–everything. (*She steps down.*)

(*Silence in the hall.*)

SALVATION ARMY OFFICER: (*coming forward.*) You have heard the testimony of our sister. Her soul offered itself to her. She did not turn it away. Now she can talk of it with joy. Does not anyone among you feel his soul offering itself to him? Let it come to you. Let it. Let it speak and tell all, at this bench it is undisturbed. Come to the stool of repentance. Come to the stool of repentance.

(*Movement among the benches, people look round.*)

PROSTITUTE: (*elderly, right at the front, begins to speak from the floor of the hall.*) What do you think of me, ladies and gentlemen? I only came in here for shelter, because I was tired out walking the streets. I'm not a bit embarrassed. I don't know this place at all. This is my first time. Pure chance brings me here. (*Up on platform now.*) But you're wrong, ladies and gentlemen, if you think I could wait to be asked a second time. Thanks, but that's expecting too much. Well, you can see what I am—come on—look me over good and proper—size me up—use your eyes as much as you like. I'm not degrading myself in any way. I'm not a bit embarrassed. You won't get the chance to enjoy this spectacle more than this once. You'll be bitterly disappointed if you think you can buy my soul off me too. That I've never sold yet. I might have been offered a lot, but my soul was just not for sale. I'm obliged for all the compliments, ladies and gentlemen. You'll never come across me on the streets again. I've not a minute to spare for you lot—my soul gives me no peace. Thanks again, ladies and gents, I'm not a bit embarrassed, not a bit. (*She has taken off her hat. The soldier leads her to the stool of repentance.*)

SALVATION ARMY OFFICER: A soul has been saved!

(*Salvation Army band. Jubilation of the Soldiers.*)

SALVATION ARMY GIRL: (*to* CASHIER.) Do you hear it all?

CASHIER: My story. My story.

SALVATION ARMY GIRL: What are you muttering to yourself?

CASHIER: The wooden leg.

SALVATION ARMY GIRL: Are you ready?

CASHIER: Not yet, not yet.

MAN: (*standing in the middle of the hall.*) What is my sin? I want to hear my sin.

SALVATION ARMY OFFICER: (*appearing on platform.*) Our comrade will tell you.

VARIOUS VOICES: Sit down. Quiet. Let him talk.

ELDERLY SALVATION ARMY MAN: Let me tell you my story. It is an everyday story, no more. That's why it became my sin. I had a pleasant home, a contented family, a comfortable job—mine was just a normal humdrum life. When I sat in the evening at the table under the lamp and puffed away at my pipe, with my family round about me, then I was content. I never wanted my life to change. And yet it did. I don't remember what started it—perhaps I never knew. The soul can make its presence felt without great upheavals. It bides its time and takes its chance. Anyway, I could not ignore its warning. My sloth struggled against it at first, I know, but the soul was mightier. I felt that more and more. The soul alone could procure me lasting contentment. And contentment had been my goal all my life. Now I can find it no more at the table with the lamp and with the long pipe in my mouth. I find it only at the stool of repentance. That's my everyday story. (*He steps aside.*)

SALVATION ARMY OFFICER: (*appearing on platform.*) Our brother has told you—

MAN: (*coming forward ahead.*) My sin! (*On platform.*) I'm the father of a family, I have two daughters. I have a wife. I still have my mother. We all live in three rooms. It is quite cosy at our place. My daughters—one of them plays the piano—one of them does embroidery. My wife cooks. My mother waters the flowers in the window-box. It's really as cosy as can be at our place. The quintessence of cosiness. It is wonderful at our place—splendid—a real model home—so practical—like the ads. —(*Changes.*) It is sickening—horrible—it stinks—it is pathetic, absolutely one-hundred-per-cent pathetic, with the piano playing—the embroidery—the cooking—watering plants—(*Exploding.*) I have a soul! I have a soul! I have a soul! (*He staggers to the stool of repentance.*)

SALVATION ARMY OFFICER: A soul has been saved!

(*Salvation Army band. Great tumult in the hall.*)

MANY: (*standing up after the band finishes, even standing on the benches.*) What is my sin? What is my sin? I want to know my sin! I want to know my sin!

SALVATION ARMY OFFICER: (*appearing on platform.*) Our comrade will tell you.

(*Deep silence.*)

SALVATION ARMY GIRL: Do you see him?

CASHIER: My daughters. My wife. My mother.

SALVATION ARMY GIRL: Why do you keep muttering and whispering?

CASHIER: My own story. My own story.

SALVATION ARMY GIRL: Are you ready?

CASHIER: Not yet. Not yet. Not yet.

MIDDLEAGED SALVATION ARMY MAN: (*stepping forward.*) My soul had no easy victory. It had to seize hold of me and shake me up. In the end it used the strongest possible means. It sent me to prison. I had stolen from the money that was entrusted to me, embezzled a large sum. I was caught and sentenced. There in my cell I had peace. That's what the soul had been waiting for. Now at last it could speak freely to me. And I had to listen to it. The most wonderful time of my life was in that lonely cell. When I came out, I wanted only to commune with my soul alone. So I looked for a quiet place. I found it at the stool of repentance and find it daily, whenever I want to enjoy a glorious hour! (*He steps aside.*)

SALVATION ARMY OFFICER: (*appearing on platform.*) Our comrade has told you of his glorious hours at the stool of repentance. Who is there among you who longs to free himself of this sin? Whose sin is this, from which he escapes here in joyousness? Here is peace for him. Come to the stool of repentance.

ALL: (*in the hall screaming and gesticulating.*) That is nobody's sin here! That is nobody's sin here! I want to hear my sin! ! My sin! ! My sin! ! My sin!

SALVATION ARMY GIRL: (*piercingly.*) What are you shouting?

CASHIER: The bank. The money.

SALVATION ARMY GIRL: (*urgently.*) Are you ready?

CASHIER: Now I am ready.

SALVATION ARMY GIRL: (*taking his arm.*) I'll lead you there. I'll stand by you. I'll always stand by you. (*Ecstatically, into the hall.*) A soul wishes to proclaim itself. I have sought this soul. I have sought this soul. (*Din ebbs. Silence hums.*)

CASHIER: (*on platform,* GIRL *by his side.*) I have been searching since this morning. Something triggered this search off. It was a total upheaval with no possibility of return—all bridges burned. So I have been on the march since morning. I don't want to detain you with stations that did not detain me. They were none of them worth my decisive revolt. I marched on stoutly— with critical eye, groping finger, selective mind. I passed it all by. Station after station disappeared behind my wandering back. This wasn't it, that wasn't it, nor the next, the fourth, the fifth. What is *it*? What is there in life really worth sacrificing everything for? This hall! Drowned in music, packed with benches. This hall! From these benches rises up–with roar of thunder–fulfilment. Freed from dross it rises liberated aloft in praise–molten out of the twin glowing crucibles: confession and repentance. There it stands like a gleaming tower–sure and bright: confession and repentance! You cry fulfilment, to you I shall tell my story.

SALVATION ARMY GIRL: Speak. I'll stand by you. I'll always stand by you.

CASHIER: I have been on the road since this morning. I confess: I embezzled money entrusted to me. I am a cashier in a bank. I took quite a sum: £60,000! I fled with it to the asphalt city. By now I'm certainly being hunted–a reward has probably been put on my head. I am not hiding anymore, I confess. Not all the money from all the banks in the world can buy anything of real value. You always get less than you pay for. The more you pay, the less you get. Money diminishes value. Money conceals the genuine–of all frauds money is the most miserable. (*He pulls it out of his tail pockets.*) This hall is the fiery furnace, heated by your contempt for all mean things. I throw it to you, to trample beneath your feet. That's some of the fraud removed from the world. I shall pass through your benches and give myself up to the first policeman: after the confession I seek atonement. Thus it is consummated. (*With his kid-gloves he flings notes and gold coins into the hall. The notes flutter down on the bewildered company, the coins roll on the ground between them. Then fierce battle for the money is joined. The meeting becomes one struggling heap. From the platform the bandsmen abandon their instruments and dive in. Benches are overturned, hoarse shouts resound, fists punch into bodies. Finally the tangled mass heaves to the door and rolls out.*)

(SALVATION ARMY GIRL *who has taken no part in the fight, stands alone in the middle of the upturned benches.*)

CASHIER: (*looks at the* GIRL *with a smile.*) You stand by me– you'll always stand by me! (*He notices the abandoned instruments, takes two drumsticks.*) Onwards! (*Short drum roll.*)

From station to station. (*Drums a few rolls followed by single beats.*) Masses left behind us? Crowd dispersed. Vast emptiness. We've made space. Space! Space! (*Drum roll.*) A girl stands there, emerging from departing waves–upright–steadfast! (*Drum roll.*) Maid and man. Ancient gardens re-opened. Cloudless sky. Voice from the silence of the tree-tops. All is well. (*Drum roll.*) Maid and man–eternal constancy. Maid and man–fullness in the void–beginning and end–seed and flower–sense and aim and goal. (*Drumbeat after drumbeat, then endless roll.*)

(SALVATION ARMY GIRL *steps back gradually to the door, disappears.*)

(*Drum roll dying away.*)

SALVATION ARMY GIRL: (*flings door open. To* POLICEMAN, *pointing to* CASHIER.) There he is. I pointed him out to you. I've earned the reward!

CASHIER: (*letting the sticks drop from his raised hands.*) Here I stand. I stand above you. Two are too many. There's space for one only. Loneliness is space; space is loneliness. Coldness is sun. Sun is coldness. The fevered body bleeds. The fevered body shivers. Bare fields. Ice spreading. Who can escape? Where is the way out?

POLICEMAN: Are there any other doors?

SALVATION ARMY GIRL: No.

(CASHIER *fumbles for something in his pocket.*)

POLICEMAN: He has his hand in his pocket. Turn the light out. We present too much of a target.

(SALVATION ARMY GIRL *obeys.*)

(*All lights on the chandeliers out except one. Single bulb lights up the bright wires of the crown in such a way that they seem to make a human skeleton.*)

CASHIER: (*burying his left hand in his breast pocket, grabbing a trumpet with the right and blowing a fanfare to the chandelier.*) Discovered! (*Fanfare.*) Rejected amid the snow-

72

laden tree this morning–welcomed now amid the wire-mesh of the chandelier. (*Fanfares.*) I announce my arrival to you. (*Fanfare.*) My path is behind me. In steep curves I pant upwards. I have exhausted my strength. I have not spared myself! (*Fanfares.*) I have taken the difficult way and could have had it so easy–up in the snow-laden tree, when we were sitting on the same branch. You should have urged me a little more forcefully. A little spark of enlightenment would have helped me and spared me all that trouble. So ridiculously little intelligence is needed! (*Fanfare.*) Why did I climb down? Why did I take that path? Where else am I still going? (*Fanfares.*) At the start he is sitting there–stark naked! At the end he is sitting there–stark naked! From morning to midnight I chase round in a frenzied circle–his beckoning finger shows the way out—where to? (*He shoots the answer into his shirt-front. The trumpet dies out at his lips with a fading note.*)

POLICEMAN: Switch the light on again.

(GIRL *does so. At that moment all the bulbs explode.*)

(CASHIER *has fallen back with outstretched arms against the Cross sewn onto the curtain. His dying cough sounds like an 'Ecce'–his expiring breath like a whispered–'Homo'.*)

POLICEMAN: There must have been a short circuit.

(*It is quite dark.*)

73

THE BURGHERS OF CALAIS

A Drama in Three Acts

Translated by J. M. Ritchie and Rex Last

Characters

JEAN DE VIENNE leader of the Councillors
DUGUESCLINS Captain of the King of France
EUSTACHE DE SAINT-PIERRE ⎤
JEAN D'AIRE
The THIRD
The FOURTH   Councillors
The FIFTH
JACQUES DE WISSANT
PIERRE DE WISSANT ⎦
The FATHER of EUSTACHE DE SAINT-PIERRE
The MOTHER of the THIRD Councillor
The WIFE of the FOURTH Councillor
The old NURSE with the young CHILD of the FOURTH Councillor
The two DAUGHTERS of JEAN D'AIRE
The ASSOCIATE of the FIFTH Councillor
An English OFFICER
A French OFFICER
English SOLDIERS
Two hunchback SERVANTS
A LAD
Councillors–Citizens

The names of only four of the six burghers of Calais have been handed down to our time. In this drama I have avoided invented names, in order not to lock away their fertile memory behind a false inscription.

Ad aeternam memoriam

ACT I

The open town hall. A red-brick building—with wide steps that serve as seats rising towards a platform, where squat, square pillars support the invisible roof. A tribune, closed off by a door, projects into the rows beneath. On the steps stand the councillors, flowing robes draped loosely about their haggard forms—with backs turned and looking up at the platform. Only EUSTACHE DE SAINT-PIERRE, *seventy years old, is seated—front right—staring at the ground. In front of the tribune two guards, their lances crossed before the door. Nearby a clarion bell rings rapidly—the pealing of many bells in the distance. Crowding on to the outer edge of the platform the citizens, gesticulating and shouting to those below. The noise swells, new arrivals force their way through:* JEAN DE VIENNE— *fifty years old—appears. A second wave of people and shouting wells up:* DUGUESCLINS—*in black armour— enters. Behind him his standard bearer.* JEAN DE VIENNE *has turned round to await* DUGUESCLINS: *amid the commotion they exchange a fraternal kiss. An officer with a troop of soldiers has followed above—behind their crossed lances the crowd is slowly forced back. The platform is now empty. The noise fades away—dies. Meanwhile* JEAN DE VIENNE *and* DUGUESCLINS *begin to descend the steps. The ensuing violent commotion repeats the pattern of events on the platform: the councillors receive the two with outstretched hands. Then they embrace and kiss one another. Two youths—*JACQUES DE WISSANT *and* PIERRE DE WIS-SANT—*hurry across the upper steps to greet* JEAN D'AIRE—*a man in his late seventies—with extreme devotion. The clarion bell ceases, so too the distant bells.* JEAN DE VIENNE *stands below front right, opposite him* DUGUESCLINS—*his close-cropped head bared—has sat down. The councillors take their places. The standard bearer— the great banner before him—on the tribune.*

JEAN DE VIENNE: We are summoned to this hall by the clarion bell. This summons has long not been given—who still glowed

77

with the feeblest flicker of hope of hearing it again? It burned so weakly–where is there even a glimmering spark to fan the flame once more—to melt the fetters on our arms–to let the bells swing again–and ring out over the city–pealing out freedom for Calais! Cast your minds back–recall the last meeting. We came from the work to which we had dedicated our strength–as to no previous work. Go into the streets and look in the houses:–where are arms, not still trembling–hands, not still clenched as if round the work tools they wielded–or backs not bent double as if still hauling the burdens–which drove the dikes out into the sea–forced back wave upon wave–broke their rage and tempered their unrest–until the new bay rounded out–broad and smooth as on no other coast: we opened a gateway into the sea–now ships were to glide out on voyages to prosperity! I ask you–and examine this question within yourselves:–was this our goal–or something other?–Is there anyone here with some different desire in his heart of hearts?–If that is so, then I will place upon my open palm the key to the city and–bareheaded and barefoot–in the garb of the delivered penitent!–I will carry it before the gates!—England is threatened by the harbour of Calais. Darker yet their suspicion perhaps–more grievous their accusation: it is they say a gateway through which the King of France can launch a swift and easy assault on England! And this they claim is why the harbour was built!—Is this not a shallow pretext?–The ancient dismal quarrel between the King of England and the King of France–who shall rule in England–who over France–is to flare up because of the harbour! No storms have ever lashed–or clouds darkened–like those of England under sail against France. At the last moment the King of France was able to rush his Captain into the city. Calais did not fall–Calais survived the wilderness of the siege!–When did the like ever happen before? When was a battle ever waged where no sword struck–no bow snapped–no lance splintered? Outside a slothful beast idles on the sand–have any shots flashed from it–other than those of the sun's rays playing over its shimmering body? Why does it not stir–why does it not rise up and let loose the storm–to flood over the walls–and thus conquer

Calais? Why does it not raise its paws to crush its prey?—
Because the King of France is drawing near. How will the
King of England withstand him? How will he meet this threat
from the rear–if he does not save his strength–for this other
enemy?–Great is the cunning of the King of England–but he
will be demolished before he can achieve his ends!–A raging
wind has been unleashed, which has rounded up troops from
every corner. Never before has the soil of France resounded to
an army as mighty as this. Its ranks swell irresistibly. The earth
thunders beneath it–its whirling cloud of dust darkens the sky.
It marches, singing and rejoicing through day and night.
Laughing the King of France rides at it head–laughing as if in
sport–the sport of the lion who goes hunting the hamster!—
On any morning now the tall column may appear–to darken
the sun–and rock the earth beneath. Each morning I look out
for the cloud whose rumbling proclaims the King of France!—
This morning the King of England has sent word into the
city–but this time not to the man who defends the city with
the sword!—The clarion bell rings out–the bells peal forth
over the city:–today the office which we were forced to place
on the amoured shoulders of the Captain of France is restored
to us! (*In an unrestrained outburst.*) No more shall the sword
rule over Calais–Calais is delivered from it! (*With the utmost
emphasis.*) The envoy will speak here in the open hall of the
city to the Councillors of Calais!

(*Once again a brief joyful movement flows through the ranks–
then, at a gesture from* JEAN DE VIENNE, *the guard on the left
hands his lance to the one on his right, opens the door of the
tribune and enters.–He now escorts out the English officer,
whose head is shrouded in a hood of black cloth. The soldier
removes it–closes the door and stands as before.*)

THE ENGLISH OFFICER: (*Remains in an attitude of uncertainty. He turns his still half-blind eyes in a circle, then fixes
them firmly upon* DUGUESCLINS.–*Then he draws himself up to
confront the assembly.*) The King of England has crossed the
sea. His ancient, well-founded bloodright–has been violated.

79

The impudent hand of a foreigner has snatched at the crown of France. That offender had to be chastised–for thieves are punished with the whip! (A *hasty movement runs through the ranks.* DUGUESCLINS *draws his sword clattering to his side.*) The insolent thief hid–for thieves are cowardly!–and beguiled with his agile tongue–quickened to eloquence by fear!–and deceived the gullible people of France until they came crowding round to defend him and his injustice!–That is why the King of England was compelled to take up the sword instead of the rod. When justice is being carried out–it does not turn against the judge. That saying proved true–the blow has fallen:–two days ago the forces which the thief drove forward against the King of England were dashed to pieces in bloody defeat and scattered to the four winds!

(*The Councillors–with the exception of* EUSTACHE DE SAINT-PIERRE–*have leapt to their feet: in incredulous astonishment they throw up their arms in the air. Now all eyes turn to* DUGUESCLINS, *who, overcome by agitation, is about to throw himself at* THE ENGLISH OFFICER. *But he is restrained by those standing next to him.*)

DUGUESCLINS : What you say is—! —A shark has swum through the sea from England–to fling breakers against the coast of France with the thrust of its angry tail. Each dark wave coming in to break against the shore–is a lie!–A seething tide of lies: the King of France rules under false pretence. But how can a man be a thief in his own house? The one who lurks outside is the thief. Where does he come from, this man who scorns and threatens us? From England the thieving magpie lusting for the glittering crown of France!–A seething tide of lies: the people of France have been incited by cunning and deceit? But no voice called them–no banner recruited them: –and even the feeblest arm reached out for a weapon! Mere bribes cannot stir men so–only anger. A wild wave has washed up a raging beast on the soil of France–now it shall be cast back again into the sea–there to bleed to death from wounds inflicted with terrible force!–And if the King of France had taken off his crown and pawned it to the King of England for the sake of peace–the people of France would redeem it with rivers of their blood and restore it to him on bended knee!– A seething tide of lies; and now the lie that exposes these claims, the ultimate lie:– every single day the sunlight has flashed from the shimmering ring that encircles Calais. Month after month the ring has been unbroken—yesterday the light did not reveal a single gap: today for the first time one armoured figure has broken the circle–this is the figure before us. Not one of them has risen from repose–and yet the King of England is said to have wiped out the all-powerful army of France two days ago!–Are we so wearied that dust no longer pricks our eyes–are we deaf that we cannot hear the noise of battle?–The King of England calls us blind–we can show him how blind we are:–till this very moment we have seen helmet by helmet–lance upon lance unmoving on the sands of Calais!

THE ENGLISH OFFICER: Helmets are all that lie on the sands before Calais–and lances on the ground–helmets lying on the ground—if a child has not picked them up. The sunlight playing on them–is what dazzles you!

(*The Councillors sit down–as if overcome by a weakness that maims their limbs.*)

DUGUESCLINS: (*bursting out.*) Now do you see the King of England's trickery?–Is he not glittering with the glory–of unaccomplished deeds? Observe the King of England–his country's leader and its most cunning brain! Does he not provide you with proof after proof? The splendid King of England has removed me from office–the clever King of England has called you together. What do the citizens of Calais know about weapons! Ten swords are mightier than one. That is the calculation you people of Calais fail to make. This is the point of the King of England's cunning. The King of France attacks with tenfold might–how then will the King of England save himself from destruction? How will he slip out of the noose in which he became trapped outside Calais? Where is there a way out–where an open gateway through which he may swiftly and simply slip away? Now only the smooth round harbour of Calais can serve him! If he has not actually said so, does not the ringing of the bells tell us it is true:–'Go out of the city and surrender the key–for all hope is extinguished–Calais will never see its deliverer!'–Credit the cunning of the King of England–and applaud him–but let him hear this answer. A child–playing in the evening with empty helmets on the sand–can stammer the brief tale of the day that is near at hand. Has not the King of England himself presented us with the most convincing evidence? Now send him back his happy envoy. His efforts to undermine your courage have been in vain. This truth stands firm–tomorrow and for all time: as I hold high the sword over Calais–so the King of France bears it even now strong and free before the proud armies of France!

THE ENGLISH OFFICER: (*turning towards* JEAN DE VIENNE.) The King of England knows that the citizens of Calais are not familiar with weapons. They know not how to wield them–nor how to inflict heavy blows. Therefore, they will be more quickly convinced by someone whose words they do not doubt. Time is running out!

(*At his imperious order the guard on the left of the tribune obeys–as before. In the hall a deathly hush falls. The guard brings out an English soldier–similarly shrouded in a black hood: he leads close behind him, a third figure, still clothed from head to foot in a cloak, and struggling violently beneath it.*)

THE ENGLISH OFFICER: (*to the guard.*) This man first!

(*The guard removes the hood from the soldier. The* ENGLISH SOLDIER *immediately frees the figure, the* FRENCH OFFICER, *from the cloak: to reveal his blood–and dust-covered armour–his hands are bound behind his back. The* ENGLISH SOLDIER *loosens the bonds. With swift movements the* FRENCH OFFICER *jerks the hood from his bandaged head–and tears the gag from his mouth–His voice still fails him as if choking.*)

DUGUESCLINS: (*throwing himself at him.*) Godefroy!

(*Many of the Councillors rise, the others sit hunched far for-*

ward–All eyes are riveted in the utmost tension upon the two.)

THE FRENCH OFFICER: (*clasping* DUGUESCLINS *tightly in his arms.*) Save—save—the honour of France!—It is not yet lost. You still have breath within you!–You can raise it up–from the dust–into which our feet have trampled it!

DUGUESCLINS: Where is the King of France?

THE FRENCH OFFICER: Seek him among the dead. (*Almost screaming.*) Stop him among the fleeing rabble.–You will not overtake him now–for the King of France rides swiftly!

DUGUESCLINS: What happened to the army?

THE FRENCH OFFICER: Cast chaff upon your hand and then blow on it. Is your hand not empty then?

DUGUESCLINS: When did this happen?

THE FRENCH OFFICER: One day–far from Calais. Why should we worry about the enemy. We would find him before the gates of Calais. We sing songs–we chatter in the saddle–and so we ride on without a care. Then it happened. A storm burst upon us. It seized us in the flank–buffeted our rear-guard–broke through our columns–dashed us to the ground–pounced on us at every turn–shattered our helmets and our armour–!We sank down in rivers of blood—We rose up again groaning–and seized hold of any running figure–and joined him in the tumult of flight, until he shook us off with a blow, and left his sword behind with us–that he might run the faster!—That was a raging storm–it snuffed out the fame of France in a single breath–like a light that burned too brightly! –That could not have been the King of England–Duguesclins–him you held fast outside Calais!—The light is not yet out–it flickers on–for you are still standing here!–Nothing is lost–save–save the honour of France! (*In exhaustion he raises his hands towards his neck.*) Water–water—Let me drink!

THE ENGLISH OFFICER: You are free to go in the town–wherever you show yourself your appearance will tell the whole story!

(THE FRENCH OFFICER, *stumbling over the steps, reaches the platform–and disappears.* DUGUESCLINS *regains his seat unsteadily. He rests his forehead upon the pommel of his sword and remains motionless. The Councillors, whose eyes have*

83

followed the FRENCH OFFICER, *turn slowly to face the* ENGLISH OFFICER.)

THE ENGLISH OFFICER: *(after a pause.)* This morning the King of England is back besieging Calais. No enemy threatens from the rear–no walls are strong enough to withstand his assault. Calais is delivered into his hands. He can do with it as he pleases. Tomorrow it will be destroyed to the last stone–ruins will spread where once it stood–as barren as the salt sea-coast! –With just punishment the King of England will chastize the defiance that barred the city and took up the sword against him!–That sword is now splintered–the King of England summons the Councillors into the open hall of the city!– But the King of England wishes to be merciful. For the sake of the harbour which has been opened into the sea from Calais –you shall avert destruction with the merest penance:– at dawn six of the Councillors shall set out from the city– bareheaded and barefoot–clothed in penitent's garb with a rope about their necks! In this manner the King of England is prepared to accept the key!–But should the six Councillors delay at all tomorrow–then the King of England will unleash the storm and dash the city into the harbour!–

(The first to rise are JACQUES DE WISSANT–*left–and* PIERRE DE WISSANT–*right–and erect with outstretched arms they set alight the cry: 'Duguesclins!'–At their sides those nearest rise–the movement swells swiftly through the rows. The limpness has fallen from the Councillors like a loose garment from a stiffened body. As one they shout: 'Duguesclins!'* DUGUESCLINS *pulls down his helmet over his short black hair– rises. He holds his naked sword upright before him against his chest.* JEAN DE VIENNE *signals to the guard: the latter takes the hood back to the* ENGLISH OFFICER. *The shouting increasing in crescendo towards him: 'Jean de Vienne!' A clear lane up the steps is formed–arms reach out to guide the* ENGLISH OFFICER *to the platform.)*

EUSTACHE DE SAINT-PIERRE: *(goes from his seat to* JEAN DE VIENNE *and grasps his raised arm.)* Jean de Vienne–in the presence of this envoy will you seek for an answer with us?

(*The noise in the hall swiftly fades away.*)

JEAN DE VIENNE: (*after pondering for a moment—with a violent gesture towards the* ENGLISH OFFICER.) We must!

(*The two guards lead the* ENGLISH OFFICER *and the* ENGLISH SOLDIER *into the tribune and close the door behind them. Still grasping* EUSTACHE DE SAINT-PIERRE'S *hand tightly.*)

We must—with all our resources!—Does it not spring to every tongue—and burn like fire—and choke the very breath? Does it not send every pulse racing—every brow throbbing—and cast a weighty burden upon us?—Who can still speak—who can still stammer—who is not bewildered by this disgrace?—Who are we—with our shoulders—with our arms—with our hands?—What did we accomplish with our shoulders—what did we raise up with our arms—what did we hold in our hands?—Is what we have achieved invisible?—What is this work?—The sea pounds violently upon the shore. No ship, that arrives without peril—or departs without fear. No ship, that is not some day dashed to pieces. No coming—no going—not threatened by this danger. Search the shoreline now—where today do you see wrecks piled high.—The sea pounds—and no longer destroys. The waves rise and fall. Ships arrive—ships depart—what can disturb their coming and going?—We bent our shoulders to this work—and now we are to place the rope about them!— That is our deed—behind which we are to troop out—like criminals!—We must search.—Who among us can find them—words of rebuke—words of fire—words that will chastise! (*Swinging round.*) Duguesclins, stand before us!

DUGUESCLINS: —Calais was the stake in the game. The game has been won by another. Calais is lost—Calais is his prize. He weighs it in his hand—it pleases him—he wants to keep it. He toys with the good fortune he holds in his hand. He can afford to. Both are safely his. For this is his lucky day! (*With increasing volume.*) But next morning both hand and good fortune will be flung at his feet. His hand will be hewn off by this sword—his good fortune will be consumed by fire!—He will not succeed here, for his attack will not catch us unawares in drowsy torpor–he will not confound us, for we are prepared. No arm, that does not hold a weapon. We shall stand on the walls–at the gates–in the streets. Then he will have to force his way in over his own dead. Then the arm of the last man left alive will throw the torch. The flames will roar in the houses–the walls totter and burst–and in dust and smoke the city will sink into the harbour. Calais is destroyed–the sea surges over it guarding this prize against all!

(JEAN D'AIRE *first–and then others, mostly old men, have risen to their feet: their arms are outstretched as if reaching for weapons. Younger men crowd round them, grasping their lean clenched fists in approbation.*)

JEAN DE VIENNE: Duguesclins–you can see our arms outstretched towards you–for a weapon. We will stand shoulder to shoulder with you at the gates–in the streets. The weakest among us will kindle the flames. Our hands upon your hand Duguesclins–beneath your hand the sword–so we shall hold it with you!

(*The Councillors stand up in their seats, their hands outspread as if swearing an oath.* JEAN DE VIENNE *tries to place* EUSTACHE DE SAINT-PIERRE'S *hand with his own on the sword. As* EUSTACHE DE SAINT-PIERRE *resists, he turns to face him. Then, with a gesture towards the rows.*)

This is our decision. The path which we are to take lies clear before us. Duguesclins has opened it up!–It only remains for the words to be spoken that will guide our actions. Now Eustache de Saint-Pierre will speak them for us!

EUSTACHE DE SAINT-PIERRE: (*weakly–his head bowed, his arms hanging at his sides.*) We must do it! (*Seeing his dejection all noise in the hall is stilled.–He draws himself up.*) We come from the work–to which we have dedicated our strength–as to no previous one. The new bay is rounded out–new ships are to glide out on voyages to prosperity!—Jean de Vienne, did you not call for our answer–did you not try to ferret out our most deep-seated desires with this one question: What is the goal!–Is this not it? Is this not why we bent our shoulders from the very start–and why we burdened our arms?—Jean de Vienne, you threw out the challenge to us: if but one of us were troubled in his motives–this would cause you to place the key upon your open palm and go out from the city gates!–Jean de Vienne–now take the key yourself–now go–bareheaded and barefoot!–outside the city! But this decision is not yours alone: (*To the rows of Councillors.*):–it is your hands that give him the key–your desire that this should come about!–(*To* JEAN DE VIENNE.) So remove your sandals, discard your gay apparel–you will do penance for the deceit that has been unmasked today–: our true motives were quite different. You thrust the harbour into the conflict–and into its very midst. What we have achieved is in vain–the conflict is all-important!–That makes you guilty–therefore atone as you promised. Here your vow rang out–and echoes still in our ears!

(*An astonished silence reigns.*)

THE FOURTH COUNCILLOR: (*forty-five years of age–half rises.*) Eustache de Saint-Pierre–are we to submit to the will of the King of England?

EUSTACHE DE SAINT-PIERRE: (*ignoring him, addressing himself to all.*) Today we must set the seal on what we have achieved. Let us finish it today with utmost zeal–which is its own reward. One part has been done. Look at us–traces of the toil that parched our limbs are still visible. We had no time to rest–for the sea did not rest! No burden overwhelmed us–though the stone did not move. Our breath ached–our bodies bent to the task!–Our aching breath–our bent bodies forced back the sea–wave after wave it yielded–we have wrested victory from the sea. It is accomplished!—But it is not enough. Now the second stage lies before us. Now your achievement makes its demands upon you–now it makes the strongest claim. Its success so far demands your utmost dedication. Gather your strength–raise up your heads–bring your innermost thoughts into sharpest focus. Your greatest achievement becomes your most solemn obligation. You must guard it–with all your resources–in all your actions. What are you worth–if you retreat from your

87

work? Wretched penitents before your work—cast down by weariness—no more enduring than your sighs!

THE THIRD COUNCILLOR: (*urgently questioning.*) Eustache de Saint-Pierre, are six of us to suffer disgrace on the sands of Calais?

EUSTACHE DE SAINT-PIERRE: Consider this:—did laughing and singing bring about our achievement? Did not a sense of duty guide our every step towards it? Where is power ever given away—without submission to duty? A binding—a tormenting duty—which we have to carry out?—Till yesterday you submitted to this duty—can you run away now that power is accorded to you?

JEAN D'AIRE: (*speaking with difficulty.*) Eustache de Saint-Pierre, shall we trample the honour of France under foot and walk out on the sands before Calais?

(EUSTACHE DE SAINT-PIERRE *is silent. Uproar rages in the rows:* JEAN D'AIRE *is closely surrounded by the crowd.*)

DUGUESCLINS: (*striding swiftly past* EUSTACHE DE SAINT-PIERRE *to where* JEAN D'AIRE *is standing below.*) From the poor sand before the gates of Calais a tree will shoot up. One day it will blossom. Its roots will feed on blood. Its shadow will spread across all France. Among its branches there will be a humming as of bees:—the glorious name of Calais that will save the honour of France!—(*He turns to address* EUSTACHE DE SAINT-PIERRE.) The King of England will spare the city—for the sake of the harbour. Should we make the harbour an object of barter—if the honour of France is the price?

EUSTACHE DE SAINT-PIERRE: (*slowly.*) We saw the coast towering high—we saw the boiling fury of the sea—we did not seek the fame of France. We sought what our hands might achieve! (*Confronting the increasing agitation.*) A man is come, goaded on by rage. That rage is kindled by a craving. He attacks greedily—and seizes everything in his path. He piles up a mountain of broken fragments—higher and higher still—and on its uppermost peak he disports himself;—burning in his fever—rigid and convulsed—the sole survivor of the destruction!—Who is he?–A man who today is gripped by a craving which to-morrow will moulder with him–is your worth to be measured by such as he–or his life the measure of yours?—(*Here and there a Councillor leaps to his feet and turns to his neighbour with a gesture of disgust towards* EUSTACHE DE SAINT-PIERRE, *who speaks to each of them in turn.*) You want to destroy your work–for the sake of this man who waxes and wanes with the passing hour?–Is a day longer than all time? What have you learned from the work, on which you spent day after day–till a day was no more than a drop in the sea? Were you suddenly caught up in delirium–or were you bound to your work more coolly?–Are you going to recant today? Are you going to shrug aside today your guiding and controlling light?—A stranger hesitates outside the city for the sake of this harbour:–surely you too will hesitate?—

(*More and more Councillors are rising to their feet–with the same violent gestures.*)

EUSTACHE DE SAINT-PIERRE: (*undismayed.*) Are you not consumed by that other shame:–at having done this work?–Do these hands which worked on it not disgust you? Do these bodies which bent to build not repel you?—You drove back the sea–and built as on solid ground. Your achievement now stands–a beacon of light to draw others on. Now warm rivers of energy flow from it into every arm! Already men are naming the new land to be carved out of the desert–already they are measuring the mountains they intend to level–already digging the canals to control the swell of the water. Now any obstacles can be overcome–since you have achieved the conquest of the sea!

(*Now everyone is on his feet.*)

EUSTACHE DE SAINT-PIERRE: (*with the utmost emphasis.*) But today your work becomes your crime!–Did you not lie with this work–more grievously than with words? Was not the zeal of all kindled by this promise–a zeal set aflame and still burning with impatience to succeed in its own achievement?–You ventured to do what no one has attempted before you–and

89

you have given birth to a wave of emulation!–Will you now stand calmly on one side–and let cheap scorn pour from your lips?–You dared to achieve–what no one else had–only to make others lose heart–and deceive all similar efforts:–blind rage lies always in wait–our lust wells up–with sharp thrusts destroys the meaning of our work!—Would you not rather avoid such deceit? Are you prepared to bear this blemish which clearly marks you out–and can never be effaced?—

(*Councillors flood across the steps:–*JACQUES DE WISSANT *and* PIERRE DE WISSANT *bear down on* JEAN DE VIENNE *and* DUGUESCLINS *together and gesture to others to lead the two away with them.*)

THE THIRD COUNCILLOR: (*bursting out.*) Eustache de Saint-Pierre–with these hands we sought out our work.–(*To all present.*) Are we the tool? Are we the doers?–Eustache de Saint-Pierre–is this achievement then not to be the source of our greatest pride?

(EUSTACHE DE SAINT-PIERRE *remains silent.*)

THE FOURTH COUNCILLOR: The cliffs tower up–the sea storms wildly–we forced it back from the cliffs!—The waves lifted us on to their crest–Eustache de Saint-Pierre–are we to be shaken by cowardly deceit?

(EUSTACHE DE SAINT-PIERRE *remains silent.*)

JEAN D'AIRE: (*coming down one step.*) We did not seek fame–now fame is flung at our feet! Eustache de Saint-Pierre–is it wrong to pick it up–and put it on as our coat of many colours?

(EUSTACHE DE SAINT-PIERRE *stares at the ground.*)

DUGUESCLINS: That is why the harbour was dug out so deeply–that honour and fame might drown in it–together with your courage!

EUSTACHE DE SAINT-PIERRE: (*turns sharply towards* DUGUESCLINS, *takes a few steps in his direction. Slowly he masters his emotion and speaks.*) Does your courage flare up at the thought of this battle into which you will dash tomorrow?

–What else does this battle tomorrow demand of you?–
Tomorrow you will take up your sword–strike many down
about you–and in turn many will overpower you!–Is this
conflict not already decided before it begins?–Is there a glimmer
of doubt–have you any other choice? What else is there for
you to do?—You pull the peak of your visor down over your
eyes and are blind and deaf behind its shield. Exactly as you
stand here too, blinded and deafened! You are enveloped in a
darkness that hides your deed from you. This way you cannot
see it–this way it shrivels up–this way the deed becomes small
–no longer too frightening to attempt it!—

(JACQUES DE WISSANT *and* PIERRE DE WISSANT *take up position in front of* DUGUESCLINS.)

Where is courage, when the will to act is parted from the deed
itself?—I can see none!–Where is courage if it does not
carry out its deed?–What is this act still worth if it compels
you blindly? If today you lay waste all the streets about you–
will your path tomorrow be strewn with praise?–It costs you
no courage:–you *must* take this path–there is no other!
You hurtle breathlessly along it–as a fugitive pants for breath
in flight!–fleeing towards your deed. The deed awaits you
there–to save you from the desert around you–to raise you up
from the void. Perhaps to strike you down–: you are safe!—
Your deed becomes mere cowardice–as you hanker after it
today!–The courage falls from it and swiftly shrivels on the
ground. It rustles about your feet–ground to dust by our bare
soles–and blown into the sea by the wind from our robes!–
Where will your torch of courage be tomorrow? Suffocated by
thick smoke! Smouldering dully from the hot embers–stagnat-
ing out of your blood beneath your rigid armour!–Today you
and your blood lie dead before your deed–but shall we not live
on in our flimsy robes until the brightness of a new dawn?—

(*The citizens come back onto the platform. They press forward
slowly and in silence: under the weight of fear their arms
hang limp–their shoulders are bowed. Now the crowd reaches
the edge of the platform. There it alters its attitude: heads
crane forward–eyes search the space beneath: an inflexible*

demand is given expression—unashamed and unabashed.—The Councillors look up at them: they stand erect and motionless watched by the eyes above—ringed by the throng that fills the breadth and depth of the platform.)

DUGUESCLINS : —I will mock that courage of mine which places the sword in my hands. For the little there is of it would be put to shame were there one man here prepared to put on his grey humiliation and wear it out of the city at dawn. That is a greater courage! (*He returns to his place.*)

JEAN D'AIRE : (*pointing with one arm towards the platform— with the other towards* EUSTACHE DE SAINT-PIERRE). Eustache de Saint-Pierre—you are troubled about the harbour. Is it not only natural that you above all should be tormented with anxiety? For are you not the richest among us? Are not your warehouses the largest—are they not crammed with goods to the very roofs?—Of course you tremble—of course you are prepared to beg for the sake of your riches!

A CITIZEN : (*on the platform.*) Jean de Vienne, step forward. Search—ask your question. Let it ring out in the hall. Let it call for one of us. Let it thunder forth once only—let its shame burn our ears only once! (*He points with outstretched arms to the Councillors below. They point back; hastily regain their places and sit down. Among the rows and on the platform there is breathless silence.*)

JEAN DE VIENNE : (*without leaving his seat—his voice solemn.*) The King of England is master of Calais. He can do with it as he pleases. Now he makes this demand: six Councillors shall bear the key out of the city—six Councillors shall stride out of the gate—bareheaded and barefoot—in penitent's garb— a rope about their necks.—(*He raises his head.*) Six shall set out from the city at break of day—six shall deliver themselves up in the sand before Calais—six times shall the noose be tied—: thus we shall make amends and save Calais and its harbour!—(*After a pause.*) Six times the question will ring out—six times must an answer be given:—(*With the utmost effort.*) Where are the six—who will rise up—leave their places —and come forward together?—

(*For a moment the question weighs heavily on them; at first only some slight movement and turning of heads is perceptible; then the noise swells in a crescendo of scorn.*)

EUSTACE DE SAINT-PIERRE: (*rises from his seat and goes to the middle of the floor. His hands move to his robe at the neck as if about to remove it.*)—I am prepared to go!

(*Silence descends among the crowd.* JEAN DE VIENNE *stares in astonishment at* EUSTACHE DE SAINT-PIERRE. *There is a murmur on the platform:* 'Eustache de Saint-Pierre!' *A* FIFTH COUNCILLOR *on the right, almost directly behind* EUSTACHE DE SAINT-PIERRE'S *place—and the same age as the* THIRD *and* FOURTH COUNCILLORS—*rises; he walks with deeply bowed head and hands crossed over his breast—and without uttering a word takes up position next to* EUSTACHE DE SAINT-PIERRE. *The* COUNCILLORS *stare in breathless astonishment. From the platform there comes the murmur:* 'The second!' *Then the eyes of the* COUNCILLORS *sweep across the rows: they look questioningly at those around and above them.*)

THE THIRD COUNCILLOR: (*on the left leaps to his feet and cries out, his fingers clawing at his neck.*) I—will go!— (*Breathless and panting he joins the two in the middle. Above on the platform the murmuring counts them:* 'The Third!' *The heads turn more sharply in the rows.*)

THE FOURTH COUNCILLOR: (*on the left—rises, and, as if surrendering to an inner compulsion, goes—unhurried and with head held high—to join the others.*) —I will go!

(*On the platform the murmuring grows louder:* 'The fourth!' *Many of the* COUNCILLORS *half rise in their seats, in order to gain a better view of the rows. Up above the murmuring becomes louder still.*)

JEAN D'AIRE: (*on the right—on his feet: he sways under the impact of his decision—descends the steps unsteadily and has to support himself against* EUSTACHE DE SAINT-PIERRE, *pressing his forehead against the latter's back.*) Eustache de Saint-Pierre, I ask to be permitted—to follow in your footsteps!

(*Above voices count and heads nod in satisfaction:–'The fifth!'* JEAN DE VIENNE, *standing in* JEAN D'AIRE'S *way trying to stop him flings out his arms appealingly towards the rows, to stop* JACQUES DE WISSANT *left–*PIERRE DE WISSANT *right, who have already risen to follow* JEAN D'AIRE *with gestures of anxiety and horror. Groaning and with hands clenched they hesitate still–each hidden from the other by the projecting tribune. From the platform there comes an astonished pointing at them both and curious glances move from one side to the other. Now the two descend the steps simultaneously. Having come down beneath the tribune they catch sight of one another. They stop short–then each attempts to outstrip the other and both grasp* EUSTACHE DE SAINT-PIERRE'S *hands at the same moment and speak with one voice: 'I will go!' All the* COUNCILLORS *are now on their feet at their places.*)

EUSTACHE DE SAINT-PIERRE: (*turning his head towards* JEAN DE VIENNE.) Jean de Vienne, will you now give our answer to the envoy?

JEAN DE VIENNE: (*pulls himself together. He gestures to the guards. They throw open the doors. The* ENGLISH OFFICER *emerges; behind him the soldiers. Indicating the group in the middle to him.*) Tomorrow six Councillors will carry the key out of the city. Tomorrow six will deliver themselves up–in the garb of the penitent with a rope about their necks. The King of England demands that six atone–and six have answered his call. The price of Calais and its harbour is paid six times over!

THE ENGLISH OFFICER: (*with a fleeting glance at the group.*) The King of England awaits the six in the grey light of the coming dawn. But should they delay at all–then in that very hour he will unleash the storm and dash the city into the harbour! (*He turns to face the soldier. As he is about to take his leave–his armour clattering in the silence–*DUGUESCLINS *stops him with a gesture.*)

DUGUESCLINS: (*comes down below the tribune. He grasps the standard and pulls it towards him. He kisses it passionately and long. Once his eyes rest upon the group in the centre–*

then he unbuckles his sword.) The keenness of the sword is blunted—its brilliance dulled—the hand that bears it weary. My arms reach out towards new deeds.—(*Almost screaming.*) I cannot—I will not understand!—(*Calmly.*) The King of England has lands across the sea. The King of England shall send me where my sword can still be of service! (*He offers it to the* ENGLISH OFFICER. *The* ENGLISH OFFICER *accepts it—with a shrug of the shoulders—and gives it to the soldier. Then he gestures curtly to* DUGUESCLINS *to follow him. The three exeunt.*)

(*The Councillors in the rows and the citizens on the platform draw back in awe. Now there comes from the platform, riveting the attention of all—a shouting which grows more and more distinct, directed at the group below: 'Seven'! Eventually culminating in one crescendo: 'Seven ! !'* JEAN DE VIENNE *is about to approach* EUSTACHE DE SAINT-PIERRE.)

EUSTACHE DE SAINT-PIERRE: (*after a swift glance at those standing round him—quickly making up his mind, turns to* JEAN DE VIENNE, *speaking almost joyfully.*) This afternoon the drawing of lots will grant the seventh among us life!

(*A deep silence spreads. The standard bearer stands as before: but the cascading folds of the standard obscure the doors of the tribune—the pole juts up like a broken tower.*)

ACT II

The main chamber of the city hall: a long, shallow rectangle. In the righthand wall a low door. An enormous tapestry hangs down on to a raised step to close off the whole rear portion of the chamber. Its three panels depict with the vigorous forms and colours of an earlier age the construction of the harbour of Calais: on the left the steep cliffs tower up, the sea lashing wildly against them—on the right can be seen the bustling activity during construction—the broader middle section shows the completed harbour: with warehouses along the straight line of the quays and in the distance the opening into the broad calm bay.

95

EUSTACHE DE SAINT-PIERRE–*richly clad*–*and* JEAN DE VIENNE *are standing front centre.*

JEAN DE VIENNE: It is good that the moment of decision has arrived. The unrest has mounted with every hour of this day–now it has reached its peak, and must fall away, sparking off–who knows!–what kind of trouble, with terrifying and unpredictable results. This is a real danger. We can only avert it once the seventh, freed by the drawing of lots, shows himself on the balcony of this hall. His appearance alone will convince them that we are truly saved.–(*After a silence.*) It is remarkable that–in this short time and without the slightest struggle–the citizens are beginning to lose the stolid patience and near indifference with which they endured the long siege. I seek the reason for this:–what excites them more violently–disturbs them more deeply–to cause this wild outburst!–than the grievous sufferings of the past ever could?–I have found the answer, and the right one: uncertainty has shattered their previously unshakeable calm. The long wait for an end to the proceedings in the hall stings them with sharpest anguish. It renders this torment–and it is torment!–intolerable.
And I venture to say this: Whatever the end may be–would it were here already–if you alter your decision at the eleventh hour, that is, abandon it and set the seal upon wholesale destruction!–they will express their gratitude with a sigh of relief. For you will have saved them from the greater suffering! –(*He falls silent again.*) I admit that I too suffer from this feeling of oppression. Although I want six of you to be delivered up–the burden of anxiety will only lift when I see the seventh depart from this hall.–(*Quickly.*) And must it not distress you a hundred times more deeply?–Are you not at the same time free and lost–as long as the choice wavers? As the burden that weighs you down become heavier and heavier–do you not have to strengthen your resolve time and again–which from the very first threatens to fade? If you delay until this afternoon you are stretching the deed you propose to do beyond all reason. Save your strength–by deciding upon the seventh now!–For tomorrow a greater task awaits you!

–(*After a pause.*) We have drawn the bow too tight–we must remove the arrow from the bowstring before it is sent flying to strike home–perhaps–with deadly effect. We should have shown them the six this morning in the open hall–then the violence with which they now shout for the seventh and pour scorn upon you–would not fall like a shadow over your deed. For that I stand in shame before you! (*Bursting out.*)–I beg of you–it is a greater thing to turn from us this terrible disgrace! That is why I am not afraid to demand this of you:–hurry–and send out the seventh without delay!

(*He takes* EUSTACHE DE SAINT-PIERRE'S *hand–is about to continue speaking–but turns away and goes off to the right. When he opens the door, a torrent of muffled sound can be heard. He looks round towards* EUSTACHE DE SAINT-PIERRE, *who answers his anxious expression with a smile–then hurriedly exits through the door.* EUSTACHE DE SAINT-PIERRE *mounts the step and goes through an opening in the tapestry From the right come the* FIFTH COUNCILLOR–*richly clad–like* EUSTACHE DE SAINT-PIERRE *and later the others. Behind him his old associate.*)

THE FIFTH COUNCILLOR: (*hesitating near the door.*)–Even now I feel unable to initiate you into my most secret plans. I could be the one to come out of here a free man. Then–if I have spoken to you too soon–I should go back drained and useless to my affairs. It would be as if I had given you my plans–my hopes, in fact my whole self–and you would fill my position as well as I. Luck would instantly desert my projects. For this is how they work: to reveal them is to destroy them. They become arid and void–founder and come to nothing. Only as long as we keep them to ourselves–as the earth must long conceal the seed in its womb–will they be nourished by our faith–enlarged by our daring–impelled by our will–often in error–but always to fulfilment. Greatest delight is stunted if its buried roots are brought to light–even before one's closest associate!–And you are mine.–(*He sighs.*) I do not know how my fate will be decided in this hour. If I did–then in a flash everything would be clear and simple. But this makes it all dark and difficult.–(*He gives his hand to his* ASSOCIATE. THE ASSOCI-ATE *grasps and kisses it.*) Now the night before us is too short to say everything. Why did we not have the long day? (*The business* ASSOCIATE *bows deeply over* THE FIFTH COUNCILLOR'S *hand.* THE FIFTH COUNCILLOR, *smiling.*) Because one of us can win long life!

THE ASSOCIATE: (*in a whisper.*) You will be that one!

THE FIFTH COUNCILLOR: Can you see the lot between my fingers?

THE ASSOCIATE: Your plans–your projects cannot come to grief. They will force the lot into your hands.

THE FIFTH COUNCILLOR: The seventh is among us–

THE ASSOCIATE: You will be counted as the seventh!–

THE FIFTH COUNCILLOR: Each of us is–yet none of us is! (*He leaves him–goes off through the tapestry. The associate departs without looking up.*)

THE THIRD COUNCILLOR: (*comes–leading his mother by her out-stretched arms–to the centre of the stage. After a pause–in a muted voice.*) Mother!

THE MOTHER: (*choking.*) Son–!

THE THIRD COUNCILLOR: (*anxiously.*) Will you wait here?

THE MOTHER: I–cannot wait!–I have waited long enough–I have not spared myself. I have not weakened–I have not lost heart–I have not rested–I have not yielded one inch–: I have stumb-led my way here–a hundred times since morning!–I have placed my feet among the thorns–that lie strewn in my path! I have withdrawn the sword from my heart and thrust it in again–a hundred times–now all the blood has flown away–my knees tremble–my strength drains from me–I tried to stop it! (THE THIRD COUNCILLOR *looks at her in silence. She draws herself erect.*) What is pain compared with this:–to stammer words–that are empty!–like the fluttering of grey moths!

THE THIRD COUNCILLOR: Mother–I understand!

THE MOTHER: (*violently.*) How can they come to me? How can they be liberated–these words from within me that press so to be born?— (*More calmly.*) You render me poor in this hour–you steal my love from me–it is as if you stifle my lips and choke my heart!–You go with me–you stand here beside

98

me–I touch your hair and stroke your robe–at once I am beyond care–(*Looking at him almost in wonderment.*) The child is quite unharmed!–What is happening then?–And your richest robes!—Why are you wearing them today? What special day have the bells decreed?I am not dressed up like you–nor is anyone else in the streets of the city–they are not celebrating a feast—(*Stiffens.*) Is your hand cold– or hot?–Is it still warm or– (*With increasing vehemence.*) It is stiff–and horribly cold–it will not lift to loosen–to tear off– the noose about your neck–it does not hurl away the rope– now I truly understand!–Now I am no longer paralysed–I can throw myself upon you–and embrace you tighter than ever before!—I am dumb no longer–the cry bursts out from me, that would waken the very dead:–you are my son–I am your mother! (THE THIRD COUNCILLOR *tries to free himself. She clasps him tightly.*) Now darkness descends–it lifts me up– and soothes my anguish. No blow can shake me–no terror can haunt me–for what more is there to fear?–I am safe in my grief–grief takes me under its wing–grief is my refuge–grief the peace that gently stifles all doubt!

THE THIRD COUNCILLOR: Mother, you must hold on to the hope of my escape–that hope still exists!

THE MOTHER: (*looks at him. Then, brightly.*) I bore you in pain–suckled you with laughter–suffered you with tears of rejoicing–throughout your days!–you have grown away from me and yet have come back again–every time!–yesterday– as before–and today again you will return–neither the first nor the sixth lot will be yours–you will place the seventh into my lap–(*Closing her hands round an imaginery object*)–and I will laugh and spin it round in play like a ball!—(*She turns away.*) Now I can wait–now I am strong–now I can raise my head again and go on my way. What concern is this business of mine? (*Bowed down and with dragging steps she reaches the door–Exit.*)

(THE THIRD COUNCILLOR *straightens his shoulders and strides across the step through the tapesty.* THE FOURTH COUNCILLOR *–and his wife enter, together with the old nurse carrying their* *young child.* THE FOURTH COUNCILLOR *and his* WIFE *advance to the middle of the stage.*)

THE FOURTH COUNCILLOR: (*with one foot already on the step, cheerfully.*) It is no more than any walk outside the gates on a fine summer's day. The hot air shimmers over the sand, but from the sea a cool breeze blows. Gentle ·warmth and cooling chill–are not both present in this hour?–This handshake means we must part–but soon it will mark our reunion. The two are so close together that they cannot be separated. All will be in the balance, until the scales settle. Does not good sense bid us be happy? (*The* WIFE *looks at him smilingly.*) Let us not try to be too clever and haggle out what meagre time is left us. Who would play for pennies when the debts are piled high? Even here on the threshold we take a backward glance. That way we can cancel out some of our debts. Was the time we've had not abundant in riches. Do not our years together reach back unbroken like the links of a shining chain? Every morning bright–and every evening joyful? Now we are so weighed down by that shimmering burden about our shoulders and bodies that we can scarcely move. We are bound by a shining chain–like debtors! (THE WIFE *holds up her hand to bid him stop.* THE FOURTH COUNCILLOR, *astonished.*) Is it wrong to put it into words–to express thanks? (THE WIFE *shakes her head.* THE FOURTH COUNCILLOR *comprehending.*) Now you are the cleverer of us. As a woman you are more cautious. You see to the larder and carefully share out the food for each day. Because tomorrow we may be hungry again! (THE WIFE *nods.*) Tomorrow perhaps–who knows! Today let us be spendthrift–today we cannot be prudent–today let us drown under a wave of riches–but what of tomorrow. Could we ever be content with what it has to offer?–(*More strongly.*) If we now open out the whole picture–and if in one all-embracing glance the fullness of our life together burns in a single flame? Will tomorrow not be blinded by the blaze? A day creeping in the dark beneath the fire our eager hands kindle? A day–like the others to come–forced to scratch a meagre living from the merest scraps? It is folly for a man to give thanks before the final repose at the end of what life has to offer. We should render the next gift paltry–and we who are the receivers become the poorer with each subsequent offering! (THE WIFE *gazes steadily up at him.*)–Is it not more of a burden for you– to wait in silence? Who knows what change the coming hour will bring? How it will alter us? It may be late before it is all over–arriving at the decision can make us dull and silent. Then we shall have missed our chance–our last chance–to say our farewells! I shall have no time to tell of my ardour, to let its light penetrate the life you must now live alone–to say that I have deserted you, as one who creeps away under cover of night from home and loved ones!–that I am making you destitute–that I am not heaping up treasures before your door–you will go hungry–you will freeze–you will drift about the streets! I have nothing to offer you–nothing any more– can you understand that now:–I am a mere empty shadow suspended in time! (THE WIFE *places her hand upon his robe and points towards the nurse.* THE FOURTH COUNCILLOR *smiles and takes her over towards the nurse.*)

THE WIFE: Your child–my child!

THE FOURTH COUNCILLOR: (*overcome and drawing the child quickly towards him with a protective gesture–in a choking voice.*) For your sake–for your sake–! (THE WIFE *sinks at his feet. Taking hold of her shoulder with his free hand he raises her to her feet.*) I shall return–I shall return.–(*He gives the child back to the nurse; pressing his wife closely to him.*) I– shall return!

(*Swiftly reaches the opening in the tapestry and vanishes without looking back to say farewell.* THE WIFE, *leaning on the nurse–exits. From the right–*JEAN D'AIRE–*on one side clinging to his arm his two daughters, who hold each other in tight embrace–on the other* JACQUES DE WISSANT *and* PIERRE DE WISSANT *walk side by side.*)

JACQUES DE WISSANT: (*grasping* JEAN D'AIRE'S *arm.*) You must not go in. You must turn back. Stop here and send us in in- stead!

(*To* PIERRE DE WISSANT.) Give me your support–and implore him to agree. Is it not enough if two leave our circle?

JEAN D'AIRE: Are you trying to make me the murderer of the others in there?

PIERRE DE WISSANT: (*shaking his head.*) That is not it!

JEAN D'AIRE: Is there not one hope left in every head–a mirage we all tightly cling to–even though our better selves struggle against it!–The will to live is strong–I look back on a long life and find it all too much. You cannot feel the same as I!

JACQUES DE WISSANT: (*looking at* PIERRE DE WISSANT–*and like him shaking his head.*) That is not it!

JEAN D'AIRE: Your desires spur you on–and you rush to where great deeds are beckoning. Such is the rashness of your youth. You see the goal–the goal eclipses the path. But the path is often more important than the goal–and at the same time more difficult.–(*Turning his attention to his* DAUGHTERS.) There are many things by the wayside–but you hurtle headlong past. Ought you to ignore all other possibilities already?–You yearn towards this deed, which will place you among the highest and imbue your names with a glory that will never die! (JACQUES DE WISSANT *and* PIERRE DE WISSANT *shake their heads more vigorously.*) You are called (*Referring to his* DAUGHTERS.)–while they are swamped by the mighty wave. Here deed and sacrifice are inextricably entwined!–(*More strongly.*) Why send me away–where is the advantage in dismissing me? What am I giving up–what use am I now? What do I still possess that is painful to part with? What more has a man to cling to–who is prepared to surrender his daughters to men's embrace–into your embrace?–It is such a small thing that I ask of one of you–if the seventh lot is played into my hands–I beg of you to take it! (*His* DAUGHTERS *cling to him tightly.* JACQUES DE WISSANT *and* PIERRE DE WISSANT *stare at the ground.*) You fail to understand me. I am going past you–it is a pity this last opportunity should be wasted. For afterwards every man will be wrapped up in himself–and you will lose contact with each other–there will be no holding back. I warn you now!

PIERRE DE WISSANT: (*straightening himself.*) You must turn

back–you can go away–you are older than any of us. None
but you can still do it. And were there one man here–if not you
–another–or yet a third!–who had any right to leave–we
should accompany him to the door and kiss the hem of his
robe!

(JEAN D'AIRE *looks at him in astonishment*.)

JACQUES DE WISSANT: (*bursting out*.) Then there would be an
end to this day–that torments us with indecision!
PIERRE DE WISSANT: (*heavily*.) That leaves so little time–to
find words!
JACQUES DE WISSANT: (*violently as before*.) They burn on our
tongues–they scorch our lips–but we may not cry out!
PIERRE DE WISSANT: We have to wait–and time is slipping by!
JACQUES DE WISSANT: (*distraught*.) And one of us may yet
go out as a laughing-stock–with the seventh lot!
JEAN D'AIRE: (*having understood, smilingly*.) Are you trying
to find words? Are you not in love? Can words seek out a
desire–and fulfil it? Do not place the blame on the uncertainties
of this day–for they have buoyed you up. You have not yet
learned–that words reduce the value of things. And do you
not cherish your love above all else?–Why haggle with this
day? Is it worth a jot to you? To bride and bridegroom?–The
hope of being seventh among seven is unreliable–so rejoice in
this certainty at least:–you will in this last night celebrate
your wedding feast! (*He pushes forward his* DAUGHTERS *towards the two, turns round and goes through the tapestry*.)
JACQUES DE WISSANT: (*embracing the* FIRST DAUGHTER *and
stammering*.) I will not be the seventh!
THE FIRST DAUGHTER: Now I shall wait for you!
PIERRE DE WISSANT: (*has pulled the* SECOND DAUGHTER *close
to him*.) For the sake of this night–I will cheat myself of the
seventh lot!
THE SECOND DAUGHTER: Tonight I will live!

(*The sisters slowly walk away from them–their heads turned
back towards* JACQUES DE WISSANT *and* PIERRE DE WISSANT
and, waving to them faintly, reach the door. Exeunt. JACQUES

103

DE WISSANT *and* PIERRE DE WISSANT *stand on the step: as they turn round the tapestry is drawn back. The room now revealed has considerable depth. High walls and the broad ceiling are encrusted with decorative minerals and stones from all corners of the earth and with glittering sea shells. A table–near to the step–is laid for a meal: seven silver cups, plates. In the middle of the table a bowl covered by a blue cloth. Two unsmiling* HUNCHBACKS–*servants–have pulled the tapestry right back and go from the sides of the stage to a door left front. Along the back of the table sit:* EUSTACHE DE SAINT-PIERRE *in the middle, on his left the* FIFTH COUNCILLOR *and then the* FOURTH COUNCILLOR–*on this side there is an empty chair; on the right the* THIRD COUNCILLOR *and* JEAN D'AIRE; *here too a chair is empty.*)

EUSTACHE DE SAINT-PIERRE: (*gesturing* JACQUES DE WISSANT *towards his left.*) Jacques de Wissant, take your seat there!– (To PIERRE DE WISSANT.) You are to be at the furthest end of the table, Pierre de Wissant. We must seat you brothers apart from each other, so that you do not again break the circle which once already has been all but closed!–(*Again to* PIERRE DE WISSANT.) You are the nearest to the door. (To JACQUES DE WISSANT.) You are furthest from it. (To *the others.*) Between these two the rest of us shall reach it earlier or later. (*With a sudden burst of cheerfulness.*) Earlier or later –why should we rush the few steps that we have yet to take. We still have time–we know our duty–By tomorrow midday we shall have more leisure than anyone! (*The* TWO HUNCH-BACKS *have brought to the table bowls heaped with purple grapes, green figs and yellow apples.*) Let us enjoy the supper. Fruits!–Who will leave this table without taking his fill?– The eye feasts upon them–the palate savours the sweet juices distilled in a land far beyond our sight. And now the ripe fruit rolls into our hands!–Is it not a fitting reward for the zeal with which we bridged the sea from coast to coast to gain these luscious fruits?–Enjoy them! (*The others hesitate, silent and unmoving. The* HUNCHBACKS *bring the jugs filled with wine and put them down. Now they take up position behind*

EUSTACHE DE SAINT-PIERRE.) Wine—! Whose thirst is so small that he will not linger at this table? Who will rise and push his chair and turn round and go away?—I beg you—sample their sweetness!—(*He looks round the table—then takes a fruit from the bowl.*) We are sitting round this table—pursuing the same goal—all of one mind—and so we share the same food! (*He slices the fruit into seven pieces. He gives the plate to one of the* HUNCHBACKS, *and both of them go round the table: starting from the right, the* SECOND HUNCHBACK *places a portion before each in turn—excepting* EUSTACHE DE SAINT-PIERRE, *before whom the plate is placed once more with the remaining portion on it.* EUSTACHE DE SAINT-PIERRE *pours wine into his cup.*) We all eat of this fruit—and now savour the same wine! (*The* FIRST HUNCHBACK *carries the cup over to* PIERRE DE WISSANT. *The latter drinks, gives it back to the* HUNCHBACK. *With the exception of* EUSTACHE DE SAINT-PIERRE *all drink,* EUSTACHE DE SAINT-PIERRE *receives the cup last of all and drinks from it.*) We have drunk—now eat! (*He eats his portion of fruit. The others—bent over the table—do likewise. The door right front is opened—*JEAN DE VIENNE *enters and stands holding it open: the muffled noise of the crowd outside penetrates into the room.* EUSTACHE DE SAINT-PIERRE, *smiling.*) Jean de Vienne, we are enjoying our supper. The fruit and wine are refreshing us!

JEAN DE VIENNE: (*closes the door and moves front centre.*) Anxiety has driven me into this room. The distress lessened by the appearance of the first—burst out again as the last of you entered here. Already they are muttering and shouting for one of you to appear. He must step forth and show himself before them—and put an end to this uncertainty! The people of Calais have been changed and transformed almost beyond recognition by this fever of theirs:—in which they will believe in their deliverance only when the seventh steps out from among you. It is not that they doubt the strength of will of one of your number—they are not yet reproaching you with that! —their own strength has been drained by waiting since early morning. Now it wells up irresistibly as the moment of decision draws near!—Eustache de Saint-Pierre, I know what I am asking of you–of you all! Eustache de Saint-Pierre, send them certainty, answer their demands–for them it means much–for you it is only a small thing: do not haggle out this brief moment of time!

EUSTACHE DE SAINT-PIERRE: You bring with you into this room the raucous voices from outside. We can hear their muffled murmuring and shrill hissing–they rumble in our ears–they are not a product of our imaginations. But the deed we have to do is tomorrow not now–must we not control our impatience? (*Quickly.*) Our meal is ended. Tell that to the citizens outside. But tell them quickly, Jean de Vienne! (*At his gesture the* HUNCHBACKS *begin to clear the table.* JEAN DE VIENNE *waits for a moment, then goes off quickly to the right. The* TWO HUNCHBACKS *having finished their task withdraw towards the left at the rear. On the table only the covered bowl remains.*) The table is empty–now the talk can go round the table. And the meal be brought to a fitting end. Who will not wisely share both food and talk, so that each may be enjoyed to the full? You ate in silence–now you are doubly ready for talk. Now each will be ready to reveal his innermost thoughts–so we must talk openly of the grievous burden this day placed upon us!–(*He turns to the* FIFTH COUNCILLOR *at his side.*) What was it that occupied you above all else between early this morning and coming here?

THT FIFTH COUNCILLOR: (*staring before him.*) I have an old business associate, whom I brought with me to the very door of this room. I wanted to acquaint him with my plans. I wanted to initiate him into my projects–my secret aspirations.–I could not do it. My lips were sealed. Was this really to be the last time I should speak to him? Would I not be divulging unnecessarily what was dearest to me? Or should I not take this chance in order not to lose it. One possibility spurred me on–the other held me back. And out of these contradictions arose the torture of this day:–the uncertainty of the final outcome! (*The others have raised their heads and look at him in bewildered astonishment.*)

EUSTACHE DE SAINT-PIERRE: (*turning quickly to the* THIRD COUNCILLOR *next to him, amazed.*) What could be worse than rising from your seat in the open hall and stepping forward in the presence of all? Was not the decision to discard your bright robes—and with them any hope of a long life—the most difficult part? Is there anything more bitter than this?

THE THIRD COUNCILLOR: (*nods solemnly.*) My old mother accompanied me. She bore the news of her son's decision this morning with unfailing courage. Here she clung lamenting to my breast!—(*Looking up.*) Did I not deprive her of the final parting? Did I not stop the cry with which she drew me back to her once more? Did I not slip away like an empty shadow? Only to return grief-stricken to her bosom? Did I not worsen the pains by returning again and again?—In the same breath she said farewell and welcomed me back. We were spun round in a raging whirlpool of confusion. And uncertainty made her stammer—distorted her words—until she could find no more and crept away from me—empty and poor—robbed of the riches that she could no more place before me!—(*Supporting his head on his hands.*) She suffered my pain—she gave voice to my lamentations. To stand up and go forward before all present—that is easy. It is not that deed which weighs me down.— (*He spreads his hands over the table.*) This deed—where is it? —

(*The unrest round the table indicates agreement with the* THIRD COUNCILLOR.)

EUSTACHE DE SAINT-PIERRE: (*bending over towards the* FOURTH COUNCILLOR.) You came after these two. Did you walk more slowly, because this hour had become the most precious in your life? Did you measure it out with your footsteps—as fingers value the links of a golden chain slipping through them? Did the shadow of your decision loom darkly? Do you drink more thirstily the eternal light that still shines upon you?

THE FOURTH COUNCILLOR: I went from my house—and she who has always been by my side—went with me. We walked side by side, unhurried, unhesitant—as on a fine summer's eve outside the city. Our pulses did not quicken—nor did they fail us. It is a day like any other. (*More to himself.*) Yesterday was suffused with light—as it had been from the beginning of our time together. No shadow ever eclipsed it—no darkness ever raged round it–no desire went unanswered–no happiness not shared by us. Is it not right that a black cloud should loom overhead tomorrow?–Must I not walk into it–weighed down by my debt of gratitude? Do I not cry out my gratitude–yes, gratitude –as it crushes me with its might?–Do I not long for it– do my lips not ache–do my arms not reach out to clasp tightly the woman whom I must thank–with words of fire–in the closest embrace?–Are her lips not opened–her white hands not stretched out towards me–is not her body eager for the ultimate ecstasy? Are we not drawn towards each other–yet unable to move?––Our arms fell limply at our sides–our mouths were silent–we stood like strangers–Who will voice his gratitude before the final gift is bestowed? Who will reject further gifts because of past delight? Who will give and receive without fear of excess?–That hour was darker than the deepest night. I have but one burning desire–to leave this darkness behind. Set free or delivered up–it is one and the same. To be delivered up is no hardship–to be set free offers no temptation: one or the other will at last offer me the gift of certainty.

(JACQUES DE WISSANT *and* PIERRE DE WISSANT *have leapt to their feet simultaneously and stretch out their arms towards the covered bowl.*)

EUSTACHE DE SAINT-PIERRE: Jacques de Wissant–Pierre de Wissant, are you not brothers? This morning when you all came down together from your places making one too many, your common blood prevented each from standing aside to save himself at the cost of the other's life. Are you set at odds with each other by noon? Does not one of you want the other to draw the life saving lot any more? Does each of you want to snatch at it?–(*Anticipating an answer, to* JEAN D'AIRE.) What makes the path into this room so long and dark for you?

JEAN D'AIRE: I do not have far to go any more. Every way is short–the goal is near. I can see it so close before me, no dust can obscure it. All around me is light–the darkness has faded away: I know where I am going. My time is spent–my treasures portioned out. I hold nothing more in these shrivel-led hands!–What can my share be of the deed for which I

108

am preparing myself? Am I not a parasite with little right to the praise that thunders about you? Am I not the fool in cap and bells–beside you? I may swell with pride–but all that will happen to me is the inevitable. I come down from the lowest step of my old age–there is no other beneath it–why should my feet hesitate? I see it all–what still lies before me is clear as crystal. Whether I draw the seventh lot–or not, it makes no difference. So forgive and respect the shame I feel at sitting here among you!–(*More cheerfully*.) You are worthy –for you suffer torment. You have a difficult choice to make. You have to renounce–I am already empty. You have to close your eyes against the bright light of day–I am already blind. you are to choke the very breath in your throats–my breast is already dead. The most difficult of tasks is demanded of you–but such a summons is no longer for me:–I am secure against all passions–beyond doubt over the outcome–my lot is the same– one way or the other–advanced age has turned me to ice– hence I am at rest amid the unrest–in my perfect certainty.

(*With* JEAN D'AIRE'S *last words the movement around the table has increased: hands grasp towards the cloth over the bowl*.)

PIERRE DE WISSANT: (*on his feet, his clenched fists pressed against his brow*.) Tomorrow I will go out of the city the first among you–I will not turn my head to look back at you–I will stretch out the rope before me and fervently tighten the knot–and laugh and curse–(*Bursting out*.) I do not want the seventh lot–let me have my own!

JACQUES DE WISSANT: (*stammering*.) I do not want the last– nor the first–I do not seek to live beyond this night!–(*Bursting out*.) I will have mine–let me have my own!–(*Choking*.) The other leads to madness!

THE FOURTH COUNCILLOR: (*to* EUSTACHE DE SAINT-PIERRE.) Pass the bowl round the table!

THE FIFTH COUNCILLOR: (*more urgently*.) Eustache de Saint-Pierre–pass the bowl round the table!

JACQUES DE WISSANT–PIERRE DE WISSANT *and the* THIRD COUN-CILLOR: (*screaming in unison*.) Pass the bowl round the table!

JEAN DE VIENNE: (*Enters hastily from the right. Leaving the door open he goes swiftly to the middle of the room. Sounds from outside fill the room: shrill shouts, whining howls, shrieking and discordant whistling.*) Eustache de Saint-Pierre, they will wait no longer. They demand the seventh. They are shouting me down—I can no longer persuade them to wait even a little longer!—I have posted guards outside the entrance—but I place no reliance upon their small numbers. Your delaying brings the revolt nearer. We shall be unable to suppress it. The consequences will be terrible for everyone! Eustache de Saint-Pierre, I am no longer afraid to ask—I implore you:—send out the seventh!

EUSTACHE DE SAINT-PIERRE: You have come a little too soon—

JEAN DE VIENNE: It will be a little too late!

EUSTACHE DE SAINT-PIERRE: (*unmoved.*)—and you disturb us here in this room: can you not see that every hand is outstretched? —(*Vehemently.*) Do you want to shatter the calm that unites us round this table as for a solemn ceremony? Is it not vital to us?—You force your way in bringing uproar from outside:—aren't you all out there in the sunlight—does not the mild air caress your every brow?—Spare us your babbling and whining!—Bask in your warmth and sunshine—while we choose cold and darkness!

JEAN DE VIENNE: Eustache de Saint-Pierre, I will wait here and go out with the seventh!

EUSTACHE DE SAINT-PIERRE: (*even more insistently.*) You are a stranger among us—for you have not partaken of the meal at this table—you have not drunk with us—you are set apart from us, like all those on the far side of a deep abyss!

JEAN DE VIENNE: Eustache de Saint-Pierre, how much longer?

EUSTACHE DE SAINT-PIERRE: We are ready now! (*With head bowed* JEAN DE VIENNE *goes off to the right. Breathless silence reigns.* EUSTACHE DE SAINT-PIERRE *draws the covered bowl towards him.*) The blue ball is cold to the touch—and casts a deathly chill. To whom will it fall—to whom will it not? Now I am as curious as you!—Jacques de Wissant—Pierre de Wissant, you caused this game to be played—so begin it now. This time may the first ball part you, lest you confuse the outcome again!—(*He hands the bowl to the* FIFTH COUN-

CILLOR *next to him, the latter gives it to the* FOURTH COUNCIL-
LOR.–*The* FOURTH COUNCILLOR *offers it to* JACQUES DE WIS-
SANT. *The attention of the others is riveted upon him.*
EUSTACHE DE SAINT-PIERRE *stares straight ahead across the
table.* JACQUES DE WISSANT *lifts the cloth with his left hand
and inserts his right. He removes it, his fingers tightly clenched–stretches his arm out for a considerable time across the
table–and opens his cupped hand to reveal a blue ball,* EUSTA-
CHE DE SAINT-PIERRE *stares straight ahead across the table.*
JACQUES DE WISSANT *presses his hands, the ball held between
them, to his breast. the* FOURTH COUNCILLOR *returns the bowl
to the* FIFTH COUNCILLOR–*and reaches for a ball: which he dis-
plays: it is blue. Then he supports his head on his folded hands.
the* FIFTH COUNCILLOR *hands the bowl to* EUSTACHE DE SAINT-
PIERRE *who looks up fleetingly and chooses quickly: the blue
ball, which he takes out, he places before him on the table–
takes the bowl and holds it out to the* FIFTH COUNCILLOR. *The*
FIFTH COUNCILLOR *hesitates in amazement–then he too draws a
blue ball. He opens his outstretched hands and flings back his
head.* EUSTACHE DE SAINT-PIERRE *turns with the bowl–without
looking up–to the* THIRD COUNCILLOR. *the* THIRD
COUNCILLOR *shows his blue ball, places it on the table–in order
to offer* JEAN D'AIRE *the bowl.* JEAN D'AIRE *looks at* PIERRE
DE WISSANT, *smiles–and chooses slowly from under the cloth.
Again he glances at* PIERRE DE WISSANT *and opens his hand
–without himself looking at it–to reveal the blue ball.*)

PIERRE DE WISSANT: (*bends forward–and rises.*) I am the one!

(*At the sound of his voice they all turn to face him–the* THIRD
COUNCILLOR *puts the bowl down.*)

EUSTACHE DE SAINT-PIERRE: (*quickly.*) Have you chosen your
lot?

PIERRE DE WISSANT: One remains–you hold six blue balls!

EUSTACHE DE SAINT-PIERRE: (*shakes his head.*) The bowl is not
empty–shall one of the hunchbacks have to empty it afterwards?

(*He pushes the bowl nearer to him, the* THIRD COUNCILLOR
slides it across the table right in front of him.)

PIERRE DE WISSANT: (*shrugs his shoulders, pulls the cloth back —stops short and slowly lifts out a blue ball–stammering.*) The last ball–is blue! (*Round the table there is silence.*)

JACQUES DE WISSANT: (*holding out his ball.*) This one–is blue!

THE THIRD COUNCILLOR: (*as* JACQUES DE WISSANT.) This is– like that one!

THE FIFTH COUNCILLOR, THE FOURTH COUNCILLOR: (*first singly.*) These–(*Then together.*) are like yours!

JEAN D'AIRE: (*calmly.*) Eustache de Saint-Pierre, have the hunch-backs mixed up the bowls?

EUSTACHE DE SAINT-PIERRE (*countering their stares with a smile.*) I know the reason. I arranged it so that you should all draw the same! (*Their eyes, filled with amazement, rest upon him.* EUSTACHE DE SAINT-PIERRE *continues, more spiritedly.*) Does this surprise you? Does the solution escape you–does not the puzzle fall into place? (*He looks from one to the other; they remain motionless. Then he nods.*) The confusion of this day rages within you–and you cannot see what is before your eyes!–(*Sitting upright.*) Therefore one of us must take the lead–I shall bring you out of confusion to the goal!–(*Emphatically, speaking to left and right in turn.*) Who thrust himself forward this morning in the open hall? Did he not come in coat of shining armour–did not the sword stab high from his mailed fist? Did not upright valour flash from the crest of his helmet? Did not the bravery of his deed dwarf all others? Hacking sword, blows of battle–were these not the things haloed in a fiery glow–conferring the ultimate in glory, and drawing the best men? What could stand up to them? Did not shame slink away and cower into a corner?–(*After a pause.*) I did not slink away–I stood up to him and weighed my deed against his–and struck the sword from his hand and stripped the gaudy standard to shreds. He yielded–I remained firm! (*The others listen hunched far forward over the table.*) How did I strike the sword from his hand? How did I demolish his deed–and the chain of such deeds that reach back to the beginning of recorded time? How did I diminish them in his presence –and show them up in their true light? Did I attack him as I was entitled to–did I abuse him with ill-measured words as I ground his courage into the mud? How could he be ablaze with courage tomorrow if he hurtles into a battle that has been decided today?—And is his courage today so great—when the battle has not even begun? Surely his is a blind leap—: leaving him in heady unawareness of all the implications!—Does he not turn his deed into an act of cowardice by deciding on it today? Does he not bring it into disrepute because he does not pursue it to the end? Today he pulls down the visor—thick darkness wells up behind it and chokes the air—tomorrow after many blows a feeble thrust will fell him—for even before the last blow of his sword he is already dead! (PIERRE DE WISSANT *has gone from his place and—leaning against* THE THIRD COUNCILLOR—*is close by* EUSTACHE DE SAINT-PIERRE *listening. The others sit, their chins cupped in their palms.* EUSTACHE DE SAINT-PIERRE *continues, laughing to himself.*) He gave his sword away—and climbed across the many steps and himself carried upwards—step by step—the burden which he lifted from my shoulders. I sighed with relief as he went up out of sight. Had I not caught him in a cunning mesh? And did he not free himself with a shake of the shoulder and cast the net at my feet? Did I not outstrip his courage in this way—and that—in every way? Was not my decision—(*To some of them individually.*)—yours—yours—and yours—taken today by you yourselves? Were not you—(*As before.*)—you—you each able to take your leave and shut yourselves off from the world, so that tomorrow no light—or life—will torment you any more?—(*Looking round the table.*) Are you not separated from your deed—as he was? Have you not removed the sting of your deed—as he did? Are you not afraid that to-morrow a child will see through your cleverness—and fasten fool's bells to the rope about your necks? (*Some of them nod slowly. Gesturing with one finger.*) We were on the verge—of bringing our work to shame with this cleverness of ours!—(*Running his fingers through* PIERRE DE WISSANT'S *hair.*) Then you came—you and your brother—to my aid! (JACQUES DE WISSANT *goes over and places his arm round* PIERRE DE WISSANT. EUSTACHE DE SAINT-PIERRE *speaks to each of them in turn.*) You exceeded the required number and again burst open our

113

circle which was all but closed. One of you restored freedom of choice to us all and so released us all. Now each became superfluous–the seventh–the extra man–(*To the others.*) Who was it to be? Could not you–you–or you–be turned away? You as easily as the next? Might you not leave us–only to be forced to rejoin us? Was your deed not taken away from you and handed back to you again–in swift alternation? Could you lose it for the space of a breath–or conceal yourself within it–in its urgency with no means of escape? It remained open to you–the gateway was not barred against you!–(To PIERRE DE WISSANT *and* JACQUES DE WISSANT.) Thus the man who fled across the steps could not fling back my reproaches in my face: they were justified by you two when you stood there. For then our decision was postponed until the afternoon!––

THE FOURTH COUNCILLOR: (*looking up at him.*) Surely it is–tomorrow!–that this deed is demanded of us? Have we not been granted this space of time–from this afternoon till early tomorrow, which is long enough–to let me bury myself deep and secure against all anguish?

EUSTACHE DE SAINT-PIERRE: (*cheerfully.*) Look at the lot–it did not fall to you!–(*Quickly to counter the movement round the table.*) I played this game of drawing lots with you. I invented it out of the experiences of this day. Did I not charm it out of the very words you spoke round this table?–(To the FIFTH COUNCILLOR.) What has been heaviest for you to bear since this morning? Try to remember! (Now to the FOURTH COUNCILLOR.) What drove thorns into your flesh? Conceal nothing!–(To the THIRD COUNCILLOR.) What deep anguish raged within you? Speak openly!–(To JACQUES DE WISSANT *and* PIERRE DE WISSANT.) What tormented you? Speak out! Do not hesitate!–(To JEAN D'AIRE, *pausing suddenly.*) What made you so profoundly glad? (*Emphatically.*) You were lulled by certainty–the others were agitated by uncertainty. Racked by this fever–you became fainthearted–: you are betraying the deed that glows within you! (PIERRE DE WISSANT *and* JACQUES DE WISSANT *go to their places; round the table all is still. With more vigour:*) Today you seek the decision–today you deaden your resolve–today you let fever overwhelm your

will to act. Thick smoke swirls about your heads and feet and shrouds the way before you. Are you worthy to tread it? To proceed to the final goal? To do this deed–which becomes a crime–unless its doers are transformed? Are you prepared–for this your new deed?–It shakes accepted values–disperses former glory–dismays age-long courage–muffles that which rang clear –blackens that which shone brightly–rejects that which was valid!–Are you the new men?–Is your hand cool–your blood calm–your zeal devoid of rage? Will you judge yourselves by your deed–do you measure up to it? The deed is but one half– the doers are the other–one destroys without the other–are we now criminals?–(*The others stare intently at him across the table*.) You court this deed–before it you discard your robes and sandals–it demands you naked and new-born–around it no battle clashes–no fire flares–no cry shrieks. You cannot kindle it with burning ardour or with raging desire. It burns a clear, smokeless flame–cold despite its heat–gentle in its blinding light. Thus it towers up high–thus you go your way–thus it accepts you :–unhalting, unhasting–cool and bright within yourselves–happy but unfevered–bold but not delirious–willing but not angry--the new men of the new deed!–Deed and doers already fused into one–as today in the morrow! Why should you want to separate today from tomorrow, if your deed and your will to act are one? If you can bear it simply and resolutely to its conclusion, in which you are delivered up or set free? What more is there to tempt you? Or trouble you? Is your impatience not blown away–to sound in the distance like the discord outside this room? (*He has raised his voice to counter the growing noise outside, which swiftly penetrates into the chamber. The door right front is thrown open:* JEAN DE VIENNE *at the head of several* COUNCILLORS *bursts in.*
JEAN DE VIENNE: (*cries out.*) Eustache de Saint-Pierre, the guards have been driven back from the entrance–we have bolted the gates–which are still holding out against them!

(*The sound of persistent battering against the gates re-echoes in the chamber.*)

A COUNCILLOR: They are rushing the door!

(Immediately outside the sound of the door crashing in—followed by a shout of triumph.)

ANOTHER COUNCILLOR: The stairway is open before them!

ANOTHER COUNCILLOR: They are running up the stairs!

ANOTHER COUNCILLOR: They are entering the room!

ANOTHER COUNCILLOR: They want to take one of you by force!

JEAN DE VIENNE: Eustache de Saint-Pierre, who was freed by the drawing of lots?

EUSTACHE DE SAINT-PIERRE: *(on his feet, loudly.)* There was an error—the balls were mixed up in the bowl. We have tormented ourselves to find a solution—now we lack the strength to repeat the game!—*(Louder still.)* Let us rest until the morning—*(speaking also to those round the table.)* —: at the first sound of the bell each of you will set out from his home—and he who is the last to arrive in the middle of the market place—will go free!

(All are shocked and silent.)

JACQUES DE WISSANT *and* PIERRE DE WISSANT: *(run round the table to him.)* Eustache de Saint-Pierre—

PIERRE DE WISSANT: *(continuing alone.)* Both of us will leave the same house tomorrow—are we to create renewed confusion by arriving together at the market place?

EUSTACHE DE SAINT-PIERRE: Are you still worried about to-morrow? Are you not able to run ahead of the others on your young legs and be the first to arrive at the goal?—*(He stands up.)*

JEAN DE VIENNE: Eustache de Saint-Pierre, are you prepared to go and face the tumult outside?

EUSTACHE DE SAINT-PIERRE: *(beckoning to those at the table.)* Not alone—for we are seven:—should it not calm them that there is still one too many? Is it not possible that one of us, in his agitation, may waver in the coming night? Is it not wise of us to be one too many?—Let us make that clear to those outside!

(The seven come down from the raised part of the room and

go past JEAN DE VIENNE *and the* COUNCILLORS, *to whom they give no sign of acknowledgement, out of the door and into the noise, which swiftly fades and dies away.* JEAN DE VIENNE *and the* COUNCILLORS *stare at one another in amazement.*)

ACT III

The market place. Steps rise up to the church door which—its pointed façade carved with many figures—takes up the whole background, except for two narrow side streets leading off into the distance on either side. Objects and people are hardly visible in the grey light of the early morning: crowded ranks of citizens line the side streets and even reach the edges of the market place— their faces recognizable as pale patches against the darker background. In the centre the COUNCILLORS *are moving to and fro.*

JEAN DE VIENNE: Here is the key of the city. I have known it well for many years—my fingers better than my mind know its every curve and unevenness—but this morning it feels strange in my hands. Its intolerable weight drags down my arms— wrenches at my shoulders—and threatens to force me to the ground!—The heat of my body does not warm it. The icy frost from it chills my whole body. This tiny scrap of metal is freezing me!—I can hardly keep hold of it. (*The* COUNCILLORS *stand motionless round him.*) I hesitate to place it in another's hands. I fear it will break even the strongest—snap the most pliant will of any man. Will he not carry with him a twofold burden: that which I give him here—and that already placed on him by his decision to be one of the six? I do not know whom I should ask to suffer such intolerable strain!—(*Silence reigns. He stiffens.*) Are you clear in your mind which one I should send out with the key at the head of all the others?

A COUNCILLOR: Surely, Jean de Vienne, the man who was the first to come forward in the open hall yesterday—must lead them out today?

ANOTHER COUNCILLOR: Is it not the responsibility of the man— who encouraged the others by coming forward?

117

JEAN DE VIENNE: (*looks up.*)–May not Eustache de Sainte-Pierre be the last to arrive? (*Renewed silence.* JEAN DE VIENNE *continues after a pause.*) I will name no one. How can we know how any one of them will come out of this night? Who has seen just one of them making his way here? If you make your choice now you may well be deciding upon the weakest of them!–(*More strongly.*) We breathe in the morning breeze–the brightness of the sun shall not fail us–it is easy for us to criticize–I do not want to single out anyone yet!—

ANOTHER COUNCILLOR: (*resolutely.*) Jean de Vienne, by deciding this for them we are only trying to free their last morning from dispute:–give the key to the first to arrive here!

JEAN DE VIENNE: (*slowly.*) Whose home is the shortest distance away? (*Pointing to the sides of the stage with increasing violence.*) Have they not counted already the number of steps he will take? Has their curiosity not run ahead and dragged him through the streets–a hundred times already? Or their pitiless fervour slackened since yesterday? Did the stony ground not echo wildly throughout the night to the hard clatter of nimble feet? Did it not sound like a hail of pebbles hurled against a window pane?–They have turned it into a shameful game to while away their impatience–now they await its conclusion, so that each can boast to the other he judged the distance more accurately!–I have not the power to turn them away from the edge of the market place–but I begrudge them this spectacle!–(*To the* COUNCILLORS.) Can you not hear–can you claim not to have given a single thought to the least and longest distance:–who is the nearest to this place?

SOME OF THE COUNCILLORS: (*indistinctly, hesitatingly.*) Eustache de Saint-Pierre–(*Then several speak out.*) Eustache de Saint-Pierre!

JEAN DE VIENNE: You all name him alone. Again you pick him out. His is always the name that rings out. It lured us yesterday–and may well lead us astray again! You are right, he is the nearest. Yesterday he thrust himself forward–and now he will be the one to rush on ahead of the others. He will be the first of them–with his swift feet–his confident strength. He will demand this of me: to lead out the others and bear on his outstretched arms the burden that weighs me down as if it were the merest featherweight. Now all fear has left me—this game and the goal no longer matter—before Eustache de Saint-Pierre all uncertainty disappears!

(*Arms stretch upwards from the throng at the sides of the market place—and more arms reach up to join them: the pale gleaming hands point emphatically upwards. A slender beam of light catches the tip of the church façade. The* COUNCILLORS *raise their eyes.*)

JEAN DE VIENNE: (*with a violent gesture.*) The time has come—we must prepare their robes! (*The strident note of a bell rings out at long intervals. The arms slowly fall. Some of the* COUNCILLORS *bend down and gather up dark bundles. The bell stops ringing.*)—They have set out—the streets are being shaken by a movement such as they have never known before!—(*Speaking after a pause.*) Let us go and meet the first. We all know which route Eustache de Saint-Pierre is taking! (*He goes to the right, some follow him—including one bearing a bundle. From the left the sound of steady regular footsteps; at the same time from back left a whisper runs through the crowd. On the right some are still pointing hesitantly—then arms swiftly point across the square—the hissing swells in volume: 'The first one!' the* FIFTH COUNCILLOR *comes from the left. He halts his purposeful steps in the centre of the market square. He pauses stiffly for an instant—then his eyes sweep round in a wide circle to right—and left. Breathless silence has fallen. the* FIFTH COUNCILLOR *looks down at the ground—and steps out of his sandals. Then he raises his eyes and with steady hands begins to untie his robe at the neck. His shoulders and arms are bared—now he gathers the robe to his breast and waits. A* COUNCILLOR *comes forward, unrolls the bundle and withdraws a short length of rope. He takes up position immediately behind the* FIFTH COUNCILLOR, *raises the drab sack-cloth and slips it over his head: it hangs heavily about him, enveloping his arms and dragging round his feet.—Now he slackens the noose—and places it round his shoulders, allowing the loose end of the rope to hang down at the back. The* FIFTH COUNCILLOR *takes a step to one side. The* COUNCILLOR *bends down, picks up the discarded shoes and the robe, and deposits them on the steps.*)

JEAN DE VIENNE: (*had turned round sharply at the arrival of the* FIFTH COUNCILLOR. *Some of the* COUNCILLORS *have been standing in* JEAN DE VIENNE's *path gesturing violently at the* FIFTH COUNCILLOR. *Now* JEAN DE VIENNE *brushes them aside.*)—I can see him. He was the first to join Eustache de Saint-Pierre in the hall. He walked hurriedly. So he arrives before the one we expect to be first. Eustache de Saint-Pierre is coming from his house and does not hurry. He knows how long it takes. Eustache de Saint-Pierre will be the next—the second in the market place! (*He turns back to the right. Again deep silence reigns. From the left the ring of footsteps as before. The same whisper as before runs round the market place:* 'The second one'—*and dies away, the* THIRD COUNCILLOR *makes his way over to the* FIFTH COUNCILLOR *without pausing anu after a fleeting glance takes up position next to him. A* COUNCILLOR *performs the same ceremony—and withdraws.*)

JEAN DE VIENNE: (*without moving, in astonishment.*) Who is it?

ANOTHER COUNCILLOR: The one who stood up after the other two and came forward!

JEAN DE VIENNE: After him—and whom else?

ANOTHER COUNCILLOR: After him—and after Eustache de Saint-Pierre!

JEAN DE VIENNE: Eustache de Saint-Pierre—! (*shrugging off his astonishment.*) Who can gauge how quickly or slowly a man will come when setting out on a walk such as this? One man will rush out of his house and dash headlong through the streets—another will pause to snuff the lamps and turn the lock in his door. It does not depend on the feet—theirs is the least important part I nearly raised my voice to reproach him—and now the reproach falls heavily back on me. I am ashamed to face him if he is the next to arrive. Let us stand aside for Eustache de Saint-Pierre!

(*He moves quickly away from the right. From the right comes the sound of slow dragging footsteps. On the left of the*

market place heads crane forward. From the right the whisper-
ing swells up: 'The third one!'—and flows further towards
the left. JEAN D'AIRE *comes out of the righthand side street,*
pauses and glances across the market place. Then he nods,
starts walking and reaches the centre. He looks searchingly at
the two in the middle—and sets about removing the robe from
his lean body. A COUNCILLOR *provides him with the sack-*
cloth and rope then removes the bright robe and shoes.)

ANOTHER COUNCILLOR: (*stepping in front of* JEAN DE VIENNE.)
That is not Eustache de Saint-Pierre!

ANOTHER COUNCILLOR: (*speaking to other* COUNCILLORS.)
Eustache de Saint-Pierre has still to come!

ANOTHER COUNCILLOR: (*to* JEAN DE VIENNE.) It is the one who
stepped forward before Jacques de Wissant and Pierre de Wissant.

ANOTHER COUNCILLOR: (*to* JEAN DE VIENNE.) He is the oldest of
them!

JEAN DE VILLE: (*excitedly.*) He is weaker than any of the
others—then Eustache de Saint-Pierre! His weary footsteps have
dragged through the streets—past Eustache de Saint-Pierre's
house! None of the others find walking such an effort—surely
the slowest taking the same route would overtake him!

ANOTHER COUNCILLOR: (*to other* COUNCILLORS.) Eustache de
Saint-Pierre has not yet set out!

MANY COUNCILLORS: (*to one another.*) Eustache de Saint-Pierre
has not yet set out.

(*These voices mingle with the murmur that circles the market*
square from left to right: 'The fourth one!' the FOURTH COUN-
CILLOR *comes—and quickly counting those already there—joins*
the group in the middle. A COUNCILLOR *assists him to change*
his garments against a background of noise caused by the con-
tinuing commotion among the COUNCILLORS.)

A COUNCILLOR: (*almost in a whisper to* JEAN DE VIENNE.) This
man was the fourth to come forward in the open hall!

JEAN DE VIENNE: (*stammering.*) Are four gathered here? And
Eustache de Saint-Pierre is not among them?

ANOTHER COUNCILLOR: Eustache de Saint-Pierre is still not among
them!

JEAN DE VIENNE: Eustache de Saint-Pierre is still missing—

ANOTHER COUNCILLOR: Still two of the six to come!

SEVERAL COUNCILLORS: (*crowding in front of* JEAN DE VIENNE.) Still two of the six to come!

ANOTHER COUNCILLOR: (*confidently.*) One of them will be Eustache de Saint-Pierre!

ANOTHER COUNCILLOR: Eustache de Saint-Pierre will be the last!

ANOTHER COUNCILLOR: He will take the key from you, Jean de Vienne: that is why he is saving his strength so that he will not have to wait here long with the others for the last one to arrive!

JEAN DE VIENNE: (*in an angry outburst.*) Are you unable to count—your eyes not blinded by this pale shaft of light?—Work it out—work it out: who is yet to come?—How can you begin—to unravel this knot of confusion? Does it not become all the tighter—and weave itself into a thick tangle? Tie the knot—tighter and tighter!—Who will be the next to come?—You think it will be Eustache de Saint-Pierre? Will he join the others to become the fifth?—The fifth who will break the circle the fifth who will burst open the ring—the fifth who— (*Breaking off, even more excitedly.*) Jacques and Pierre de Wissant are setting off from the same house! They are brothers—so surely they will arrive together—and then seven will stand here! Will it not all finish as it began—a beginning without an end? (*More and more powerfully.*) Will I have to send them all back to play this game again—to make them repeat this terrible walk? Must we torment their bodies—with change upon change of their garments? Must we bruise their feet—warm one moment—cold and bare the next? Must we tighten and slacken the noose time and again?—Time is running out—the executioner already awaits them! It is getting lighter—the morning is passing! Perhaps we are letting deliverance slip through our fingers? (*Falteringly.*) And if Eustache de Saint-Pierre delays and comes last of all—the seventh—Eustache de Saint-Pierre, who called upon the others encouraged them to join him!—drove himself harder than any of them—if he does not come.—(*Clutching himself.*) Do not try to work it out—do not try—at every turn—you will destroy yourselves–: do not allow–your heart–or your mind–to dwell upon it—(*Drawing others with him towards the back of the market place.*) Let us not ponder–let us not seek–let us not listen for a weary footstep–nor the steps of two together–we must wait and watch!

(*Once more absolute silence falls. From the right the firm sound of two men approaching. No whispering, no pointing.* JACQUES DE WISSANT *and* PIERRE DE WISSANT *arrive, their arms tight about each other. In the centre they pause–and count. Then they kiss each other and take up their positions to the far left and right respectively. Two* COUNCILLORS *perform the ceremony. Light falls upon the church façade and lights up a group of statuary high above. The citizens have surged forward out of the side streets, encircling them. Slowly the crowd presses forward, closing in at the centre spreading over the steps so that left- and righthand groups are joined. From the crowd comes an indistinct murmuring– contented and decisive: 'The six are here!'*)

JEAN DE VIENNE: (*in boundless astonishment.*) Is Eustache de Saint-Pierre deaf? Surely his ears heard the shrill note of the bell? Is he lame that his limbs did not tremble at the footsteps passing before his door? Was the whole city not shaken by this movement in the streets? Did it not send our blood racing– our heads ringing?–winds rushing and beating about us–so that we had to fight to keep our feet? Did not every footstep pound through us and drag us in its train–six times to this place–six times a thousand footsteps to the market? Have we not been running this race time and again since yesterday –spurring on the chase–keen and hard–and arriving here– from the farthest corners of the city–before time–on time–each early–each fully prepared:–each stripped to the task–each set- ting forth—! —: is Eustache de Saint-Pierre not coming?!
A COUNCILLOR: (*crying out.*) Eustache de Saint-Pierre is not coming!
ANOTHER COUNCILLOR: (*similarly.*) Eustache de Saint-Pierre is not coming! (*The shout echoes forth. Louder and stronger*

123

comes the reply–arms point from the steps down towards the centre–: 'Six!' Renewed silence.)

A COUNCILLOR: (*Beside himself with rage.*) Eustache de Saint-Pierre has played the foulest trick on us! (*His words come pouring out.*) One of the six raised his voice in the open hall–and drew attention to Eustache de Saint-Pierre's tremendous wealth that causes him so much anxiety!–Who has warehouses like his by the harbour? Crammed high to the beams with merchandize? Who has freight in countless merchant ships? Was he who spoke out in the open hall–a brazen slanderer?–Surely his scorn was too temperate–surely he spoke out too mildly! What could he know of the twists and turns of cunning by which Eustache de Saint-Pierre avoided the drawing of lots that would destroy him?–Did he not come forward and take his place–the first, prepared to die for Calais? Was he not fully aware–what use one would be? Six are necessary–and where there are six men of daring many more will come forward! So seven stood together–one too many! How did his nimble brain slip out of the danger–how did he manage to turn the extra man to his advantage?–Who has forgotten the events of that long day yesterday? How did he keep all seven together until the afternoon? And how did he put off the decision yet again–the decision that could make him one of the six?–Did not his brazen tampering make a crude swindle of the drawing of lots? Did his cunning brain not avoid the decision–and send them all out of the room–referring them to this morning–and this morning's walk here, thus he parted company with the six–and saved his own neck from the rope?—He shuts himself up in his house–and becomes a free man!—Are we blind—stupid–would a child not see through the deception and babble out how Eustache de Saint-Pierre treacherously escaped from death?—Now he is sitting behind locked doors, his shoulders hunched over the table and mocking us–we who believed him like fools and followed him blindly like sheep!

(*From the sides of the market place and from the steps the noise increases building up to a shrieking cry:–'Six!'*)

ANOTHER COUNCILLOR: (*running forward to right front.*) Does your breath not catch in your throats–your pulse throb so in

124

your very mouths–that you are choking for shame?–Are you counterfeiters buying with false money–clinking your dud coins and yet insisting on the deal? Will you not cast this false currency from your fingers and trample it into the mud at your feet?–Do you expect them to set out–do you demand their shameful death?–have you lost all sense of value–does treachery no longer mean anything to you?–Are you not sickened by the cries from your tongues–burned by the babblings of your mouths?–Will you gorge yourselves on stolen food–devour weeds and filth like worms of the earth? Are you not wearied by your greed–your limbs not weakened by last night's frantic chase through the streets of the city? Do you still want another game? One is promised–prepared to the last detail–: now search the market place–spy out the man who concocted it all–and you will not find him–not in the light–not in the dark! Go now and seek out your rights, scream for satisfaction! (*Round the market place the cry is raised, and burst harshly forth in unison:*–'Send out the six.')

ANOTHER COUNCILLOR: (*running forward.*) I will not be a citizen of a Calais founded upon this deceit!–I will not be an accessory to treachery within its walls–I will not creep timidly about its streets! I will not profit from this betrayal–I will hold back my hands from this stigma that marks them–I will not endure such a stain upon my body!–(*He stands there with stiffly outstretched arms.*)

ANOTHER COUNCILLOR: (*running to join him, grasping his arm calls out to those behind him.*) Who will demand that the six men be sent to a shameful death? Who will burden one of them with the key? Who will throw open the gates of the city before them? Who will deliver them over this morning?– (*Strongly.*) Will anyone among us be party to this deceit? (*Among the* COUNCILLORS *there arises an uneasy movement: some are advancing–others holding back. Threateningly and more strongly from the sides:* 'Send out the six!')

ANOTHER COUNCILLOR: (*loudly.*) Calais shall not surrender–!! (*Into the now diminshed noise he speaks hurriedly.*) Neither today–nor tomorrow–shall we be at the end of our strength! We suffer no hunger–we lack nothing! Our bodies bear no wounds–the blood flows strongly in our veins–our shoulders are firm–our arms grasp the lances tightly–and the sword –We stand behind the walls–we fill the streets–the banner of France blazes out over the city–the Captain of France at our head–and before the Captain of France—(*He pauses. Deep silence.*)

ANOTHER COUNCILLOR: (*breaking out.*) Duguesclins has left the city!

ANOTHER COUNCILLOR: Eustache de Saint-Pierre has sent Duguesclins out of the city!

ANOTHER COUNCILLOR: Eustache de Saint-Pierre has betrayed us all!

ANOTHER COUNCILLOR: Eustache de Saint-Pierre prevents the city from being saved!

ANOTHER COUNCILLOR: Eustache de Saint-Pierre sought to betray us from the very start!

(*Around the market square the cry is taken up again:* 'Send out the six!!')

A COUNCILLOR: (*Flailing his arms about his head.*) We shall fetch Eustache de Saint-Pierre out of his house!

ANOTHER COUNCILLOR: We shall drag Eustache de Saint-Pierre from his table!

ANOTHER COUNCILLOR: We shall drive Eustache de Saint-Pierre before us to the market square!

(*One group of* COUNCILLORS *surges to the right and is held back by the thick crowd.*)

A COUNCILLOR: (*from the front of the stage.*) Eustache de Saint-Pierre alone shall do penance!

ANOTHER COUNCILLOR: We shall bind the key of the city to Eustache de Saint-Pierre's back!

ANOTHER COUNCILLOR: Eustache de Saint-Pierre shall drag the key out of the city on his knees! (*A new group surges towards the right.*)

A COUNCILLOR: (*from the front.*) Eustache de Saint-Pierre shall be disgraced in the open market place!

ANOTHER COUNCILLOR: We shall sit in judgement over Eustache de Saint-Pierre in front of the six!

ANOTHER COUNCILLOR: (*urging them on.*) Find Eustache de Saint-Pierre!

MANY OF THE COUNCILLORS: Find Eustache de Saint-Pierre!

(*To the right at the back of the market place the resistance of the crowd has so far been unbroken: but now it yields to the overwhelming pressure and the* COUNCILLORS *flood into the side street. The cry rings out sharply: 'Find Eustache de Saint-Pierre!'* JEAN DE VIENNE *stands alone–tired, broken. From the sides the citizens close in on him–yelling: 'Send out the six! !' In the side street the din ceases–slowly the crowd of* COUN-CILLORS *recedes–gesturing in wonderment to each other. Around the market square the uproar diminishes–those who have pressed forwards move back to the sides.* JEAN DE VIENNE *advances quickly to question the* COUNCILLORS. *They reply by pointing to the far end of the side street:–they stand wait-ing in silence–forming a pathway from the near end of the street that stretches almost to the centre of the market square. The sound of very slow footsteps approaches:–the two deeply bowed* HUNCHBACKS *are carrying a bier shrouded in black. A short distance behind* EUSTACHE DE SAINT-PIERRE'S FATHER– *a bald, haggard old man–follows; a whispy beard flutters about his face, raised upward in the manner of the blind–all his senses concentrated into his groping hands. A slim boy leads him by the waist. The* HUNCHBACKS *place the bier on the ground in the centre of the stage. The* COUNCILLORS *press closely round the six.*)

THE FATHER OF EUSTACHE DE SAINT-PIERRE: (*words forming mysteriously from his unceasingly moving lips.*) I am a cup–that overflows–– (*The boy leads him in front of the six.*) Are they standing together–? (*He runs his hands over the garment and rope of the first.*) Coarse robe and smooth rope–one!– (*as before in front of the second.*) Roughly clad and prepared–you! (*Moves on.*) You a prisoner of your harsh robes–: (*Moving on.*) You ready like the one before–! (*To the remaining two.*) More–more–next to you–the final one! (*Nod-ding his head.*) He said that six were left–waiting on the market square–the hour of their departure is come–take me to them there. They must hurry--if they want to follow me, he said--for I have gone on before!--(*He turns round, feels for the cloth covering the bier and draws it to one side.*) My son!-- (*The* COUNCILLORS *bend over him; some of them cry out:* 'Eustache de Saint-Pierre!' EUSTACHE DE SAINT-PIERRE'S FATHER *takes no notice of them.*) My mouth is overflowing-- the words that pour out are his--Mine are silent--forced back by the outpourings of this night. I am merely the bell, struck by a hammer. I am the tree, another the soughing of the wind. I am stretched out before you--he who lies here is stand- ing on my shoulders and far above your shoulders beyond all of you!--(*Turning to the six.*) Does his voice reach you from this height--does its flow press hot on your bodies--bare beneath their coarse robes? Do your leaden feet wrench themselves from the stony ground and soar up through the noose about your necks?--Can you still feel any pain--the thorn and spur of torture?--He bent and blunted them--healed the wound in your flesh from their stab! (*The six stand by themselves next to the bier.*) You are standing close to him--but he is far away --and yet closer than any one of you. You are where he is resting--he summons you with his beckoning finger. Is it not easy to go where someone calls? The chores are gay with the words of a promise--he calls it out in rejoicing--draws the last of you into the boat. Six oars dip--the keel furrows straight and true:--your goal steers you more surely than the helm. Now he waits for you--for you will arrive after him!--He has preceded you--who will now turn and look back? Whom do you watch out of sight--who has left you--and taken the brightness with him--and left the rest of you in shadow? Who has removed the light from your deed--and made it dark about you?--Your deed becomes overcast and dull!--He kept you mindful of this deed that you might be worthy of it! He drove on and on to ward off sleep from your eyelids--discovered ways and means to draw you closer and closer together--sustained you until this morning! Did he even once let you slip back into weary slumber? Did he deprive you of the short night hours? Was he not watching over you? Are you not standing here fully prepared for your deed and facing it with steady gaze?--

128

(*He takes a deep breath.*) He has thrown open the last gateway before you. He has cleared the darkness of terror and you can pass–with unfaltering steps–and unerring feet. Your deed burns about you with a clear flame. There is no swirling smoke of passion–no smouldering embers. You press onwards–bathed in cool clear light. Fever does not harry you–frost does not cripple you. You move your limbs freely in your robes. You set off as one body–for who will desert? Is your number not round and perfect like a sphere, with no distinction between beginning and end? Does it matter who is first–or seventh–where now is the stab of impatience, the sting of uncertainty?—He fused them into a smooth rounded circle–now you are one united body unmarked and unblemished!—(*Raising one arm towards them.*) Go in search of your deed–and the deed will seek you out: for you are the chosen! The gates stand open–and the surge of your deed can sweep onward. Do you carry it along–or does it carry you? Will one of you cry out his own name–to snatch immortality for himself? What manner of man is the author of this new deed? Is any one of you seized with the ambition to heap glory on himself alone?—If that is so, the new deed will shun you!–You will be engulfed by the rolling wave of your deed. Who are you then? Where are you drifting with your arms–and hands?—The wave rides up–held high by you–arched over you. Who will throw himself beyond it–and shatter the smooth circle? Who will destroy the work? Who will hurl himself higher and rage against such wholeness? Who will sever limb from limb and ruin such perfection? Who will shatter the work that rests on each one of you? Is your finger greater than your hand, a limb greater than your whole body? For the body calls all limbs into its service–the hands of a single body are creating your work. Your work flows through you–you are the way and the walkers on the way. All things and nothing—in the greatest the least–in the least the greatest. So share out your weakness among all–strong and mighty in the soaring flight of unity!–(*His words ring out over the market place. With visionary excitement.*) Stride out–into the light–and out of this darkness. The day of light has dawned–

darkness is dispelled. The sevenfold silver brightness shines from every corner–the awesome day of days awaits you!— (*Stretching one hand over the bier.*) He prophesied it–and extolled it–and waited joyful and carefree for the bell to ring out the feast—then he raised the cup from the table with steady hands and calmly with steady lips consumed the burning draught—(*He draws the boy closer to him.*) I come out of this night–to go into night no more. My eyes are open never again to be closed. My blind eyes are sound–what I have witnessed I shall never forget: I have seen the New Man–This night He was born!—Why should it now be difficult–to go out of the city? Already in my ears is the rushing wave of those coming in their turn. I feel the turbulent flow of creation–about me–above and beyond me–unending! I am one with the stream of new life–in it I live on–and stride forth from today into the morrow–untiring in all things–in all things enduring—(*He turns round, the boy guides him carefully to the right, their footsteps echo slowly down the side street.* TWO COUNCILLORS *go over to* JEAN DE VIENNE, *who has approached those standing near the bier. One of them places his hand on* JEAN DE VIENNE's *shoulder; the other points to where the growing daylight has lit up almost the whole of the church door.*)

JEAN DE VIENNE: (*looks questioningly up at them–then stiffens, pointing to* EUSTACHE DE SAINT-PIERRE's *body.*) This man has gone on before you–is it hard for any of you to follow?– (*More loudly.*) Will any of you stagger under the weight of the key–if I place it upon your hand?

(*The six stretch out their arms towards him.*)

JEAN DE VIENNE: (*handing over the key to the one nearest to him.*) Which of you is the first–which the last? Who can distinguish between you? The hands of one single body take hold of the key–and carry it out!–The morning is bright–now we send out six–the seventh lies here.–Patiently and quietly we shall stand beside this man who is one of your number–we shall be standing as if with you at your goal! (*He completely removes the cloth from the bier. In the absolute silence of the* market square the six set out–their bare feet patter gently across the cobbles. The side street to the left is open before them; and from it comes the rapid echoing of approaching feet.)

THE ENGLISH OFFICER : (*in splendid armour, followed by a soldier–bars the way of the six with upraised hand.*) Jean de Vienne, the King of England sends words to you this morning !

JEAN DE VIENNE : (*calling out to him.*) We have not missed the appointed hour : at daybreak six of the Councillors are to set out from the city and deliver themselves up on the sand before Calais. And we stand here ready !

THE ENGLISH OFFICER : (*to the six.*) Delay your departure !– (*Going over to* JEAN DE VIENNE.) The King of England sends this message on this morning to the city of Calais :–last night was born to the King of England a son in the camp before Calais. For the sake of this new life the King of England will on this morning take no other life. Calais and its harbour are saved from destruction without need for penance ! (*Deep silence reigns.*) On this morning the King of England will give thanks in a church. Jean de Vienne–open the gates–the bells shall ring out for the King of England !

(*Out of the lefthand street pour English soldiers–in resplendent armour, pennants flying from their lances; they quickly create a pathway that reaches across the market and opens out on the steps before the church door.*)

JEAN DE VIENNE : (*draws himself up to his full height. His eyes run over the six, who, standing in the middle of the path have drawn closer to him.*) Raise up this man and place him inside on the uppermost step :–the King of England–when he prays before the altar–shall kneel before his conqueror !

(*The six raise the bier and carry* EUSTACHE DE SAINT-PIERRE *on their stiffly outstretched arms–high above the lances–across the steps and into the wide doorway, from which the blare of tubas rings out. From above the bells peal forth incessantly. The citizens stand silent. Nearby the blast of trumpets.*)

THE ENGLISH OFFICER : The King of England !

131

(JEAN DE VIENNE *and the* COUNCILLORS *stand waiting. Light floods across the church façade above the door: its lower part represents a deposition from the cross; the frail body of the dead man lies limply in the sheets–six stand bowed over his litter–The upper part depicts the elevation of the dead man: he stands free and untrammelled in the sky–six heads are turned up towards him in wonder.)*

THE CORAL

Play in Five Acts

Translated by B. J. Kenworthy

Characters

MILLIONAIRE
SON
DAUGHTER
SECRETARY
MUSEUM CURATOR
DOCTOR
Ship's CAPTAIN
SINGER
The GENTLEMAN in GREY
The MAN in BLUE
The LADY in BLACK
The DAUGHTER in BLACK
The YOUNG LADY in TAFFETA
FIRST ⎫
SECOND ⎭ Examining Magistrates
The CHAPLAIN
The Two FOOTMEN
The CLERK
The Two WARDERS
The YELLOW STOKER
The COLOURED MANSERVANT
SAILORS

ACT I

An oval room: 'the warm heart of the world.' The doors are set invisible in very light panelling: two at the back, one left. In the centre only two armchairs in white elephant hide stand facing one another at a little distance; the one on the right with a signalling device on the outside of the arm.

In this chair the SECRETARY is seated: in an indefinable way, the profile suggests unobtrusive energy. Stiff reddish hair runs down in a narrow strip almost to the chin. His body, in a suit of the coarsest material, is slight; yet he derives weight and significance from a certain sustained aggressive alertness, that is controlled only with an effort. In the other chair the YOUNG LADY IN TAFFETA.

SECRETARY: I wonder if you would–

THE YOUNG LADY IN TAFFETA: Oh, I understand:–if I'd be brief. I'm not the only one who wants to get a hearing. People are crowding in the waiting-room–and perhaps their wishes are more justified. Who can tell? There is misery in every corner of the globe. Now, whether the corner, in which fate has seen fit to put me, is a particularly draughty one–

SECRETARY: To judge that, I must know where fate has put you.

THE YOUNG LADY IN TAFFETA: In hell, sir!–Yes, hell. I'm not using an exaggerated expression. That is not my way. Or could one describe it better by–one is a human being–one has a mother–one believes in God–no, sir, I haven't lost this ability– not by and large!—and–I can't say it out loud–: I earn my bread with my body.

SECRETARY: Are you seeking admission to a Home?

THE YOUNG LADY IN TAFFETA: Where the windows are bright with flowers!

SECRETARY: (takes a pad from his pocket–writes.) You have two years to think about the foundations of a new life.

THE YOUNG LADY IN TAFFETA: Two—

SECRETARY : (*gives her the sheet of paper.*) Any Home for Fallen Women is open to you.

THE YOUNG LADY IN TAFFETA : (*at once seizing his hand and kissing it–hysterically.*) I had not sold the faith of my childhood–God was not for sale–now he seeks me out with his messenger–the messenger of my God–I greet you–kneeling, receive my ardent thanks. More–more: God is walking among us once again–we are all redeemed–alleluia ! Amen !

(SECRETARY *presses on the signal panel. Immediately* TWO FOOTMEN–*Herculean figures in yellow livery–enter from the left. They pick up the* YOUNG LADY IN TAFFETA *and lead her back towards the door.*)

THE YOUNG LADY IN TAFFETA : (*ecstatically.*) Into a Home for Fallen Women–I shall become a new being–a new being—!

(*The three go off.* THE MAN IN BLUE *is admitted by the* FOOTMEN *and led to the chair. The* FOOTMEN *exeunt.*)

SECRETARY : Would you–

THE MAN IN BLUE : (*speaking jerkily.*) My chest–

SECRETARY : Are you seeking admission to a sanatorium?

THE MAN IN BLUE : (*burying his head in his hands.*) Dismissed –after all my strength had been worked out !–Am I an old man? I'm in my prime–and look like an old man. This suit sags round me, and I used to stretch it at the seams. The system has been the ruin of me–

SECRETARY : Are you a labourer?

THE MAN IN BLUE : The system ruins everyone–the inhuman exploitation of labour. The competition is fierce enough–that is why you have to be expended quickly–to make room for the next man !

SECRETARY : You can find no employment in factories?

THE MAN IN BLUE : They turn me away before I'm past the gates. For two weeks I've been wandering the streets and I've spent everything I had. Now–

SECRETARY : We have agricultural settlements.

THE MAN IN BLUE : We have them, yes. But they are right out in the country. I can't walk that far.

SECRETARY: The settlements can be reached by train.

THE MAN IN BLUE: I–haven't the money for the fare!

SECRETARY: (*takes out the pad and writes. Giving him the paper.*) Show them this note outside.

THE MAN IN BLUE: That is more–than the fare! (*Stammering.*) I have a wife and children–I can take them with me–I was going to leave them!

(SECRETARY *presses on the signal panel. the* TWO FOOTMEN *enter.*)

THE MAN IN BLUE: (*already running off left.*) My wife—my children! (*Exit.*)

(THE FOOTMEN *close the door after him—open it and admit the* LADY IN BLACK *with her* DAUGHTER. *The* DAUGHTER *carries a violin-case.*)

THE LADY IN BLACK: (*to the* FOOTMEN.) Thank you–I'll stand. (THE FOOTMEN *go off.*)

SECRETARY: (*stands up.*) Would you–

THE LADY IN BLACK: (*calmly.*) As the mother of my daughter I resolved to come here. I lost my husband a few months ago. He left me virtually nothing. I have managed to find a job that will keep me. But I should never be able to earn enough to provide for my daughter's training. I have reason to believe that my daughter's talent will assure her future. I have refrained from bringing certificates and recommendations. The best evidence for her ability is her playing. May she play?

SECRETARY: I think it will also give your daughter greater pleasure after she has completed her training.

THE LADY IN BLACK: May I assume from that–

(SECRETARY *writes.*)

THE LADY IN BLACK: (*to her* DAUGHTER.) Kiss his hand.

SECRETARY: (*gives the paper to* THE LADY IN BLACK.) Collect this every month until she finishes her studies.

THE LADY IN BLACK: (*without reading.*) You will find thanks tedious, you hear it too often. People must seem pitiful to you, you make so many happy. For us it remains only to marvel at the miracle: that there is someone who does not turn a deaf

137

ear when we come to him with our troubles. To listen to us all shows great courage–as granting our requests is itself untold kindness!

(SECRETARY *presses on the signal panel. The* FOOTMEN *come and show out the* LADY IN BLACK *with her* DAUGHTER. *On the signal panel a bell buzzes.* SECRETARY *immediately presses another knob. Only* ONE FOOTMAN *from the left.*)

SECRETARY: (*to him.*) Wait!

(*The* FOOTMAN *exit. Through the door back right, which reveals thick padding on the inside, the* MILLIONAIRE *comes in quickly. The full description of the* SECRETARY *given earlier was aimed at the* MILLIONAIRE: *the* SECRETARY *is nothing less than his counterpart down to the last detail. The correspondence is complete even in speech and gesture.*)

MILLIONAIRE: The passenger-list of the *Freedom of the Seas.* Drawn up after sailing yesterday and reported here this morning by radio. My son is not named among the passengers.

SECRETARY: (*reads the sheet of paper.*) Only his companion.

MILLIONAIRE: The list is incomplete!

SECRETARY: Reports from the ship are usually completely accurate.

MILLIONAIRE: Where is my son, if his companion is on the steamer? He must be travelling on the *Freedom of the Seas.* It was my wish. The papers had printed the names of the first-class passengers, my son's first and foremost!

SECRETARY: I do not believe in any error.

MILLIONAIRE: He must be on board. There is no other ship he can travel on. It was the explicit instruction that I sent to his companion: to use this fastest and finest of steamers! There is a mistake in the report. Get in touch with the shipping office. Ask where the mistake was made. Whether on board– or in compiling the list.!

(SECRETARY *hesitates.*)

MILLIONAIRE: Wait on the telephone for an answer.

SECRETARY: It will prevent me–

MILLIONAIRE: Doing what?

SECRETARY: It's 'open Thursday' today—

MILLIONAIRE: (*thoughtfully*.) 'Open Thursday'—

(SECRETARY *waits*.)

MILLIONAIRE: (*curtly*.) Go and find out. I will carry on here.

SECRETARY: (*gives him the writing-pad*.)

MILLIONAIRE: Mark the request urgent and come straight back with the answer.

(SECRETARY *goes off through the door back left*. MILLIONAIRE *sits down in the arm-chair, presses on the signal panel. The* FOOTMEN *admit the* GENTLEMAN IN GREY: *of powerful build, in a loose-fitting, light-grey suit, whose pockets are stuffed with newspapers and pamphlets. Round, red head, cropped hair. Sandals.*)

THE GENTLEMAN IN GREY: (*aiming a blow with his travelling-cap at the* FOOTMEN, *who are trying to lead him towards the chair*.) Gently. Easy. Get our breath back. (*As the* FOOTMEN *wait*.) You go and keep order outside–I'll do things in my own time here. (*To the* MILLIONAIRE.) You'll grant me that. I shall rivet your attention with a couple of words. (*To the* FOOTMEN.) I'm not a wild beast.

(*The* FOOTMEN *withdraw at a gesture from the* MILLIONAIRE.)

MILLIONAIRE: Would you–

THE GENTLEMAN IN GREY: (*looking about him*.) So this is the room of Promise–the source of great sympathy–the shrine from which loving kindness and succour emanate–(*With an eloquent gesture*.) A vaulted circle–significant shape–'the warm heart of the world'!

MILLIONAIRE: Now tell me–

THE GENTLEMAN IN GREY: Impressive, this bareness: two armchairs–and room for complaints and lamentations. Surprising that the panelling hasn't darkened with all the cries of distress that have bounced off it!

(MILLIONAIRE *gropes for the signal panel*.)

THE GENTLEMAN IN GREY: (*noticing it*.) Don't ring for the

footmen. I know this 'open Thursday' is precious to the people waiting. Every wasted minute seals someone's fate.

MILLIONAIRE: What do you want me to help you with?

THE GENTLEMAN IN GREY: I–(*leaning right forward.*)–want to help you!

(MILLIONAIRE *involuntarily reaches for the knob.*)

THE GENTLEMAN IN GREY: Don't ring. I'm not ill–and what I have to say I have long pondered over. I have studied the matter –worked it out–and have reached conclusions–a solution of ridiculous simplicity. The whole dispute–this gigantic struggle, waged with an enormous deployment of measures and counter-measures–collapses–dissolves–is over!

MILLIONAIRE: What dispute?

THE GENTLEMAN IN GREY: The only one that rages everlastingly: between rich and poor!

MILLIONAIRE: The one–

THE GENTLEMAN IN GREY: –that I propose to settle!

MILLIONAIRE: (*scrutinizes him with a sudden flash of interest.*) Why have you come to me?

THE GENTLEMAN IN GREY: You were taken by suprise. But I had to catch your attention from the first moment. Otherwise my opportunity was lost. Your footmen would not have let me in a second time. There's no joking with those two. (*Churning newspapers and pamphlets out of his pockets.*) Now I'll develop what I previously reduced to its simplest terms. This is the material that provides the final answers. Socialist papers, periodicals, pamphlets–the whole armoury of the militant proletariat. Appeals–commendations of measures that guarantee success–lists–tables–statistics: a flood of literature. Literature–and nothing more. It doesn't get you a step further– the gulf only gapes even wider, for it is built up on mortal hatred. (*Stuffing it all back into his pockets.*) Wasted effort. Pointless excursions down blind-alleys. It all comes to nothing. Do you understand?

MILLIONAIRE: I do not understand you.

THE GENTLEMAN IN GREY: What are you doing here? Giving away money with both hands. Everyone gets what he asks for. Whether it is large or small. Your millions permit it. They are behind this 'open Thursday'. Anyone can come and get his gift. Misery comes crawling over this threshold and dances out happy. On the lips of the oppressed this oval room becomes paradise: here beats the heart of the world–warm and merciful. Not for a minute does the pulse-beat slacken–it gives and gives. What makes you do it?

MILLIONAIRE: My millions–

THE GENTLEMAN IN GREY: No!

MILLIONAIRE: But?

THE GENTLEMAN IN GREY: Your wealth disgusts you!

(MILLIONAIRE *raises his head*.)

THE GENTLEMAN IN GREY: Not that you are aware of it–but for me there is no other explanation. Take it from me. I didn't discover it overnight. I trudged down all the blind-alleys –until I found here the open road which alone leads to the goal.

MILLIONAIRE: What is this goal?

THE GENTLEMAN IN GREY: The end of the struggle between rich and poor. What no party, no catch-word can bring about, you can achieve with a stroke of the pen. That will make all the rest of it unnecessary: your 'open Thursday'–'the warm heart of the world'–the collection of misery in the waiting-room. Anyway, you are only pouring drops into the sea of wretchedness. But through this stroke of the pen you are announcing eternal peace. Sign this declaration!

MILLIONAIRE: (*does not take the paper*.) What am I to declare?

THE GENTLEMAN IN GREY: That you regard the enrichment of the individual as the most infamous scandal!

MILLIONAIRE: That I–

THE GENTLEMAN IN GREY: You must say it. You–the millionaire of millionaires. Your lips will lend it weight. It will throw a blinding light over the battlefield where the adversaries, armed to the teeth, are ranged against each other. It is the white flag of truce being hoisted. Parley–agreement. The struggle becomes superfluous, the cause of war is removed: you did not want to be rich–you were only compelled by circumstances to become rich. Now the way to change these conditions can be discussed –a solution found, because it is sought in brotherhood!

MILLIONAIRE: I am scarcely–

THE GENTLEMAN IN GREY: You alone are!–You want to give your money away because you must. Something in you compels you to. At present you are doing it in a small way–now you know of something greater: now you will be glad to sign! (MILLIONAIRE *rises*.)

THE GENTLEMAN IN GREY: You are not going to call the footmen, are you?

MILLIONAIRE: I–(*Stands pondering behind the chair.*)

THE GENTLEMAN IN GREY: I knew it!

MILLIONAIRE: –will make my declaration to you.

THE GENTLEMAN IN GREY: Your signature!

MILLIONAIRE: (*once more on the defensive.*) And you shall tell me whether I can sign.

THE GENTLEMAN IN GREY: But you must!

MILLIONAIRE: (*returns to his seat.*) As you are more or less set on uprooting the foundations of the world, I must try to build up for you the foundations of my world. Do you know my origins?

THE GENTLEMAN IN GREY: In your own strength!

MILLIONAIRE: In my own weakness!

(The GENTLEMAN IN GREY *stares at him in amazement*.)

MILLIONAIRE: Or let us say: timidity–fear. Weakness and fear are inter-dependent. But you won't be able to grasp it in just a word or two. My career–I suppose that's what it's called–has already found its way into the school-books. So I am merely repeating a well-known story. I give the same dates–only my interpretation is different. My father was a workman in the same factory that now belongs to me. Whether he stoked a boiler or was a porter I don't know. He can't have earned much, since we led a miserable existence. One Monday–pay-day –he didn't come home. He'd been sacked, because he was worn out–and had gone off with the last of the money. In any case, he wouldn't have been able to feed us. That evening my mother took her own life. I heard a scream somewhere in the house–I didn't run to see what it was–I knew everything –I was eight years old. In that moment terror was implanted in me. It stood before me like a grey wall that I had to get over, in order to escape from the horror. Horror stemming from my father's failure to return with his pay coupled with my mother's scream--that set me on my way--that drove me to flight. It stood behind me as I worked--I got a job at the works! --It never left me for a second--I ran and ran—and I am running because it is still somewhere there behind me!

THE GENTLEMAN IN GREY: You worked your way up with astonishing speed.

MILLIONAIRE: Restless energy--restless flight. Nothing more. I had to keep going on, so as to increase the distance between myself and the horror. There was no quarter given, I'd realized that. It hounded me onwards. Fear that froze in my limbs made me inventive. The machines there: they sucked my father dry--they hanged my mother behind the door--they will crush me, if I don't subject them to my will. The plant--with its machines--with its people placed between me and the horror: that brought me peace for the first time!

THE GENTLEMAN IN GREY: (passes a hand across his brow.) What's this all about—an experience that happens a hundred times every day--the father disappears--the mother—

MILLIONAIRE: It struck me down because I was particularly frail. I must have been, or else I should have withstood it better. But I ran away for all I was worth. Does that tell you enough?

THE GENTLEMAN IN GREY: (confused.) I cannot accept--

MILLIONAIRE: The weakling before you?

THE GENTLEMAN IN GREY: You must treat your fellow-men mercilessly!

MILLIONAIRE: When you're running away you've no wish to see those you trample over!

THE GENTLEMAN IN GREY: (looks at him--pleased.) And you contradict yourself:--'the warm heart of the world'!

MILLIONAIRE: Yes--I don't want to hear about misery that might remind me too powerfully of the horror. That is why I have set aside one day each month: the 'open Thursday'. That way I know when I have to hide.

THE GENTLEMAN IN GREY: But you are sitting here and listening to it all yourself!

143

MILLIONAIRE: Wrong–: my secretary sits here.

THE GENTLEMAN IN GREY: (*after a pause–sharply*.) Is that your social order?

MILLIONAIRE: Not mine–it is *the* social order.

THE GENTLEMAN IN GREY: The classes are fugitives who have run shorter or longer distances?

MILLIONAIRE: Everyone is on the run.

THE GENTLEMAN IN GREY: And those who run fastest–who–

MILLIONAIRE: Are the most frightened cowards–

THE GENTLEMAN IN GREY: Are the winners!

MILLIONAIRE: People like me!

THE GENTLEMAN IN GREY: (*groans. Then ironically*.) So I can only hope for a human race that no longer numbers cowards among it.

MILLIONAIRE: People are always being born who are more deeply terrified. The cause is no longer important. It has always been the lever which applies itself. Progress–the point is not where to–but: what from!—Are you beginning to have your doubts about other things as well? I'm putting your conjectures into plain words. These ideas are more familiar to me. Where do the great men come from who conquer the world? They rise up out of the darkness, because they come from the darkness. They experienced horror there–one way or another. They are hideous meteors that flare up–and fall!

THE GENTLEMAN IN GREY: (*sarcastically*.) And when–do you fall?

(MILLIONAIRE *smiles and shakes his head*.)

THE GENTLEMAN IN GREY: How have you insured against a meteoric fate?

MILLIONAIRE: I have a son.

(*The* SECRETARY *re-enters*.)

MILLIONAIRE: (*leaves his chair–towards the* SECRETARY.) Is the mistake cleared up now?

SECRETARY: The list was complete.

MILLIONAIRE: Without my son?

SECRETARY: He was not aboard the *Freedom of the Seas*.

MILLIONAIRE: But his companion is travelling on the *Freedom of the Seas*!

SECRETARY: He must have left him.

MILLIONAIRE: When he was not to leave his side by so much as a step?

(SECRETARY *remains silent.*)

MILLIONAIRE: I want an explanation. Why, at the moment I don't know where my son is!–Speak to his companion by radio. Have him report what has happened. Something must have happened. I don't understand how he could travel without my son!

SECRETARY: Your son is young–

MILLIONAIRE: (*smiling.*) Bonds of love that–? We shall soon know the reason.

(SECRETARY *goes off again.*)

MILLIONAIRE: (*returning to his chair.*) Did I give you such a shock just now?

THE GENTLEMAN IN GREY: (*had jumped up when the SECRETARY entered. He still stares at the door through which the SECRETARY has departed. Then to the MILLIONAIRE.*) Am I seeing double? Is that you sitting here? Did you just go out the door? Were you talking to yourself?

MILLIONAIRE: No, I was discussing something with my secretary.

THE GENTLEMAN IN GREY: Your secretary!–Are you brothers? But even that would be–

MILLIONAIRE: It *is* possible, you see.

THE GENTLEMAN IN GREY:(*falling back in his chair.*) Appalling!

MILLIONAIRE: A joke which nature frequently permits itself. You will find a duplicate for every human being. If you look, that is. I started searching–and I admit fortune favoured me.

THE GENTLEMAN IN GREY: Fortune–?

MILLIONAIRE: It gives me great advantages. I can be here and there without the trouble of going. And on the 'open Thursday', too, I am here in my well-known person–and am perhaps relaxing with my fishing-rod by some distant water.

THE GENTLEMAN IN GREY: And do you yourself still know who you are?

MILLIONAIRE: Yes, I think so.

THE GENTLEMAN IN GREY: And everyone else takes the Secretary for you?

MILLIONAIRE: Except the two footmen, who look after my personal safety.

THE GENTLEMAN IN GREY: No one could tell the difference.

MILLIONAIRE: That's why some unobtrusive little sign is needed. A piece of coral worn by the Secretary on his watch-chain. The one with the coral is the Secretary.

THE GENTLEMAN IN GREY: And only the footmen know about it?

MILLIONAIRE: They are detectives.

THE GENTLEMAN IN GREY: Supposing I betray your secret?

MILLIONAIRE: Who would believe you? Just another fairy-tale about me.

THE GENTLEMAN IN GREY: (shakes his head violently.) You haven't got the coral on your chain—or did you have it before. I didn't notice—

MILLIONAIRE: No, I was speaking for myself all along. And if you want to hear the conclusion as well—

THE GENTLEMAN IN GREY: (laughing.) The end of your flight. Headlong from horror! Or isn't there one?

MILLIONAIRE: In my son. I have a daughter, too, but the deeper affinity is with one's son. Have you any children? No. Then you'll have to take my word. You find a continuation of yourself in your son—while he is himself a beginning. That is a law inherent in our blood. I know with the greatest certainty that it holds good! Isn't every father's wish: may my son have a better time of it. That's how they generally express it.

THE GENTLEMAN IN GREY: He's not to know the horror, as you call it.

MILLIONAIRE: Need I say more? It is all so obvious.

THE GENTLEMAN IN GREY: And you've protected him?

MILLIONAIRE: I am letting him lead a carefree life. He has no contact with all the things that scream and wail in your pamphlets. I have kept him apart.

THE GENTLEMAN IN GREY: Where do you keep him hidden?

MILLIONAIRE: I don't keep him hidden. The earth has so many sunny coasts!

THE GENTLEMAN IN GREY: Where you dream and escape the horror!

MILLIONAIRE: Where you make yourself a happier past!

THE GENTLEMAN IN GREY: Rest from flight in blissful peace!

MILLIONAIRE: In Paradise!

THE GENTLEMAN IN GREY: You have found yourself your outward double–the Secretary.

MILLIONAIRE: Is that still bothering you?

THE GENTLEMAN IN GREY: No, there is method in it.

MILLIONAIRE: How do you mean?

THE GENTLEMAN IN GREY: Now you are creating the inward double–your son.

MILLIONAIRE: Perhaps I have a passion for interchanging myself.

THE GENTLEMAN IN GREY: When one has such sound reasons.

MILLIONAIRE: Is so timid.

THE GENTLEMAN IN GREY: And so powerful!

MILLIONAIRE: Do you still want to help me? With this declaration of yours that I'm to sign?

THE GENTLEMAN IN GREY: (*stuffs his papers etc. still further into his pockets, sighing.*) You have confused me. The air here is heavy. It makes you sweat from every pore.

MILLIONAIRE: Think it over quietly.

THE GENTLEMAN IN GREY: It's too absurd: 'the warm heart of the world'–the 'open Thursday'—and all that follows from it!

MILLIONAIRE: What follows from it?

THE GENTLEMAN IN GREY: Chaos comes again!

MILLIONAIRE: It has come again--so let who can find a safe refuge.

THE GENTLEMAN IN GREY: (*almost shouting.*) You won't find a refuge!

MILLIONAIRE: I have a son.

THE GENTLEMAN IN GREY: Let me out. Ring for your footmen. I can't see the door. Go on, ring!

(MILLIONAIRE *presses the button. The* TWO FOOTMEN *enter.*)

THE GENTLEMAN IN GREY: (*shaking his fist at the*

MILLIONAIRE.) You have shattered my world–and from beneath its ruins I curse you—curse you!

(The FOOTMEN *seize him roughly and take him out.*)

SECRETARY: (*re-enters.*) A radio message from your son.

MILLIONAIRE: From the continent?

SECRETARY: No–from on board.

MILLIONAIRE: Is he travelling–

SECRETARY: (*reading.*) Just sailed–

MILLIONAIRE: On the *Freedom of the Seas*, you mean?
(SECRETARY *shakes his head*)

MILLIONAIRE: Is there a sister-ship afloat, then, that has luxury
cabins like the *Freedom of the Seas?*

SECRETARY: (*goes on reading.*) On the *Albatross.*

MILLIONAIRE: *Albatross?*–What sort of ship is that?

SECRETARY: A–collier.

MILLIONAIRE: A—collier? Does he give any explanation?

(SECRETARY *hesitates–hands him the telegram.*)

MILLIONAIRE: (*reads it over.*)—As a stoker!—(*Staggering to
the chair.*) What can it mean: my son—on a collier—
stoker?!

ACT II

Under the awning on the MILLIONAIRE'S *yacht. At the back a
section of the railing. The calm of a heat-shimmering sea.
In white-lacquered cane-chairs: the* MILLIONAIRE, *his* DAUGHTER,
the MUSEUM CURATOR, *the* DOCTOR, *the* CAPTAIN–*all in white. A*
NEGRO *is setting down iced drinks. The voice of the* SINGER *at a
little distance.*

SINGER: (*sustaining the last note of the aria and letting it
die away, comes in at the back and focuses her camera on the
group. She stops singing and snaps at the same time.*) Thank
you. (*Now the others look up surprised.*) For purposes of
publicity. On the high seas–aboard the world's most fabulous
yacht–and this audience: I just had to get a snap of that. All
the opera-houses in the world will be outbidding each other
with contracts. (*Sitting down in a chair beside the*
MILLIONAIRE.) If–you were listening to me in raptures–or am

I mistaken? Now do tell the truth. I have the pictures in my camera, remember!

MILLIONAIRE: (*slightly embarrassed.*) No, no, really extra-ordinary–(*The others clap.*)

SINGER: (*quickly takes a photograph.*) Picture number two: the applause. (*Handing the glass back to the negro.*) Hot lemon.

DOCTOR: That is what I was just going to recommend for you.

SINGER: You see, Doctor, I am everything in one: singer, impressario, personal physician.

MUSEUM CURATOR: That means you put two people out of a job.

SINGER: Isn't that the whole secret of success?

MUSEUM CURATOR: You have good strong nerves!

SINGER: The worst possible!

DOCTOR: Would you explain that a bit more clearly to me, as a doctor?

SINGER: I see ghosts.

DOCTOR: What ghosts?

SINGER: Ghosts!

DOCTOR: Well, I've never seen any.

SINGER: Because you haven't a sensitive nature. And artists have sensitive natures–so they see ghosts.

DOCTOR: So only artists see ghosts, then.

SINGER: We could ask everyone. That makes an amusing game at sea. In turn. (*To the* MILLIONAIRE.) Do you see ghosts?

MILLIONAIRE: I don't think we have enough time left–(*To the* CAPTAIN.) Oughtn't the *Albatross* to have been sighted by now?

CAPTAIN: These boats don't hold a steady course.

MILLIONAIRE: Would you mind–?

(CAPTAIN. *Exits.*)

DOCTOR: What sort of ship is this *Albatross*, anyway?

MILLIONAIRE: My son discovered it. It must have exceptional advantages. Perhaps the yacht of some friend he made on his travels.

DAUGHTER: We'll arrange a race with the *Albatross*.

SINGER: Marvellously exciting. I haven't got enough film.

DAUGHTER: The loser gets rammed.

149

DOCTOR: Crew and all?

DAUGHTER: Five minutes are allowed for getting into the motor-launch. (To the MILLIONAIRE.) Shall I tell the Captain to prepare for the race?

MUSEUM CURATOR: And suppose we lose to the unknown *Albatross*?

DAUGHTER: I'll stay on the bridge. I'll give the orders to the engine-room. We'll get up the last ounce of steam.

DOCTOR: In a temperature like this.

DAUGHTER: On the bridge the wind will whistle as we race through it.

DOCTOR: I was thinking of the engine-room.

DAUGHTER: (*stamping her foot.*) I only know about the deck.

MILLIONAIRE: I don't believe the *Albatross* is faster than we are. So the contest loses its appeal.

DAUGHTER: With my brother travelling on it?

MILLIONAIRE: We'll let him decide–after all, he knows the *Albatross* and us.

(CAPTAIN *returns.*)

MILLIONAIRE: Sighted?

CAPTAIN: Not yet.

MILLIONAIRE: (*to his* DAUGHTER. You see, it is moving slowly. (*To the others.*) Let's do something else to pass the time.

SINGER: So it is to be the ghost game.

MILLIONAIRE: (*briskly to the* MUSEUM CURATOR.) Is the Tintoretto really without any qualities?

MUSEUM CURATOR: Great qualities–the greatest.

MILLIONAIRE: And you refused my gift.

MUSEUM CURATOR: Christ Bearing the Cross.

SINGER: Do you find the subject offensive?

MUSEUM CURATOR: If I expand it into a principle–yes.

DOCTOR: Then you'll have to exclude pretty well all old art from your gallery.

SINGER: You tell them all about it, Curator, and I'll snap your listeners at the climax of your talk.

MUSEUM CURATOR: In this new museum that I'm to be in charge of I'm propagating a breach with the whole past.

DOCTOR: And what is left?

SINGER: Empty walls.

MUSEUM CURATOR: Empty walls, and I have virtually nothing to cover them with.

DOCTOR: A queer museum.

DAUGHTER: Covered tennis-courts.

MUSEUM CURATOR: It is to be a stimulus to new achievement. An emphatic beginning. That certainly does not imply any adverse criticism of past achievements–in fact, my appreciation is unbounded. We are all of us still sitting in their shadow. That torments us somehow. This is how it strikes me. It weighs us down like a cross–this burden of the past, which we shall only throw off with violence and crime–if need be!

DOCTOR: Is that possible–without self-deception?

MUSEUM CURATOR: I don't know.

DOCTOR: I fear that bearing this cross is inescapable.

MUSEUM CURATOR: One must desire the future relentlessly.

DOCTOR: That may be possible in your gallery.

MUSEUM CURATOR: More than that I do not claim.

DOCTOR: In life, I think, no one will be able to leap over his own shadow.

(A SAILOR *enters and gives a message to the* CAPTAIN. *Exit.*)

CAPTAIN: (*rises; to the* MILLIONAIRE.) The *Albatross* is just to starboard of us.

MILLIONAIRE: (*excitedly.*) Send over the motorboat! (*Exit* CAPTAIN.)

DOCTOR: Now we shall soon see what this fabulous ship is like.

SINGER: The champion.

MUSEUM CURATOR: The suspense is terrific.

DAUGHTER: I'll radio them the challenge to a race.

MILLIONAIRE: (*keeps her back. To the others.*) You go on and we'll follow you.

(SINGER, MUSEUM CURATOR *and* DOCTOR *exeunt.*)

MILLIONAIRE: There's something I want to talk to you about.

DAUGHTER: Now?

MILLIONAIRE: Just a question I want to ask you.

DAUGHTER: What is it?

MILLIONAIRE: Could you make up your mind to–marry the Museum Curator?

DAUGHTER: I–don't know!

MILLIONAIRE: I'm pressing for your decision because–

DAUGHTER: But I hardly know him.

MILLIONAIRE: And I–

DAUGHTER: Then how can you try to persuade me?

MILLIONAIRE: When he was talking just now he impressed me in a way no other person has ever done.

DAUGHTER: He refused the gift. Did that impress you?

MILLIONAIRE: His attitude impressed me. This intellectual independence of his–and for him there exists only the future–which obliterates the past–

DAUGHTER: I was not listening to him.

MILLIONAIRE: You would make me happy–

DAUGHTER: Then there is nothing more for me to think over!

MILLIONAIRE: (shakes her hands.) Now let's go and wait for your brother. (They both exeunt.)

(Ship's bell and high-pitched siren. SAILORS open up the railing at the back and winch down the boarding-steps. They all re-enter, leaning over the railing; handkerchief-waving and halloing.)

DOCTOR: (stepping under the sun-canopy.) Why, it's a hulking old barge.

MUSEUM CURATOR: (following him.) It lives up to the name Albatross.

DOCTOR: Did you manage to discover any other passengers over there?

MUSEUM CURATOR: Maybe that was the charm of the voyage.

DOCTOR: Not for me, thank you.

SINGER: (approaches them, holding her camera behind her back.) Discretion–a family scene!

(SON–in a grey suit–climbs up the boarding-steps and is greeted tempestuously by the DAUGHTER. The CAPTAIN stands saluting.)

SON: You were lying in wait for me?

DAUGHTER: For two days we have been cruising in the same spot. A fantastic bore.

MILLIONAIRE: I wanted to give you a surprise.

SON: And you were entirely successful. Your guests?

MILLIONAIRE: Only the most intimate circle.

(SON *goes from one to the other, shaking hands without a word. Then he stops by a chair. An embarrassed silence reigns.*)

DAUGHTER: (*throwing herself into a chair.*) This is too solemn for me.

MILLIONAIRE: (*indicating the chairs.*) Won't you sit down?

(*They all sit–*SON *follows hesitantly.*)
(CAPTAIN *enters and sits down.*)

SON: (*to* him, *in surprise.*) Aren't we getting under way?

MILLIONAIRE: I thought we might stay another two or three days at sea.

SON: If that was your wish–

MILLIONAIRE: On your account.

SON: Why?

MILLIONAIRE: After that trip–

DAUGHTER: The Albatross–I didn't see it in the excitement. Has it got class? How many knots?

(MUSEUM CURATOR *and* DOCTOR *laugh.*)

SON: What's all this about the Albatross?

DAUGHTER: We were going to challenge it. Was it a tough opponent?

SON: It'll make you laugh.–No, the Albatross is not an opponent in that sense.

DAUGHTER: (*astonished.*) Then why aren't you travelling on the Freedom of the Seas?

MILLIONAIRE: (*uneasy, changing the subject.*) Your impressions of the great cities of the earth–

SINGER: Did you go to the opera everywhere?

SON: We can soon settle the character of the Albatross: it is a collier!–Captain, you must surely know about the ships that are at sea?

153

CAPTAIN: I should never have guessed that this was the Albatross.

SON: Why not?

(CAPTAIN *smiles.*)

SON: (*to the others.*) Is that so wonderful? Don't other people travel on such ships?

CAPTAIN: They are not equipped for passengers.

SON: Not for them—but surely the crew—the stokers are human too?

MUSEUM CURATOR: (*after a silence.*) You show some sublety in devising pleasures for yourself.

SON: What pleasures?

MUSEUM CURATOR: Only in the contrast between that collier and this yacht is the real opportunity to appreciate its luxury presented.

SON: Or to—(*Breaking off and turning to the* MILLIONAIRE.) Has my companion informed you?

MILLIONAIRE: I have spoken with him.

SON: He must have arrived two days ago?

MILLIONAIRE: I've been lying out here for two days.

SON: Are you dissatisfied with him? I am to blame. He certainly did everything he could.

MILLIONAIRE: (*evasively.*) Wouldn't you like to change your clothes?

DAUGHTER: Why, you're wearing your ordinary suit.

SON: It is better protection against swirling coal-dust. Moreover, it was less conspicuous—and if you're sensible you fit in.

MILLIONAIRE: Then fit in with us—and put on white from head to foot.

SON: You must leave me my pleasures.

SINGER: (*with her camera.*) Very interesting and effective picture.

SON: Is that all it is to you?

DOCTOR: With this excessive temperature white clothing is to be recommended from considerations of health.

MILLIONAIRE: You hear what our solicitous doctor says.

SON: (*with restrained sharpness.*) Would your medical advice be followed in the engine-room as well?

154

DOCTOR: Scarcely.

SON: It wouldn't be accepted. For the reason that they are dealing with black coal.

DOCTOR: Exactly.

SON: So health can suffer down there–and be pampered up here?

MUSEUM CURATOR: It appears that you have seen more on your travels than you–

SON: Once you are on the way, you open your eyes wider.

DAUGHTER: Did you meet any princes?

SINGER: Do tell us!

SON: Daily.

DAUGHTER: You made friends? Will any of them be visiting you?

SON: On my collier I could introduce you to five, even ten. Come with me next time.

MUSEUM CURATOR: Are you going to–

SON: Devise some more subtle pleasures for myself?

(A SAILOR *comes with a message for the* CAPTAIN. *The* CAPTAIN *goes to the* DOCTOR *and whispers to him. All three exeunt.*)

SON: Are we sailing after all?

MILLIONAIRE: I have given no instructions.

SON: Why has the Doctor gone with the Captain?

SINGER: Perhaps an accident among the crew.

SON: Don't you want to take a picture?

DAUGHTER: We really could sail, just to get some air. The heat is unbearably oppressive.

SON: We live on deck!

SINGER: Is it cooler somewhere else?

SON: No–it's hotter.

SINGER: Is that possible?

SON: Climb down to the stokers!

MILLIONAIRE: Now I'll arrange for us to sail!

MUSEUM CURATOR: (*ironically.*) Mind you don't overtax the stokers.

SON: Do you know what it's like standing in front of the furnaces?

MUSEUM CURATOR: I have not sought the opportunity to do so.

SON: And you can't work up any interest in a description?

155

MUSEUM CURATOR: A life-like description by an expert–

SON: I am an expert!

MILLIONAIRE: (to his DAUGHTER.) Tell the Captain–

DAUGHTER: Full speed ahead!

SINGER: The ladies are taking command!

DAUGHTER: We'll set a new record. It will be radioed to the papers this evening, and tomorrow the world will burst with envy! (Exit with the SINGER.)

SON: Aren't you going to stop this nonsense?

MILLIONAIRE: The yacht hasn't yet shown its top speed.

SON: Then please let me get off the boat first.

MUSEUM CURATOR: You aren't used to speed after the collier.

SON: To frivolity!

MILLIONAIRE: You always enjoyed such games.

SON: I am ashamed that I came to my senses so late.

MILLIONAIRE: What do you mean?

SON: That I—(Emphatically.) I can come on this record-breaking trip only in front of the furnaces!

MILLIONAIRE: (to the MUSEUM CURATOR.) Don't keep the ladies waiting on the bridge.

(MUSEUM CURATOR exits.)

MILLIONAIRE: (slowly.) You really travelled on that tub as a stoker?

SON: I hadn't the stamina to keep it up–and had to remain a passenger.

MILLIONAIRE: You were anxious to–

SON: The boat is the least of it.

MILLIONAIRE: You were surprised by a lot of things on your travels?

SON: Like scales it fell from my eyes. All the wrongs we do became obvious to me. The rich like us–and the others choking in smoke and torment–and are human beings the same as we are. We haven't the faintest right to do it–why do we do it? I ask you, why? Tell me an answer that absolves you and me?

MILLIONAIRE: (stares at him.) You ask that?

SON: I am asking you–and shall not stop asking I am grateful to you today as I have never been before in my life. You gave

156

me this trip–without which I should still have been blind!

MILLIONAIRE: You will forget again.

SON: Forget what is in me–fills me through and through? I should have to obliterate myself first.

MILLIONAIRE: What–is in you?

SON: Horror at this life with its torment and oppression.

MILLIONAIRE: Your experiences on your trip are insufficient–

SON: Insufficient?

MILLIONAIRE: You are exaggerating chance happenings.

SON: They are burning in my blood! And on top of everything else the most striking image: there beside the quay lies the *Freedom of the Seas*. Beflagged, music. On the deck passengers in bright clothes promenading–chattering–gay. A few feet lower down: hell. There, in scorching pits, people are burning, their bodies convulsed, in front of hissing stokeholes. So that we can enjoy a quick, easy voyage!–I had already set foot on the *Freedom of the Seas*–but I had to turn back–and not until I was on this *Albatross* did my conscience rest easier!

MILLIONAIRE: And now you have got over these shocks?

SON: Here they have been vastly intensified! Here–on your luxury yacht! Shame impels the blood beneath my brow! We laze in chairs–and groan about the heat that comes from the sun. We gulp down iced water and are not irritated by dust in our throats! Here below the soft soles of your white shoes fever seethes. Half-dark reigns!–Rip open this wall of planks–it is so thin, and yet divides so cruelly!–and look down –look down all of you–and feel how the words with which you thought to exalt yourselves above any one of those down there stick in your throats!

(*The* DOCTOR *saunters in.*)

SON: (*quickly to him.*) What's happened, doctor?

DOCTOR: A Chinese stoker has collapsed.

SON: Dead?

DOCTOR: (*shakes his head.*) Heat-stroke.

SON: Where have you put him?

DOCTOR: I've had him put beside the ventilation-shaft down below.

SON: Not brought up on deck?

DOCTOR: No.

SON: (*curtly.*) Wait here. (*Exit.*)

DOCTOR: (*flops into a chair—to the* NEGRO.) Iced water. (*To the* MILLIONAIRE.) I find being at sea for some time like this is extraordinarily soothing to the nerves. I should like to prescribe it for you for five days every two months.

(MILLIONAIRE *stands motionless.*)

DOCTOR: I can foresee that this treatment will do great things for you.

(MILLIONAIRE *silent.*)

DOCTOR: True enough, the special attraction of waiting for your son will be lacking in the future, but your daughter will show her inventiveness in thinking out surprises of a more moderate sort. I'll have a word with her to that effect.

(*Voices and footsteps approach.*)

DOCTOR: (*setting down his glass.*) Is there a deck-game going on? (*Sailors bring the half-naked Chinese stoker.*)

SON: In here!

DOCTOR: (*getting up.*) What's all this?

SON: Push some chairs together. Doctor, catch hold. A life is at stake. (*To the* SAILORS.) Lay him down. (*To the* NEGRO.) Iced water. (*To the* DOCTOR.) Come, on, Doctor, you know more about this than I do. Bathe his chest. (*To the* MILLIONAIRE.) I take it you've no objection to your personal physician lending a hand? (*To the* DOCTOR.) Is there any danger?

CAPTAIN: (*enters—in a low voice to the* MILLIONAIRE.) I was not able to prevent any of it.

(MILLIONAIRE *shakes his head violently.* DAUGHTER *and* SINGER *enter.*)

SON: (*to the* DAUGHTER.) Won't you help us? A man may be dying here!

(DAUGHTER *comes closer.*)

SON: Dip your hands in the iced water and lay them on his burning chest. It is your duty. I summon you to it!

(DAUGHTER does so.)

SON: (beside himself, to the DOCTOR.) Doctor, you must save him—otherwise I am a murderer!

MILLIONAIRE: (stares at the group—moves his lips—finally mutters.) The horror!

SINGER: (focuses her camera—to the CURATOR.) I've never yet taken anything like this. (She clicks her camera.)

ACT III

Square room, whose back wall is glass: the MILLIONAIRE'S office. On the walls right and left, reaching from floor to ceiling, huge brown-tinted photographs showing factory buildings. Broad desk with cane chair; a second chair to one side. Outside chimneys, serried and sheer as columns of solidified lava, supporting mountainous clouds of smoke.

MILLIONAIRE: (at the desk.) How many dead?

SECRETARY: (standing beside the desk.) The exact number of casualties could not be ascertained, as the rescued ran away, as soon as they were brought to the surface, and, up to yesterday, had not reported in.

MILLIONAIRE: Why did they run away?

SECRETARY: Their sufferings during the three days they were trapped below ground must have been horrible.

MILLIONAIRE: And they are still running further and further away from them?

SECRETARY: They came up distracted, as though from the grave, shouting and shaking.

MILLIONAIRE: Those not reporting for work by the day after tomorrow will not be re-engaged.

SECRETARY: (making notes.) By the day after tomorrow.

MILLIONAIRE: How did the meeting go? Did I meet with opposition? Did they let me speak uninterrupted?

SECRETARY: No.

MILLIONAIRE: Was my life in danger?

SECRETARY: It was indeed.

MILLIONAIRE: How did I protect myself?

SECRETARY: I had the military called in, and drawn up in front of me ready to shoot.

MILLIONAIRE: Were there any actual incidents?

SECRETARY: One man shouted interruptions.

MILLIONAIRE: What did he say?

SECRETARY: Murderer.

MILLIONAIRE: Couldn't he be found?

SECRETARY: The crowd hid him.

MILLIONAIRE: He must be discovered. Threaten to take steps if he is not handed over.

(SECRETARY *notes it down*.)

MILLIONAIRE: Is everything calm now?

SECRETARY: They have been down the mine again today.

MILLIONAIRE: How did I achieve that?

SECRETARY: I announced the shut-down of the whole plant.

MILLIONAIRE: Thank you. (*A green lamp lights up on the desk.* MILLIONAIRE *lifts the receiver. In surprise.*) Who?–My daughter?–Here?–Yes. I'll expect her. (*To the* SECRETARY.) Take my place in factory twenty-four. There has been an explosion, and I've told them I'll be there in the afternoon.

(SECRETARY *makes a note*.)

MILLIONAIRE: Thank you.

(SECRETARY *goes off through a door set invisibly in the photograph.* MILLIONAIRE *rises, takes a few hurried steps towards the right-hand wall, recollects–returns to his chair and buries himself in his work. One of the* FOOTMEN *opens an invisible padded door on the right. The* DAUGHTER *enters. Exit* FOOTMAN.)

MILLIONAIRE: (*looking round*.) Your first visit to the paternal place of business.

DAUGHTER: (*looking about her*.) Yes–it is the first time I've seen this.

160

MILLIONAIRE: An unknown world!–Is it so urgent that you can't save it up for the evening fireside?

DAUGHTER: I can only explain it to you here.

MILLIONAIRE: Am I to prepare myself for the good news?

DAUGHTER: What is that?

MILLIONAIRE: I asked something of you, when we were waiting for your brother. That time on the yacht.

DAUGHTER: (*shaking her head.*) I've not thought any more about that.

MILLIONAIRE: (*suppressing his agitation–gaily.*) Haven't you really?

DAUGHTER: The impulse first came to me on the yacht.

MILLIONAIRE: Which set you on the road to supreme happiness?

DAUGHTER: To my inexorable duty!

MILLIONAIRE: (*defensively raising his hands towards her.*) No— not that!

DAUGHTER: (*calmly.*) When I took my hands off the burning chest of the Chinese stoker, they bore the stigma. The stigma has sunk into my blood and into my very heart. I no longer have any choice. I sense my destiny. And I accept it willingly. You shall show me the place where I can fulfil it.

MILLIONAIRE: What do you want to do?

DAUGHTER: Send me to the most wretched of those who lie ill. Who were injured in your factories. I want to nurse them.

MILLIONAIRE: You don't know what you are saying.

DAUGHTER: I do. Only my actions can convince you. I will go to the pit where the disaster happened.

MILLIONAIRE: What disaster do you mean?

DAUGHTER: You quelled the disturbance yourself.

MILLIONAIRE: Who's been telling you that?

DAUGHTER: Reports in newspapers are suppressed. You are powerful, all right.

MILLIONAIRE: (*stares at her–after a pause.*) Don't do it. (*Rises, goes close to her.*) I won't beg you with words. You have a hundred words against mine. It's an unequal contest. Father and daughter–that in itself decides the outcome. (*He takes her hands, looks at them.*) No–no. So small–so weak. (*Countering her objection with a shake of his head.*) Yes, yes–strong and hard–and only I know for what:–to topple a tower–heap up ruins–burying the casualties. Shall I tell you who will be a casualty?

DAUGHTER: I don't understand you.

MILLIONAIRE: Do you want to make a casualty of me?

(DAUGHTER *looks at him in surprise.*)

MILLIONAIRE: Then turn back. You will find your mission nearer home. It seems trivial to you–I think it important, because it concerns your father.

DAUGHTER: (*withdraws her hands from his.*) I have no right, while others–

MILLIONAIRE: Father and daughter–there's no arguing. Only give and take.

DAUGHTER: I thank you today for years of carefree youth–

MILLIONAIRE: With a bright future!

DAUGHTER: (*firmly.*) Which lights up my new duty! (*She rises, holds out her hand to him.*) My decision has become so easy for me. Do you want to make it difficult for me, by asking me to change it?

MILLIONAIRE: (*does not take her hand.*) Where are you going now?

DAUGHTER: To my brothers and sisters.

MILLIONAIRE: (*in a flat voice.*) You are going down there—

DAUGHTER: Will you know me among the poorest of the poor?

MILLIONAIRE: (*clutching the desk.*) Down there–

(DAUGHTER *still hesitates–turns towards the door. The* FOOT-MAN *opens it. Exit daughter.*)

MILLIONAIRE: (*falteringly–with a timid gesture.*) Down there —down—down—(*Then he pulls himself together–rings.*)

(SECRETARY *enters.*)

MILLIONAIRE: Have the pit closed!

(SECRETARY *notes it down.*)

MILLIONAIRE: No! (*Putting his hand to his brow.*) Here or there–you can't blow it away–no one has the power! (*Firmly to the* SECRETARY.) My daughter is going to devote herself to good works. You will meet her at the pit and wherever there are accidents in factories. Ignore her–I do not know my daughter!

SECRETARY: Does your daughter know about the coral?

MILLIONAIRE: No, no one apart from the two Footmen. (*Businesslike.*) We were interrupted just now.

SECRETARY: (*reads from his note-book.*) In the afternoon I am representing you in factory twenty-four.

MILLIONAIRE: At midday tomorrow I shall be present myself at the meeting of the Missionary Society, when I am to be elected Honorary President. You will come in the car at two o'clock. I shall leave the meeting on the pretext of fetching a brief-case. Then you will return in my place and read out the donations I am making. I'll give you the brief-case. (*He looks for it in a desk drawer. The green light flashes.*)

SECRETARY: A telephone call.

(MILLIONAIRE *quickly up–stares at the light.*)

SECRETARY: What about the brief-case–

MILLIONAIRE: (*vehemently.*) Stay here!–Go. Yes, later.

(SECRETARY *exit.*)

MILLIONAIRE: (*slowly lifts the receiver.*)—Who?—(*It slips from his nerveless fingers on the desk. With unsure lips.*) My son. (*The* FOOTMAN *shows in the* SON, *right. Exit* FOOTMAN.)

MILLIONAIRE: (*straightens up and goes stiffly towards him.*) I have not seen you for the last few days.

SON: Since–

MILLIONAIRE: I'm not inquiring where you've been. The time for me to watch over you is past. Justify whatever you do in your own eyes. You are grown up.

SON: You make it easy for me–

MILLIONAIRE: Perhaps it was important to tell you this. Is that why you came?

SON: The reason–

MILLIONAIRE: I won't press you about that either, now. Sit down. There is in this strictly businesslike room–

SON: From which you have jealously excluded me.

MILLIONAIRE: Are you anxious to take my place?

SON: Not yours!

163

MILLIONAIRE: I'm not offering it to you. I'm not tired yet. The reins lie taut in my fingers. I want to work–and I can. My successor is presenting himself too soon. You will not depose me today or tomorrow.

SON: I have not come with that intention.

MILLIONAIRE: But it will help you to organize your life.

SON: You are limiting my scope.

MILLIONAIRE: That is the only possible thing for you. Work is my portion.

SON: I know how you want to continue.

MILLIONAIRE: As you see, the gates are firmly barred.

SON: And since I am compelled to, I quieten my conscience?

MILLIONAIRE: You are under a compulsion as well!

SON: (after a pause.) Will you give me an answer to questions that are consuming me?

MILLIONAIRE: Once we have made our positions clear–yes.

SON: Your actions are riddled with such deep contradictions.

MILLIONAIRE: Have you been thinking about me?

SON: I can no longer think of anything else.

MILLIONAIRE: What made me a matter of such sudden interest to you?

SON: This enormous wealth you have amassed–

MILLIONAIRE: I already mentioned my energy.

SON: That isn't energy, it's–

MILLIONAIRE: Where is the puzzle?

SON: On one hand the ruthless exploitation–and on the other your unlimited charity. The 'warm heart of the world'—and that stone you must have within you!

MILLIONAIRE: I've no wish to solve the puzzle for you.

SON: Because you are ashamed to confess it to yourself!

MILLIONAIRE: It shall remain my secret.

SON: I am tugging at the veil you are hiding behind. You realize the wickedness of your wealth and drug yourself with this 'open Thursday'!

MILLIONAIRE: The explanation would be inadequate.

SON: Why, these gifts you distribute are ridiculous. They don't pay for the blood–

MILLIONAIRE: Do I spill any?

SON: No, it's accidents. But you threaten to spill blood if ever they cry out!

MILLIONAIRE: Did you see that?

SON: Now I must confess to you what I was almost driven to do yesterday.

MILLIONAIRE: What happened yesterday?

SON: I was in the yard near the pit when you were speaking. You had to appear yourself to put down the disturbance. I was there below in the pallid crowd—and saw you standing up above behind the threatening rifles. So cold and distant. Your words slapped down on the meeting like lumps of ice. No one dared shout out any more. Until you threatened to shut down the plant, which would deliver up thousands—women and children—to starvation. Then one of them opened his mouth!

MILLIONAIRE: It was you who—

SON: Who shouted murderer!—And that is not the end.

MILLIONAIRE: I heard nothing further.

SON: I might have forgotten that my father was standing up there—(He plunges his hand into his pocket and lays a revolver on the table.) I don't want to let myself be tempted a second time.

MILLIONAIRE: (pushes the revolver aside.) You wouldn't have hit me.

SON: I wanted to hit you.

MILLIONAIRE: (shaking his head, smiling.) Not me. So this can't cast its shadow between us. (He holds out his hand to him.) It needn't trouble you.

SON: (stares at him.) Are you brushing it aside like a speck of dust that blew on to your coat?

MILLIONAIRE: Not on to my coat.

SON: Forgive and forget?

MILLIONAIRE: As it is I've nothing to forgive you.

SON: No, not you. Nor anyone else, either. Not for that. We choose our own atonement. I want to make mine so hard that perhaps on the last day I can lift up my eyes again.

MILLIONAIRE: To me?

SON: No. You'll take me on this very day. You don't like wasting time.

MILLIONAIRE: Who are you setting up to be your judge?

SON: The lowliest of your labourers.

MILLIONAIRE: What are you trying to say?

SON: Until another man is driven by affliction into guilt, I shall be standing down there!

MILLIONAIRE: In the uproar?

SON: In the peace which will spread when I wish to be no more than others!

MILLIONAIRE: (*pushes the revolver towards him.*) Now is the time! (*He turns his face away from him.*)

SON: (*jumps up and runs to him.*) Tell me why everything is like this!–Tell me!

MILLIONAIRE: Come with me. (*Leads him over to the photographs.*) Do you see that? Grey factories. Narrow yards! (*Going over to the big window at the back.*) Do you see that? Chimneys–chimneys. Where is there earth–blades of grass–bushes?—That is where I come from!—Do you know about my life?—I have kept it from you. They read about it in schools. I have given you a different life. Not mine!—I came up from nothing, so they write in the books! I worked my way up out of every sort of affliction, that's what I'm telling you now! I haven't forgotten. Not for a moment have I let myself be lulled into a sense of security. I've surrounded myself with these pictures–kept this wall open–so that it cannot dim–: it is there to rouse me out of weariness and rest. It screams a reminder and a warning into my very blood: not down there—anything but down there!

SON: (*stepping away from him.*) You—

MILLIONAIRE: I can warn you. You will believe me. It devoured my father and mother–it was clutching at me—I escaped!

SON: You've known—

MILLIONAIRE: A single moment has upset you–it has been racking me for a life-time. Life is so terrible!—Do you want to sink down there?

SON: You are snatching from my hands the last thing left—

166

MILLIONAIRE: What's that?

SON: What excuses you: that you did not know the suffering of the others!

MILLIONAIRE: I carry the scream in my breast!

SON: Are you–a tiger?! Worse: it does not know what it is doing. You know what your victims suffer—and—(*He grasps the revolver–puts it down again.*)

MILLIONAIRE: I or someone else–

SON: Everyone is–

MILLIONAIRE: Be grateful to me.

SON: For the deception?

MILLIONAIRE: That you did not have to become what I am!

SON: (*calmly.*) Your blood is mine–

MILLIONAIRE: Do you feel that, too?

SON: It makes the task worthwhile.

MILLIONAIRE: Of saving me from the terror!

SON: Of suppressing the terrible temptation–and suffering beside the lowest of your labourers!

(MILLIONAIRE *stands rigid.*)

SON: You can have me turned away. I shall get work wherever I find it.

MILLIONAIRE: (*collapses against him.*) Mercy—Mercy!!

SON: (*coldly.*) On whom?

MILLIONAIRE: Mercy—!!

SON: Perhaps that will one day be my cry to you, when you refuse me and my comrades bread! (*He goes out right, leaving before the* FOOTMAN *can fully open the door.*)

MILLIONAIRE: (*at last rises jerkily. Feels for the revolver–thrusts it into his pocket.*) Not here—In the undergrowth among the trees!—the dying eye sees green twigs—patch of blue sky flooding down—sound of a little bird! (*With side-glances at the walls.*) Cornered?—Cut off?—Flight a failure?—Overtaken?—(*Waving his arms.*) Let me go—keep your hands off me—I'm as scared of you as a child! (*Running panting along the photographs and striking at them with his hands.*) Let me out—let me out—(*Shouting.*) Let me out!!

SECRETARY *from the left—questioning.* MILLIONAIRE *looks at him.*)

SECRETARY: (*embarrassed.*) The—brief-case?

(MILLIONAIRE *silent.*)

SECRETARY: You were going to hand over the brief-case to me.

MILLIONAIRE: (*staggering to the desk and collapsing into the chair.*) Daughter and son—down—down there—My children have deserted me!

(SECRETARY *remains silent.*)

MILLIONAIRE: (*looking up at him.*) Do you understand what it means: to work all your life for your children—and they come to their father and strike the gains from his grasp?

SECRETARY: Your son—?

MILLIONAIRE: (*his voice suddenly rising.*) Now who will cover over what I have panted to escape from? Now who will help to hurl mountains into chasms—to cover that up?!

(SECRETARY *looks up at him questioningly.*)

MILLIONAIRE: Will no one fetch me—out of the darkness of my past?!

SECRETARY: Because your achievements are so gigantic, there is no need to gloss over your past!

MILLIONAIRE: No need to—?!

SECRETARY: Your work stands out all the greater!

MILLIONAIRE: I'll let it go—I'll pay with my wealth—I'll give away my life for another life!! (*Fervently.*) Who will lend me his, that is bright from the first day on?!—I shall no longer find it in my son—down there!—Now where does the exchange beckon that I longed for in the fever of work—in the frenzy of gain—on the mountain of my illimitable gold?!—In whom can I submerge—and lose this fear and raging turmoil?— Who has a life—serene and smooth—for mine? ! !

SECRETARY: (*looking down at him with growing emotion.*) Your son is following different paths. A disappointment more bitter than any other. But its thousandfold recurrence makes it seem a law. Father and son are drawn in opposite directions.

It is always a life and death struggle.—(*After a pause.*) I also rebelled against my father. And although I felt how much it pained him, I had to hurt him.—(*After a further pause.*) I still can't understand what made me do it. I sought a life of my own—I suppose that will be the real reason. The urge for independence is stronger than anything else. (*Now continuing with greater animation.*) I grew up in a home such as you will seldom find. I can think back on a wonderful youth. I was the only son. My mother and father gave unstintingly of their infinite store of love. Under their care I saw and heard nothing of the tribulations of the rough daily round. A bright beam of sunshine lay forever in the restful rooms. Nor did death come to us. My parents—for me they are still alive today. Then I went to the little university—and the instinct of independence began to gain power over me. I loosed my ties and went out into the world.—Many is the dark hour I've known since—I was thrust hither and thither—but deep down nothing could shake me. For I had the greatest of possessions, upon which one can draw without limit: the vivid memory of a happy youth. What happened later became mere waves passing across a lake, whose clarity reflects the blue sky. Thus smooth and serene my untainted past lies spread out within me!

(MILLIONAIRE *has turned his face up towards him. He listens with the most intense excitement.* SECRETARY *keeps his eyes fixed before him.*)

MILLIONAIRE: (*searches on the desk.*) The—brief-case. (*He gives it to him. Jerks out.*) Go!
(SECRETARY *takes the brief-case—turns to the door.* MILLIONAIRE *takes the revolver from his pocket and fires.* SECRETARY *hit in the back falls.*)
MILLIONAIRE: (*stands motionless.*)—My life—for another life —that is bright—from the first day on—(*Slowly he walks across, bends over the prone figure—and slips the coral off the watch-chain. He holds it in front of him on the palm of his hand.*)—This life—that I thirst for—! each day of this life— that I hanker after—! (*Lifting his head high.*) They shall

force my good fortune upon me—they will give me everything I want—(*He slips the coral on to his chain.*—Then he jerks open the door on the right and shoots once more into the air.) (*The* TWO FOOTMEN *rush in. One stays at the door—the other bends over the* SECRETARY.)

THE FIRST FOOTMAN: (*in the doorway.*) The coral?

THE SECOND FOOTMAN: (*straightens up, shakes his head.*) Arrest the Secretary!

ACT IV

Interrogation room: blue quadrilateral with many entrances, whose doors have iron bars; behind them narrow passages disappear. An arc-lamp in clear glass lights up everything. Only a small iron table, at which a clerk—with eye-shade—is sitting.

(THE FIRST EXAMINING MAGISTRATE *stands deep in thought. The* TWO FOOTMEN *enter from the left. A* WARDER *comes from the right.*)

THE FIRST EXAMINING MAGISTRATE: (*to him.*) Switch off. (WARDER *operates the switch-board; the arc-lamp goes out. In the corners dull lights glow.*)

THE FIRST EXAMINING MAGISTRATE: (*goes to the table, lifts the telephone.*) Please send a relief. (*To the* TWO FOOTMEN.) Now you can—(*Changing his mind.*) No, just wait a little. (*He takes the record from the* CLERK, *reads—shakes his head. To the* FOOTMEN.) The Secretary never let the coral—(*Quickly.*) But it could be that even the coral was occasionally changed over, so as to—

THE SECOND EXAMINING MAGISTRATE: (*enters from the back.*) No results?

THE FIRST EXAMINING MAGISTRATE: (*hands him the record.*) At most that I'm having doubts.

THE SECOND EXAMINING MAGISTRATE: There is a touch of genius in this concealment of his identity with such consistency.

THE FIRST EXAMINING MAGISTRATE: He is certainly consistent in keeping quiet!

THE SECOND EXAMINING MAGISTRATE: He leaves blank self-evident inquiries about his earlier life–the basis of any interrogation!–as if he knew nothing himself. We had to find out the dates for ourselves.

THE FIRST EXAMINING MAGISTRATE: He really seems to be as ignorant of it as if he were today learning about his own life for the first time!

THE SECOND EXAMINING MAGISTRATE: Is he trying to have us on?

THE FIRST EXAMINING MAGISTRATE: How do you mean?

THE SECOND EXAMINING MAGISTRATE: Are we to read him a sermon about his past?

THE FIRST EXAMINING MAGISTRATE: For what purpose?

THE SECOND EXAMINING MAGISTRATE: To tire us out.

THE FIRST EXAMINING MAGISTRATE: He'll soon have managed that.

THE SECOND EXAMINING MAGISTRATE: (reads–lowers the paper.) Yet he doesn't deny that the coral was found on him.

THE FIRST EXAMINING MAGISTRATE: But he denies being the Secretary.

THE SECOND EXAMINING MAGISTRATE: Then how does he explain the coral on his watch-chain. (Reading.) He was repeatedly asked the question, and every time he gave no answer.

THE FIRST EXAMINING MAGISTRATE: (to the TWO FOOTMEN.) Couldn't it have been his plan to mislead you, too, for some special purpose?

THE FIRST FOOTMAN: No. It would have made our task impossible.

THE SECOND FOOTMAN: The murdered man was greatly concerned about the guarding of his person.

THE SECOND EXAMINING MAGISTRATE: It's quite transparent. Of course, it is a matter of life and death. So you put up a bit of resistance. But we have the evidence given by his son. During the conversation which took place between father and son shortly beforehand, the son had renounced his father's wealth. The daughter had also given up her claims. The Secretary had heard the excited talk in the next room and could not resist the temptation to secure the succession for himself. So he shot him then and there. Only he did not have time to change over the coral. Perhaps he would have liked to do that. (*To the* FOOTMEN.) But the shot brought you along.

THE SECOND FOOTMAN : I caught him just as he was going out of the door.

THE SECOND EXAMINING MAGISTRATE : Was he trying to escape?

THE FIRST FOOTMAN : We hadn't opened the door–he had.

THE FIRST EXAMINING MAGISTRATE : Why did he run away, if he claims to be the one who was attacked?

THE SECOND EXAMINING MAGISTRATE : (*puts down the record.*) This attempted flight itself is proof. The sound of the shot was too loud : he hadn't reckoned with that. In the confusion he hoped to get away, but the scheme was wrecked by the vigilance of the footmen. Now he has again remembered the part he intended to play.

THE FIRST EXAMINING MAGISTRATE : The similarity is certainly fantastic. I've never known a case of such identical doubles.

THE SECOND EXAMINING MAGISTRATE : Yes, if we hadn't got the coral we could only grope helplessly in the dark ! (*Picking up the record.*) And what about this attack which he claims was caused by the supposed Secretary–what reason does he give for that?

THE FIRST EXAMINING MAGISTRATE : He keeps quiet.

THE SECOND EXAMINING MAGISTRATE : Because it never happened

THE FIRST EXAMINING MAGISTRATE : But you said that he wanted to put himself in the dead man's place?

(THE SECOND EXAMINING MAGISTRATE *stops short.*)

THE FIRST EXAMINING MAGISTRATE : So there is a reason, after all?

THE SECOND EXAMINING MAGISTRATE : Which provoked him to the killing !

THE FIRST EXAMINING MAGISTRATE : Then he acted in self-defence !

THE SECOND EXAMINING MAGISTRATE : (*excitedly.*) But he's the Secretary !

THE FIRST EXAMINING MAGISTRATE : (*rubbing his eyes.*) I really am exhausted. The bright light–the coolness of the man, hardly defending himself–

THE SECOND EXAMINING MAGISTRATE: I am thinking of using means that will loosen him up. If showing him the coral does not work–(*He picks it up from the table.*) The thing looks like a drop of blood that has stuck to the culprit–! (*He puts it down.* To the FOOTMEN.) I don't need you any longer.

THE FIRST FOOTMAN: What time tomorrow?

THE SECOND EXAMINING MAGISTRATE: Let's hope we've done enough. The same rigmarole ten times over. I'll let you know, if not.

(*The two* FOOTMEN *exeunt.*)

THE FIRST EXAMINING MAGISTRATE: Are you expecting any greater success tonight?

THE SECOND EXAMINING MAGISTRATE: No greater than a full confession!

THE FIRST EXAMINING MAGISTRATE: (*surprised.*) How do you propose to get that out of him?

THE SECOND EXAMINING MAGISTRATE: He says he is the Millionaire. All right then, I take his children in to see him. Nature can play the judge. If he hesitates for a second to approach those whom, according to the statement of the son and daughter, their father loved above all else, then he has as good as confessed. He may resist the coral, it is a lifeless object– but under the impact of the sight of the son and daughter of his victim no individual will stand firm. And as he is no professional criminal, he'll cave in completely!

THE FIRST EXAMINING MAGISTRATE: I'm worn out, and that's a fact.

THE SECOND EXAMINING MAGISTRATE: Stretch out on the sofa and have a good sleep. If I may disturb you, I'll 'phone through our deliverance from the torment of the last fourteen nights.

THE FIRST EXAMINING MAGISTRATE: And then I shall go straight off to the country for a week.

THE SECOND EXAMINING MAGISTRATE: And I shall write a bestseller about the case!

(THE FIRST EXAMINING MAGISTRATE *exits at the back.*)

(THE SECOND EXAMINING MAGISTRATE *walks over left and presses a bell near a door. Accompanied by a* WARDER, *the* SON *and* DAUGHTER—*in black—from the left.*)

THE SECOND EXAMINING MAGISTRATE: It has now become necessary for me to carry out the confrontation after all. However much I should wish to spare you this distress, the obstinate denials, in which my colleague has not been able to shake him, force this step upon us. I can see no other way of obtaining a confession. And we really must have the confession!

SON: Give us our instructions as to how we are to behave.

THE SECOND EXAMINING MAGISTRATE: I intend to take him by surprise. He must not be allowed the least time for reflection. I would ask you to enter absolutely silently and not to betray your presence here. To begin with, stay well back in the passage, the warder will remain near the door. There is nothing unusual in that. (*To the* WARDER.) During the interrogation I'll arrange to step over to this side, so that the prisoner has his back to your door. As soon as I pull out my handkerchief, let the lady and gentleman in.

SON: Our task will be completed with this confrontation?

THE SECOND EXAMINING MAGISTRATE: Naturally I shall limit even this to the shortest time. Nonetheless, try to look him straight in the face. That's important. I should like to mention that to you especially, miss. Hold yourselves erect. Perhaps you will experience the most horrifying thing that can happen to you. You will believe you are looking at your father, who is dead.

SON: But surely it must be possible to distinguish between them!

THE SECOND EXAMINING MAGISTRATE: Then it would have been easy for us. The correspondence is exact. There is no distinguishing mark. Nature itself is playing a trick on us.

SON: Only this coral gives the clue?

THE SECOND EXAMINING MAGISTRATE: Undeniably. Therefore do not forget you have the Secretary in front of you!

(SON *and* DAUGHTER *exeunt left with the* WARDER. *The* WARDER *comes back behind the barred door.*)

174

THE SECOND EXAMINING MAGISTRATE: (*to the first* WARDER.) Bring him in.

(*The* WARDER *switches on the arc-lamp. Exit right.* THE SECOND EXAMINING MAGISTRATE *puts on a pair of blue-tinted glasses. The* WARDER *brings in the* MILLIONAIRE, *who walks in front of him, and remains by the door. The* MILLIONAIRE'S *hands are tied in front of him with thin wire-rope. He assumes a stance which has already become habitual—without any sign of emotion.*)

THE SECOND EXAMINING MAGISTRATE: (*ignores him for the moment. Then he picks up the revolver from the table and walks—interested solely in the weapon—over to the* MILLIONAIRE.) Where can this model be bought?

(MILLIONAIRE *silent.*)

THE SECOND EXAMINING MAGISTRATE: This is a type I should like. But I can scarcely pocket an object confiscated by the court.

(MILLIONAIRE *smiles weakly.*)

THE SECOND EXAMINING MAGISTRATE: (*looks at him.*) A carefully guarded secret?

MILLIONAIRE: A present.

THE SECOND EXAMINING MAGISTRATE: From whom?

(MILLIONAIRE *shakes his head.*)

THE SECOND EXAMINING MAGISTRATE: But surely not from a hand dear to you?

MILLIONAIRE: From one most dear to me.

THE SECOND EXAMINING MAGISTRATE: Come now, that's unnatural.

MILLIONAIRE: Yes—it was unnatural.

THE SECOND EXAMINING MAGISTRATE: Were you to use it? If you were unfaithful?

MILLIONAIRE: I was the target.

THE SECOND EXAMINING MAGISTRATE: Who wanted to shoot at you, then?

(MILLIONAIRE *nods slowly.*)

THE SECOND EXAMINING MAGISTRATE: Did you snatch the gun away from him?

MILLIONAIRE: He put it down on the desk.

THE SECOND EXAMINING MAGISTRATE: (*quickly.*) The Millionaire?

(MILLIONAIRE *silent.*)

THE SECOND EXAMINING MAGISTRATE: (*with a nod of satisfaction, takes up his position on the right.*) Now let's reconstruct the situation. Turn round towards me.

(MILLIONAIRE *does so.*)

THE SECOND EXAMINING MAGISTRATE: Just a moment. The metal is tarnished, but no doubt it will have been shining then. (*He takes out his handkerchief and polishes the gun.*)

(*The* WARDER, *left, withdraws through the door.*)

THE SECOND EXAMINING MAGISTRATE: That the gun was just lying on the desk is, of course, all humbug. Your tale is thoroughly confused, so there is no point in going into it. What happened is simply this: on some pretext or other you find something to do behind your victim—pull the gun out of your trouser-pocket—just as I am now, you were standing ready— the distance is the same—(*The* WARDER *has entered with the* SON *and* DAUGHTER, *they both stand motionless.*)—and now you turn your back to me!

MILLIONAIRE: (*turns round without faltering, he goes up to his* SON *and* DAUGHTER.) Children—in black? Has someone dear to us died?—Are you surprised that I know nothing about it? Well, I am out of touch with you. For the moment I'm being held in strict isolation. An unfortunate error, which still has to be cleared up. I am doing everything imaginable to allay these grave suspicions. But the courts are so fussy. Every triviality becomes important. A coral they found on me—that revolver there, which they say I was carrying. (*To the* SON.) Wouldn't you care to explain its origin with one word?

176

SON: (*mastering his emotion, to the* EXAMINING MAGISTRATE.) The gun is my property.

THE SECOND EXAMINING MAGISTRATE: How does it come into the possession of the Secretary?

SON: I put it down on the desk in front of my father.

THE SECOND EXAMINING MAGISTRATE: That, at any rate, is valuable. The revolver lying openly there was an incitement to the crime. Why did you hand it over to your father?

SON: I—cannot answer that.

MILLIONAIRE: I haven't betrayed you, either.

SON: (*sharply.*) Because you can know nothing!

MILLIONAIRE: No 'father'? Have I become a stranger to you, because I'm under suspicion? (*With a peculiarly watchful expression.*) Or do you believe that I am the Secretary? You—my own children—take me for the Secretary?

SON: (*with difficulty—to the* EXAMINING MAGISTRATE.) Do you need my sister and me here any longer?

(DAUGHTER *gives a cry—claps her hands to her face.*)

THE SECOND EXAMINING MAGISTRATE: Thank you, no.

(SON—*supporting the* DAUGHTER—*exeunt left.*)

THE SECOND EXAMINING MAGISTRATE: (*walking up and down.*) Quite incredible. The height of callousness!—Aren't you ashamed? (*Taken aback.*) You are smiling?

MILLIONAIRE: I saw my children.—

THE SECOND EXAMINING MAGISTRATE: Does the suffering of others put you in a cheerful mood?

MILLIONAIRE:—my children did not see me!

THE SECOND EXAMINING MAGISTRATE: They saw their father's murderer. That is what you are. You—the Secretary. Don't serve us up that stupid tale again. And even if the coral didn't offer the utterly conclusive proof it does, this unmasks you: those you claim with such cool impudence as your children repudiate you as a stranger!

MILLIONAIRE: (*impenetrable.*) That—is not enough.

THE SECOND EXAMINING MAGISTRATE: Are you sure? Because you haven't made a confession? We'll let you off that now.

Go on wrapping yourself in monumental silence. Now we will do the talking! (*He motions to the* WARDER.)

(WARDER *leads the* MILLIONAIRE *off, right.*)

THE SECOND EXAMINING MAGISTRATE: (*telephones.*) I'd like a relief, please. (*Loud.*) Yes–relief! (*Walks up and down in annoyance. Stamping his foot.*) It's enough to–!

(THE FIRST EXAMINING MAGISTRATE *enters quickly from the back.*)

THE SECOND EXAMINING MAGISTRATE: You thought you hadn't heard right? No, still going on the same. You can't get at the man. He stands up to the confrontation without batting an eyelid–and actually complains that they don't call him 'father'!

(THE FIRST EXAMINING MAGISTRATE *reads the record.*)

THE SECOND EXAMINING MAGISTRATE: I think we're finished!

THE FIRST EXAMINING MAGISTRATE: No!–It intrigues me. I shall put pressure on him. (*Striking his brow with his hand.*) Why, it's quite simple!

THE SECOND EXAMINING MAGISTRATE: Did you get any inspiration in your sleep?

THE FIRST EXAMINING MAGISTRATE: Am I furious!

THE SECOND EXAMINING MAGISTRATE: A condition that is scarcely conducive to a fertile mind.

THE FIRST EXAMINING MAGISTRATE: He has become so used to the part that he thinks he is the Millionaire.

THE SECOND EXAMINING MAGISTRATE: That's sure enough.

THE FIRST EXAMINING MAGISTRATE: So we shall have to get the Millionaire out of his system again–

THE SECOND EXAMINING MAGISTRATE: Hocus-pocus, one, two, three.

THE FIRST EXAMINING MAGISTRATE:–and the Secretary back into it!

THE SECOND EXAMINING MAGISTRATE: The trick you're going to use to do it?

(WARDER *enters, right, and switches off the arc-lamp.*)

THE FIRST EXAMINING MAGISTRATE: He must be born anew! —Yes, yes, I'll lay him in the cradle again and let him kick and crow contentedly. The Millionaire has not yet come into his existence—that's a later chapter, about which I'll not breathe a syllable. I shall build up his life for him up to this point without a gap and wrap him so softly and gently in youthful memories that he'll quite forget why he's standing here. (*Taking up a document.*) We have the facts here—collected down to the last detail. His past presents a strikingly bright picture— and so his heart won't be hardened either. He'll be wax in my hands when I open the book of his better days for him!

THE SECOND EXAMINING MAGISTRATE: He never flinched in face of his victim's children—

THE FIRST EXAMINING MAGISTRATE: Children stand outside. In the end we live only for ourselves.

THE SECOND EXAMINING MAGISTRATE: And I wouldn't want to part with the file without closing it, either.

THE FIRST EXAMINING MAGISTRATE: My attempt may come to nothing, like all the others so far—yet there is suggestive force in such delving into the past.

THE SECOND EXAMINING MAGISTRATE: Do you want the glasses?

THE FIRST EXAMINING MAGISTRATE: With dimmed lights this time (*To the* WARDER.) Don't switch on. Bring him in. (WARDER *off right.*) That by itself will make him feel better. And for the rest, I'll make it sound like granny telling the kiddies a fairy-tale.

THE SECOND EXAMINING MAGISTRATE: And the big bad wolf comes in at the end.

THE FIRST EXAMINING MAGISTRATE: He has to catch the murderer!

(THE SECOND EXAMINING MAGISTRATE *exits at the back.* WARDER *brings in the* MILLIONAIRE.)

THE FIRST EXAMINING MAGISTRATE: (*is absorbed in the document.*) This love of animals is charming. (*Looking up*

179

at the MILLIONAIRE.) Did it have a black spot in the middle of its head, then?

(MILLIONAIRE *raises his head, listening.*)

THE FIRST EXAMINING MAGISTRATE: The little dog you saved from drowning?

(MILLIONAIRE *leans towards him.*)

THE FIRST EXAMINING MAGISTRATE: Was the river shallow at that point? One doesn't risk going far into the water at the age of ten.

(MILLIONAIRE *breathes raspingly.*)

THE FIRST EXAMINING MAGISTRATE: I suppose the little river that runs past the town won't have a raging current. Or was the river in spate in the spring?
(MILLIONAIRE *swaying strangely with the upper part of his body.*)

THE FIRST EXAMINING MAGISTRATE: The waters went rushing by with their load of uprooted bushes and tufts of grass. Sometimes they overflowed the banks and seeped into cellars. And then the stores had to be saved. The job of salvaging them was always fun. And the things that turned up in the process! Father and mother turned to–and of course their son provided the most important assistance. He was forever getting in the way! But you were convinced that you were indispensable?

(MILLIONAIRE *nods slowly.*)

THE FIRST EXAMINING MAGISTRATE: Yes, a little town like that has its disasters. Something different every day. The wind snatches the cap off your head and carries it round the corner–(*Quickly.*) Did you have green school caps?
MILLIONAIRE: (*with a rippling smile.*) I—
THE FIRST EXAMINING MAGISTRATE: Don't you remember the colour clearly any longer?
MILLIONAIRE: —have forgotten so much!
THE FIRST EXAMINING MAGISTRATE: (*observes him closely.– After a pause.*) Don't you regret that? I should imagine people

like to think of pleasant impressions they once had. And you especially have every reason to refresh yourself with bright pictures of the past. Yes, you were fortunate in having an enviable youth. (*Turning the pages of the document.*) It's a pleasure to read it!

(MILLIONAIRE *also looks at it.*)

THE FIRST EXAMINING MAGISTRATE: It's all light–sunshine, sunshine–light. Not a shadow rears its head. (*Looking up.*) You must be inexpressibly grateful to your parents?

MILLIONAIRE: (*with almost singing intonation.*) My parents—

THE FIRST EXAMINING MAGISTRATE: They held protecting hands over their only child! Did you ever get a smack?

MILLIONAIRE: Did I–never get a smack?

THE FIRST EXAMINING MAGISTRATE: Oh, you must tell me that!

MILLIONAIRE: Oh—you must tell me!

THE FIRST EXAMINING MAGISTRATE: (*looks at him in astonishment. Then jokingly.*) All right, then, let's open the book of your past. Chapter one: Parents' home. Pleasant little town –set in green countryside. Father–vicar. Can you see him before you?

MILLIONAIRE: (*groping in front of him.*)–set in green countryside—father—vicar—

THE FIRST EXAMINING MAGISTRATE: Chapter two: the son is born and life in the vicarage revolves round him. Every attention is lavished on him. He thrives lustily.–You will scarcely remember this earliest childhood?

MILLIONAIRE: I know it–now!

THE FIRST EXAMINING MAGISTRATE: But in the next part you come into your own. Schooldays. The grammar school isn't large–few pupils, and you are the best among them. Learning comes easily to you–you meet no resistance–and so this period, too, is not a thorny one for you.–Or is there a dark cloud?

MILLIONAIRE: If–you don't know of one!

THE FIRST EXAMINING MAGISTRATE: Good, then there isn't one. Let's go on. This has sketched in the framework within which you moved in those days. Seldom have things been made so easy for a young man as they were for you from the very beginning–and your ability met your parents' plans half-way. You developed in an unusually high degree the capacity for being a happy person. No more beautiful picture than this complete harmony between man and environment. There is no shattering experience to poison the blood. Day links with day like the daisy-chains that children make!—(*With pathos.*) Doesn't it send warmth flooding through your heart to hear me telling the story of your past? Surely it must awaken in you a hankering after this paradise, in which–favoured above so many–you were privileged to walk? Watched over and loved–protected against every blow that others suffer at this age. Aren't you looking into a crystal-clear lake–you can see right to the bottom: and there, too, find nothing but round, bright pebbles?–Acknowledge your happy past–and preserve the best thing anyone can possess!

MILLIONAIRE: (*trembling as though in a paroxysm of happiness.*)—the best thing—anyone can possess–

THE FIRST EXAMINING MAGISTRATE: (*in growing excitement.*) Do you acknowledge this past?

MILLIONAIRE: (*in a whisper.*)—yes—yes—yes—!

THE FIRST EXAMINING MAGISTRATE: Now sign your statement!

MILLIONAIRE: (*his hands already outstretched.*) Yes!

THE FIRST EXAMINING MAGISTRATE: (*to the* WARDER.) Free his hands! (*To the* MILLIONAIRE.) Your acquiescence has convicted you–that past belongs to the Secretary. You are the Secretary. (*As the* MILLIONAIRE *hesitates.*) I'm telling you this so that you give the right signature: the Secretary's!

(MILLIONAIRE *writes in the air.*)

THE FIRST EXAMINING MAGISTRATE: Now what are you doing? Can't you remember your own handwriting?

(MILLIONAIRE *signs.*)

THE FIRST EXAMINING MAGISTRATE: The interrogation is concluded. I hope you won't revert to the former denials of your identity. From now on it would be useless! (*He makes a sign to the* WARDER.)

MILLIONAIRE: (*is led off right by the* WARDER.)—the best thing —the best thing—(*Exit.*)

THE FIRST EXAMINING MAGISTRATE: (*stands pensive for a moment. Then telephoning.*) Comprehensive confession!

THE SECOND EXAMINING MAGISTRATE: (*enters from the back.*) That really sounds like a fairy-tale! (*He reads the record.*) That went off smoothly. Didn't he see the trap you were leading him into?

THE FIRST EXAMINING MAGISTRATE: (*pondering.*) Don't you think that's strange?

THE SECOND EXAMINING MAGISTRATE: He was overtired.

THE FIRST EXAMINING MAGISTRATE: I didn't get that impression: he actually perked up when I told him about his past!

(WARDER *enters, right.*)

THE FIRST EXAMINING MAGISTRATE: (*quickly.*) Is there something he wants to let me know?

THE SECOND EXAMINING MAGISTRATE: Is he already saying he's the other one again?

WARDER: No.

THE SECOND EXAMINING MAGISTRATE: Has he broken down?

WARDER: He is standing there looking up and muttering something.

THE FIRST EXAMINING MAGISTRATE: As he was standing here —in a dream—

THE SECOND EXAMINING MAGISTRATE: (*after a silence.*) At all events, he'll get a rude awakening!

ACT V

Small square courtyard, sunk at the bottom of a pit of prison-walls. A scanty grass patch with a fixed iron bench. A low door left and a high narrow door at the back.

(WARDER *leads in the* MILLIONAIRE–*now a convict in a black linen smock with a red neck-band–from the left.*)

MILLIONAIRE: The forecourt of death?

WARDER: You have another hour here.

MILLIONAIRE: (*nods.*) The last hour has struck. (*Looking about him.*) Kindly custom—feet padding on grass—sky blue streaming overhead! Happiness has to wait upon the supreme penalty. (*He stands motionless.*)

WARDER: Are visitors to be admitted?

MILLIONAIRE: Is someone anxious to see me? I shan't object.

(WARDER *exit left.* MILLIONAIRE *sits down on the bench.* WARDER *admits the* GENTLEMAN IN GREY. *Exit.*)

THE GENTLEMAN IN GREY: (*has obviously undergone a transformation: his suit—in colour as before—is of impeccable cut; light spats over patent-leather boots, grey top-hat, white kid-gloves with black chenille trimmings.—Goes briskly up to the* MILLIONAIRE *and holds out his hand to him.*) Not yet too late. That's a real piece of luck. I should like to have come sooner, but—well, business—! Sulphur mine—booming proposition. Annual turn-over—But I suppose you're rather out of touch with profitability and dividends at the moment. Anyway, that's not the subject I propose to talk to you about—I wanted to thank you!

MILLIONAIRE: I can't imagine—

THE GENTLEMAN IN GREY: You've no objection if I sit down beside you—on this little bench for condemned men. At least one can have a quiet quarter of an hour. So from the bottom of my heart—thanks—thanks—and thanks again!

MILLIONAIRE: If you'd tell me—

THE GENTLEMAN IN GREY: I am the Man in Grey. You once refused to give me your signature to a manifesto that, at one stroke, was to bring harmony to the world. You took the trouble—and what I most marvel at today is that you gave up your time—I couldn't do it!—to demonstrate to me the hopelessness of my benevolent scheme. Your argument struck me like hammer blows—and I left the 'warm heart of the world' hurling after you a curse powerful enough to fell an ox. Are you catching on?

MILLIONAIRE: (*with a thin smile.*) You are mistaken.

THE GENTLEMAN IN GREY: I wished you straight to the bottomless pit!

MILLIONAIRE: Not me—

THE GENTLEMAN IN GREY: Didn't it have any effect on you?

MILLIONAIRE: Because you had that conversation with the Millionaire.

THE GENTLEMAN IN GREY: (*laughs uproariously.*) You don't need to keep up your act with me. Put the Secretary away in your pocket. Or haven't you got one in that dressing-gown for the everlasting night? (*Patting him on the shoulder.*) You're still the man for me, on your flight from the horror!

MILLIONAIRE: (*alarmed.*) Speak quietly!

THE GENTLEMAN IN GREY: Don't worry, I'm neither going to give you away nor to set you free. I haven't the least cause for such ingratitude. Are you satisfied with me?

MILLIONAIRE: You are the only one—

THE GENTLEMAN IN GREY: I did enjoy the trial. I wouldn't have interfered for anything. It was a stroke of genius to let them wangle you into being the Secretary and then scoff the sweet dish of his bright past. I could fairly hear you smacking your lips when they served up the magnificent meal. Is your stomach feeling all right now?

MILLIONAIRE: It was my salvation.

THE GENTLEMAN IN GREY: When your son—that hoped-for, happier reincarnation in peace and pleasure—took the downward path!

MILLIONAIRE: Don't speak of that!

THE GENTLEMAN IN GREY: But surely you've nothing more to fear. And, from the secure shore, one can after all derive a certain malicious satisfaction from the sight of the raging sea below. You've saved your neck—and in a few minutes it can no longer cost you your head. You're quite safe from that!

MILLIONAIRE: What are you thanking me for?

THE GENTLEMAN IN GREY: Doesn't one glance at the outer man tell you that?

MILLIONAIRE: You are dressed with a certain provocative elegance.

THE GENTLEMAN IN GREY: Only to illustrate the inner structure. I am in flight.

MILLIONAIRE: You–from what?

THE GENTLEMAN IN GREY: From your social order!

MILLIONAIRE: Don't you want to curse me again?

THE GENTLEMAN IN GREY: I bless you. Out of rosy clouds you have brought me down to earth. I am planted upright on my two firm feet. Your law holds good: we are in flight! Woe betide anybody who stumbles. He is trodden under foot–and the stampede goes rushing on over him. There is no quarter given and no mercy. Onwards–onwards!–Behind us chaos!

MILLIONAIRE: And have you already got a start?

THE GENTLEMAN IN GREY: I was an apt pupil. I am piling up riches and placing this glittering mountain between myself and the others. Enormous energies are developed when you know the law. You are still running even in your sleep, and in the morning you jump out of bed with projects ready-made. It is a headlong chase. Thank Heavens you didn't take the secret with you to the grave–now I can proclaim to mankind the true salvation!

MILLIONAIRE: Are you proposing to do that?

THE GENTLEMAN IN GREY: I have done it. My defection is stirring things up. All units are scattered, the battle is raging all along the line. Every man for himself and no quarter!

MILLIONAIRE: And can you see an objective that you're charging towards?

THE GENTLEMAN IN GREY: Ridiculous, there isn't one!

MILLIONAIRE: Oh, yes, there is.

THE GENTLEMAN IN GREY: (*looks at him in surprise.*) Don't keep me on tenterhooks!

MILLIONAIRE: It lies at the beginning!

THE GENTLEMAN IN GREY: (*with a resounding laugh.*) Yes–you are a lucky chap. You can laugh at us. Though of course you removed the cause that first frightened you into running. But it remains an isolated case: not everyone can afford such a perfect double! And there is something else I have to tell you. (*Passing his hand round his throat.*) Most people would find the price too high!

MILLIONAIRE: Do you call this price high?

THE GENTLEMAN IN GREY: (*rising.*) I expect you can estimate that best according to your own valuation. You've certainly never made a fuss when presented with a bill!–I should like to stay longer, but–your time is also limited. In any case it will give you a little pleasure that your great discovery is not disappearing with you. (*He holds out both hands to him.*) So keep your chin up!

MILLIONAIRE: As long as I can.

THE GENTLEMAN IN GREY: (*laughs–waving his hat.*) I'll be seeing you!

MILLIONAIRE: Where?

THE GENTLEMAN IN GREY: True–for a case like the present there is no form of greeting ready to hand! (*WARDER opens the door at the back, exit the GENTLEMAN IN GREY.*)

(*MILLIONAIRE sits motionless–his chin on the back of his hand. WARDER admits the SON. Exit WARDER.*)

SON: (*hesitates–then goes quickly up to the MILLIONAIRE, stretches out his hand to him.*) I have come–to forgive you.

(*MILLIONAIRE slowly looks up at him.*)

SON: Don't you recognize me?

MILLIONAIRE: –Oh yes.

SON: My decision surprises you. Perhaps it is strange that a son should do so. That is the least thing. I want to save you.

MILLIONAIRE: Have you got rope-ladders and climbing-irons with you?

SON: I will acknowledge that you are my father!

(*MILLIONAIRE rises and retreats behind the bench.*)

SON: Don't make my burden heavier than what already oppresses me. I am guilty as you are. Because I pointed the pistol at him. I had intended the bullet for him. It makes no difference who fires.

MILLIONAIRE: That is beyond me.

SON: Believe in my guilt–and don't make me dwell on these dreadful things.

MILLIONAIRE: Have you ever thought–what I have done?

187

SON: What anyone must when he sees madness prancing in power.

MILLIONAIRE: Was your father mad?

SON: Power is madness!

MILLIONAIRE: Yes–he was powerful.

SON: And guilty! Behind your guilt stands his–gigantic and ineradicable. You are his victim, as I am too–as are all with a thought in their heads!

MILLIONAIRE: Do they all want to kill?

SON: They cannot help it, the compulsion is irresistible. The temptation is created by the upstarts themselves. They reach the top by force–by force they are toppled.

MILLIONAIRE: You are making it easy for yourself–

SON: Didn't you provide me with the final confirmation? I know about your life–I read the reports breathlessly. You spent the most untroubled childhood and the most agreeable youth– where does any inclination to violence show itself?

MILLIONAIRE: You also had the most untroubled childhood–

SON: And resorted to the pistol. I wanted to punish out of a passionate sense of justice–you to enrich yourself. You were simply carried away by the sight of violence. My father, who always acted ruthlessly, set you the example–and as long as there are such examples, we shall be tempted!

MILLIONAIRE: Do you hope to wipe out all the bad examples?

SON: With your help!

MILLIONAIRE: What can I do about it?

SON: Renounce your position that raises you above others, and come down to join us!

MILLIONAIRE: For that your father would have to be alive.

SON: I will go to the judge and declare that, following this interview, I have recognized you as my father!

MILLIONAIRE: And the coral?

SON: Nothing must stand in the way. The task is enormous. There can be no holding back. The fate of mankind is at stake. We combine in the ardour of our work–and in our untiring zeal are united as father and son!

MILLIONAIRE: (shakes his head.) No–I cannot deny myself like that.

SON: When your life is at stake?

MILLIONAIRE: When the life you are offering me is at stake!

SON: It demands self-discipline. It cost me a struggle to visit you. I came for the sake of the great cause. If you serve this cause, you will banish the shadow of my father that stands behind you!

MILLIONAIRE: It can't succeed.

SON: I swear to you—

MILLIONAIRE: What?

SON: To be your son who did not lose his father!

MILLIONAIRE: (*steps close to him.*) Shall I name my condition?

SON: Any!

MILLIONAIRE: Will you be such a son to me as your father wanted?

SON: What do you mean?

MILLIONAIRE: Settle down again on the sunny shores—then I could agree to what you wish!

(SON *stares at him.*)

MILLIONAIRE: Otherwise the shadow—that stands behind me—will not be banished!

SON: What are you saying?

MILLIONAIRE: What your father would say. Has the first test been too much for you?

(SON *observes him with a startled look.*)

MILLIONAIRE: (*places his hands on his shoulders.*) It is nice that you have come once more. The eye likes to rest on people who are young. Haven't you got a sister? Was she, too, prepared to accept me as her father?—You make it tempting, but there are no longer any bridges to span the chasm. You have only convinced me all the more. Leave me in my yard. There is green here, isn't there?—Go and seek out your battlefield. Perhaps peace is the first false step towards war—but whoever surfaces from the bloodbath strives to escape it. You denied me your help—so I took my fate into my own hands. Should you be angry with me now, if I refuse you my support? (*He leads him over to the left.*) Do not revile me in any hour of your

189

busy life–for you have bold plans–and if you fail in one or another and ultimately in all of them!–do not keep alive the memory of your father with anger and recrimination: he would have shielded you from disillusionment—for reasons which, as you will understand, would take too long to disclose. (As the CHAPLAIN enters, to the SON.) There, you see, we lack the basic necessity: time!

(SON exits. MILLIONAIRE still gazes after him. The CHAPLAIN has approached the bench and is observing the MILLIONAIRE.)

MILLIONAIRE: (turns to him.) The third and last visitor?

CHAPLAIN: After the sight that just presented itself to me, my task is difficult. You received the best comfort that can be given by men: reconciliation with the son of the unfortunate father.

MIILLIONAIRE: No, you are mistaken: we parted after a disagreement. And if I saw him to the door, then it was because I was the stronger. I was supporting the loser.

CHAPLAIN: Didn't he come to visit you?

MILLIONAIRE: He laid a snare for me to get caught in. But I was on my guard.

CHAPLAIN: He forgave you?

MILLIONAIRE: Had he reason to?

CHAPLAIN: You took his father from him!

MILLIONAIRE: (sits down.) Do you believe in the right of retribution?

CHAPLAIN: Earthly retribution must run its course.

MILLIONAIRE: I only exacted retribution.

CHAPLAIN: What had he done to harm you?

MILLIONAIRE: In the end the choice falls at random. This one or that. They killed my father and mother.

CHAPLAIN: (shrugs his shoulders.) A peaceful death ended the life of your parents.

MILLIONAIRE: Then what reason did I have to kill?

CHAPLAIN: In a state of inexplicable mental confusion you reached out your hand after another man's riches.

MILLIONAIRE: (nods.)

In a state of inexplicable mental confusion–that bears the stamp of your wisdom. I won't resist any further. You are arching above me the heavens under which I shall breathe in gladness. Your gifts are too lavish!

CHAPLAIN: (*after a pause.*) You expressed a wish for the coral, so I've brought it for you.

(MILLIONAIRE *takes it and examines it.*)

CHAPLAIN: You can send me away–or close your ears to my words.

MILLIONAIRE: Speak.

CHAPLAIN: Of the refuge that opens to receive us when we step out of this life, which is like a house with black windows–

MILLIONAIRE: Tell me about this house with black windows.

CHAPLAIN: Could the light but find a wider entry–

MILLIONAIRE: (*nods.*) That's it.

CHAPLAIN: It is never too late. The infinite treasure can be gained in a second!

MILLIONAIRE: What treasure is this?

CHAPLAIN: The new life after this interlude!

MILLIONAIRE: Does it lie in the future?

CHAPLAIN: Which admits those who knock with humble hand!

MILLIONAIRE: (*shaking his head.*) Still the same old error.

CHAPLAIN: We have been given reliable pledges!

MILLIONAIRE: Flight into the kingdom of Heaven. That will bring no release from the cross and vinegar. You won't find it at the end–it stands in the beginning: paradise!

CHAPLAIN: We were driven out–

MILLIONAIRE: Does that dim the perception?—I've no wish to shake your faith and strike the tool from your hand. But the most profound truth is not proclaimed by you and the thousands like you–only the single individual ever discovers it. And then it is so overwhelming that it becomes powerless in its effect!–You seek a refuge–I could tell you that you are taking the wrong road. Your goal overtakes you a hundred times– and clubs you in the back each time. On you rush to your refuge. And you never reach it. No escape that way–not that way!

CHAPLAIN: You talk to me like this: what gives you–how else can I express it–this solemn tranquillity?

MILLIONAIRE: I have regained the paradise that lies behind us. I entered its gates with a violent act–for the angels at either side also carry flaming swords!–and now I am standing amidst the loveliest of green meadows. Overhead a flood of blue sky.

CHAPLAIN: Are you thinking of your happy childhood now?

MILLIONAIRE: Isn't it easy to find? Is it not contained in words already spoken: become as little children? Wisdom needs only a play on words.

CHAPLAIN: Why can we men not remain as children?

MILLIONAIRE: You won't solve that riddle today or tomorrow!

(CHAPLAIN *remains staring in front of him.*)

MILLIONAIRE: —Do you see this?

CHAPLAIN: Your last request–the coral?

MILLIONAIRE: Do you know how it grows up from the sea-bed? As far as the surface of the water–it reaches up no higher. There it stands, washed by currents–formed in ever-lasting union in the denseness of the sea. Fish are a minor event, creating a mild disturbance. Isn't that enticing?

CHAPLAIN: What do you mean?

MILLIONAIRE: I'm only lifting a corner of the lid that covers up the riddle. What is the best thing to do? Not come to the surface and be drawn into the storm as it sweeps towards the coast. There tumult rages and drags us into the frenzy of life. We are all driven onwards–all driven out of the paradise of our tranquillity. Pieces torn off the coral-tree down there in the dim light–with a wound from the very first day. It doesn't heal–it smarts–our dreadful pain lashes us on our headlong career!— What are you holding in your hand? (He *lifts up the* CHAPLAIN'S *hand with the black cross.*) That merely deadens the pain. (He *holds the coral in both hands against his breast.*) This delivers us from suffering!

(The *high, narrow door at the back opens.* MILLIONAIRE *rises.*)

CHAPLAIN: I–cannot go with you!

(MILLIONAIRE *walks with firm step to the door.*)

GAS I

Play in Five Acts

Translated by B. J. Kenworthy

'MILLIONAIRE: But the most profound truth–that is only ever discovered by the single individual. And then it is so overwhelming that it becomes power-less in its effect!'

The Coral

Characters

The WHITE GENTLEMAN
MILLIONAIRE'S SON
DAUGHTER
OFFICER
FIRST GENTLEMAN in BLACK
SECOND GENTLEMAN in BLACK
THIRD GENTLEMAN in BLACK
FOURTH GENTLEMAN in BLACK
FIFTH GENTLEMAN in BLACK
GOVERNMENT OFFICIAL
CLERK
FIRST WORKER
SECOND WORKER
THIRD WORKER
GIRL
WOMAN
MOTHER
CAPTAIN
Machine-gun Detachment
WORKERS

ACT I

Square room, whose rear wall is glass: office of the MILLION-AIRE'S SON. *Right and left, from floor to ceiling, wall charts covered with graphs. On the left, a broad desk with a cane chair to one side. Small desk right. Outside serried chimney stacks, belching out fire and smoke in straight lines. Dance music blaring in.*

At the desk right the young CLERK. *From the right the* WHITE GENTLEMAN *enters: noiselessly shutting the door—walking noiselessly—after looking round the room—across to the* CLERK, *touching his shoulder.*

THE WHITE GENTLEMAN : Music?

(CLERK *startled, turns to face him.*)

THE WHITE GENTLEMAN : (*listening towards the ceiling, nodding.*) Waltz.

CLERK : How did you get in—?

THE WHITE GENTLEMAN : Without any fuss. A certain noiselessness-produced by rubber soles. (*He sits down on the chair at the desk.—Crossing his legs.*) The boss—busy? Upstairs?

CLERK : What—do you want?

THE WHITE GENTLEMAN : A dance?

CLERK : (*still in stupefied haste.*) Upstairs—the wedding.

THE WHITE GENTLEMAN : (*flexing his fingers.*) The boss? Or—?

CLERK : His daughter—to the officer.

THE WHITE GENTLEMAN : Then he's certainly tied up at the moment, the boss.—The boss!

CLERK : Here there is no—boss!

THE WHITE GENTLEMAN : (*turning quickly towards him.*) Interesting! What about these subtle calculations you're engaged in—the pay-roll?

CLERK : Here there is no pay-roll!

THE WHITE GENTLEMAN : You are piling on surprises at some

rate! Right into the vortex of affairs! (*Pointing out through the window.*) This establishment of the most gigantic dimensions bursting with production–and no boss, no pay-roll?

CLERK: We work–and we share!

THE WHITE GENTLEMAN: (*indicating the walls.*) And these schedules? (*Standing up and reading the charts.*) Three grades: thirty and under, scale one–forty and under, scale two–forty and over, scale three. A piece of simple arithmetic –profit-sharing according to age. (*To the* CLERK.) An invention of the boss's–who claims not to be one?

CLERK: Because he has no desire to be richer than others!

THE WHITE GENTLEMAN: Was he rich?

CLERK: He is the Millionaire's son!

THE WHITE GENTLEMAN: (*smiling.*) He pressed forward to the very periphery of wealth and comes back to the centre–back to the heart.–And you all work?

CLERK: Each gives his all!

THE WHITE GENTLEMAN: When they share all the profits!

CLERK: That is why we work harder here than anyone else in the world!

THE WHITE GENTLEMAN: And does the product match your exceptional industriousness?

CLERK: Gas!

(THE WHITE GENTLEMAN *blows through cupped hand.*)

CLERK: (*excitedly.*) Don't you know anything about the gas we produce?

(THE WHITE GENTLEMAN *as before.*)

CLERK: Coal and water-power are obsolete. The new energy drives millions of new machines with more powerful force. We create it. Our gas feeds the technology of the world!

THE WHITE GENTLEMAN: (*at the window.*) Day and night– fire and smoke?

CLERK: The highest potential of our productivity has been reached!

THE WHITE GENTLEMAN: (*stepping back.*) Because poverty is wiped out?

CLERK: Our enormous efforts are productive!

THE WHITE GENTLEMAN: Because the profits are shared?

CLERK: Gas!

THE WHITE GENTLEMAN: (*close to him.*) And supposing the gas should–

CLERK: The work cannot stop for an hour. We are working for ourselves–no longer for others' pockets. No slackness–no strikes. Production continues uninterrupted. There will never be a shortage of gas!

THE WHITE GENTLEMAN: And supposing the gas should—explode?

(CLERK: *stares at him.*)

THE WHITE GENTLEMAN: What happens then?

(CLERK *speechless.*)

THE WHITE GENTLEMAN: (*whispering right in his face.*) The white terror!–(*Straightening up–listening to the sounds from overhead.*) Music. (*Stopping half-way to the door.*) Waltz. (*Goes off, noiselessly.*)

CLERK: (*in growing confusion–finally bends over the telephone–almost shouting.*) The Engineer! (*His glance, wanders to the doors right and left. The* ENGINEER–*in morning-coat– from the right.*)

ENGINEER: What–

(From the left WORKER–*apprehensive–in white overalls.*)

CLERK: (*pointing at him with outstretched arm.*) There–!

ENGINEER: (*to the* WORKER.) Are you looking for me?

WORKER: (*surprised.*) I was going to send for you.

ENGINEER: (*to the* CLERK.) You had already telephoned for me!

CLERK: Because–

ENGINEER: Have you had a report?

CLERK: (*shakes his head. Indicating the* WORKER.) He–

ENGINEER: –has only just come.

CLERK: –had to come!

ENGINEER: (*in some perplexity.*) What has happened?

WORKER: The gas is changing colour in the gauge.

ENGINEER: Changing colour?

WORKER: Only a trace as yet.

ENGINEER: Is it increasing?

WORKER: Visibly.

ENGINEER: The colour?

WORKER: Pale pink.

ENGINEER: You are not mistaken?

WORKER: I've been watching with complete concentration.

ENGINEER: How long—

CLERK: (*quickly.*)—ten minutes?

WORKER: Yes.

ENGINEER: Who told you that?

CLERK: Won't you have to telephone them upstairs?

ENGINEER: (*telephoning.*) Engineer–report from the control-room–gauge showing colour change–I'm personally taking charge. (*To the* WORKER.) Come on. (*Both exeunt left.*)

CLERK: (*suddenly throws up his arms and runs shouting towards the left.*) You won't save yourselves—you won't save yourselves! (*Exits.*)

(MILLIONAIRE'S SON–sixty years old–and OFFICER–in red uniform–enter right.)

OFFICER: Is there cause for serious concern?

MILLIONAIRE'S SON: I'm still waiting for the Engineer's report. In any case, it's a good thing that the two of you are leaving. I just wanted a word with you about the fortune my daughter is bringing you. (*He takes a book out of the desk.*)

OFFICER: I am grateful to you.

MILLIONAIRE'S SON: You owe me nothing. It comes from her mother. It may be considerable. I've no head for calculations of that sort.

OFFICER: An officer is compelled—

MILLIONAIRE'S SON: You love each other–and I raise no objections.

OFFICER: I shall watch over your daughter, whom you are today entrusting to me, with my honour.

MILLIONAIRE'S SON: (opens the book.) This is a list of the securities and where they are deposited. Choose a reliable banker and let him advise you. That will be necessary.

OFFICER: (reads. Straightens up in astonishment.) That will keep a banker busy all right.

MILLIONAIRE'S SON: Because it is a large capital? That's not why I said it.

OFFICER: Please go on.

MILLIONAIRE'S SON: What you have now, you have for the future as well. You can expect nothing from me. Neither now— nor in future: there will be no legacy to inherit from me. My principles are sufficiently well-known, you'll know where you stand.

OFFICER: We shall hardly get ourselves into the position—

MILLIONAIRE'S SON: You can never tell. As long as money is accumulated it will go on being lost. Circumstances based on that are always insecure. I merely wanted to tell you all this, so that I shall have no occasion to feel responsible later. You are marrying the daughter of a worker—that is all I am! —I won't conceal from you that I would rather her mother had not left her a fortune. But my power extends only to my own sphere—and I'll drag no-one into it by force. Not even my daughter.

DAUGHTER: (dressed for travelling—from the right.) Why do we have to go away?

OFFICER: (kisses her hand.) How warm you still are from dancing.

MILLIONAIRE'S SON: I wouldn't like your party to end on a discordant note. (At her startled gesture.) The danger will be overcome all right. But it demands our undivided efforts.

DAUGHTER: (towards the window.) Down there at the plant?

MILLIONAIRE'S SON: Later on I wouldn't be able to say a word of farewell to you.

DAUGHTER: Is it as serious as that?

OFFICER: Countermeasures have been taken.

MILLIONAIRE'S SON: (takes his DAUGHTER'S hand.) Enjoy your

trip. Today you have laid aside my name. Nothing is lost by that–I am a very simple man. I can't match the splendour of your new name. Must the memory of you fade when you go?

(DAUGHTER *looks at him questioningly.*)

OFFICER: How can you talk like that?

MILLIONAIRE'S SON: I shall not follow you into the frenzy of your error.

DAUGHTER: But I shall come back again.

MILLIONAIRE'S SON: I can hardly expect your return to the fold! (*Breaking off.*) Now I'll ask the guests to leave.

(*He kisses her forehead–gives the* OFFICER *his hand.* DAUGHTER *still stands perplexed–*OFFICER *leads her towards the left, both exeunt.*)

MILLIONAIRE'S SON: (*on the telephone.*) Pass the word round in the hall: an incident at the plant has put an end to the party. It is advisable to leave the works area as quickly as possible.

(*The music stops.*)

ENGINEER: (*from the left–an overall above his morning-coat–in great agitation, jerking out the words.*) Report from control station: colour of gas deepening every second. Within minutes –at the present rate–bright red!

MILLIONAIRE'S SON: Is there a defect in the machinery?

ENGINEER: Working perfectly!

MILLIONAIRE'S SON: A deficiency in the materials?

ENGINEER: Raw material never untested before mixing!

MILLIONAIRE'S SON: Then where is the failure?

ENGINEER: (*shaken by a paroxysm of trembling.*) In—the formula! !

MILLIONAIRE'S SON: Your–formula–is wrong?

ENGINEER: My formula–is wrong!

MILLIONAIRE'S SON: Are you sure?

ENGINEER: Now!

MILLIONAIRE'S SON: Do you know the flaw in it?

ENGINEER: No!

MILLIONAIRE'S SON: Can't you find it?

ENGINEER: The calculation–is correct!

MILLIONAIRE'S SON: And yet—the gauge is changing colour? !

(ENGINEER *throws himself into the chair at the desk: covers the paper with spasmodic bursts of writing.*)

MILLIONAIRE'S SON: Is the alarm working?

ENGINEER: (*without stopping.*) The bells have been hammering away for ages!

MILLIONAIRE'S SON: Is there time to clear the works?

ENGINEER: The transport trucks are racing from their sheds!

MILLIONAIRE'S SON: Is discipline being maintained?

ENGINEER: Perfectly.

MILLIONAIRE'S SON: (*in enormous agitation.*) Will they all get out? !

ENGINEER: (*jumps up, stands erect in front of him.*) I have done my duty. The formula is clear. Flawless!

MILLIONAIRE'S SON: (*as if stupefied.*) You can't find the flaw? !

ENGINEER: No-one can discover it. No-one can. No brain calculates more precisely. The final calculation is done!

MILLIONAIRE'S SON: And isn't right?

ENGINEER: Right–and not right! We have reached the limit. Right–and not right! No mathematics will penetrate beyond it. Right–and not right! The calculation continues on its own reckoning and rebounds on us! Right–and not right!

MILLIONAIRE'S SON: The gas—? !

ENGINEER: –is bleeding in the gauge!–flows red past the formula in the gauge!–bursts out of the calculation on a course of its own!–I have done my duty. My head is cool. What is happening cannot happen–and yet is happening!

MILLIONAIRE'S SON: (*gropes for a chair.*) We are delivered up defenceless–

ENGINEER: –to the explosion!

(A *hissing sound shatters the stillness outside–briefly a rending thunder crashes out: the chimney-stacks split and topple. Smokeless silence. The great window rattles into the room with a hail of splintered glass.*)

MILLIONAIRE'S SON: (*pressed against the wall—expressionlessly.*) The earth is rocking.

ENGINEER: Pressure of millions and millions of atmospheres.

MILLIONAIRE'S SON: Dead silence.

ENGINEER: Vast radius of destruction.

MILLIONAIRE'S SON: Who is still alive?

(*The door left is flung open: a* WORKER—*naked, discoloured from the blast—staggers in.*)

WORKER: Report from shed eight—control room: white cat jumped—red eyes staring—yellow mouth gaping—crackling back arched—grows round—snaps girders—lifts the roof off— and bursts in sparks!! (*Sitting in the middle of the floor and hitting out about him.*) Drive the cat away—shoo, shoo!! —hit it on the mouth—shoo, shoo!!—cover its scorching eyes —flatten its arched back—every fist on its back—look, it's puffing itself out—it's getting fatter and fatter—with gas from every pipe and cranny—!! (*Heaving himself up once more.*) Report from control-room:—the white cat is exploding!!

(*He falls full length.* MILLIONAIRE'S SON *goes to him.* WORKER *gropes with his hand.* MILLIONAIRE'S SON *grasps it.*)

WORKER: (*crying out.*) Mother—! (*Dead.*)

MILLIONAIRE'S SON: (*bowed low above him.*) People—

ACT II

The same room. In front of the big window a green Venetian blind is lowered. A long drawing-table stands there, littered with plans.

The young CLERK—*his hair now snowy white—at his desk, doing nothing.* MILLIONAIRE'S SON *leaning against the drawing-table.*

MILLIONAIRE'S SON: How long ago was it?

CLERK: Today is the seventeenth day.

MILLIONAIRE'S SON: (*looking round towards the window.*) Did sheds once raise their arched roofs there, chimney-stacks belching fiery breath reach into the sky? Wasn't that so behind this green back-drop?

CLERK: It all collapsed in minutes, pulverized into dust-heaps.

MILLIONAIRE'S SON: Didn't it all happen a thousand years ago?

CLERK: I can't forget that day!

MILLIONAIRE'S SON: Doesn't it lie too far behind you?

(CLERK *looks at him questioningly.*)

MILLIONAIRE'S SON: When you look at your hair in the mirror?

CLERK: I was in such a state–that I had hallucinations. I could feel it approaching. I saw–terror in person. That was worse than–when it actually happened. I had already gone white by then!

MILLIONAIRE'S SON: (*nodding.*) The white terror–that was needed to give us the impetus–violently–to hurl us forwards by a thousand years!—Seventeen days–you say? Seventeen days of peace and quiet!

CLERK: (*dispassionately.*) The workers are persisting in their refusal.

MILLIONAIRE'S SON: And I can't employ them in any case. The works have been razed to the ground.

CLERK: They won't return to work–

MILLIONAIRE'S SON: Until I give my permission.

CLERK: (*surprised.*) Are you postponing the rebuilding, then?

MILLIONAIRE'S SON: (*shaking his head.*) I am not postponing it–

CLERK: You're always drawing away at the plans.

MILLIONAIRE'S SON: (*bending over the drawing-table.*) I'm measuring and drawing—

CLERK: The requirements of the whole world are growing urgent. The supply will be exhausted in the immediate future. Gas shortage–!

MILLIONAIRE'S SON: (*quickly straightening up.*) I hold the fate of the world in my hands, don't I?

CLERK: You must meet the workers' demand–otherwise there will be the most shocking disaster ever!

MILLIONAIRE'S SON: (*goes across and passes a hand over his hair.*) Disaster, you all it?–you–a white-haired youth–ought to have heeded the warning. It was shocking enough, when everything here went up in the blast!–Do you want to go back into the white terror? Have your fingers already started itching again? Are you nothing more than a clerk?

CLERK: I have my calling.

MILLIONAIRE'S SON: Aren't you being called away–by more important things?

CLERK: I need the income.

MILLIONAIRE'S SON: And if that reason were removed?

CLERK: I am–a clerk.

MILLIONAIRE'S SON: Body and soul?

CLERK: I–write.

MILLIONAIRE'S SON: Because you have always written?

CLERK: It is–my calling!

MILLIONAIRE'S SON: (*smiling.*) It has buried you as deep as that. It's been shovelled on top of you–layer upon layer. And so it needed an exploding volcano to blast you all to the surface –otherwise you would never have surfaced!

(The THREE WORKERS *enter from the left.*)

MILLIONAIRE'S SON: (*to them.*) Have you tramped through the rubble again? I haven't been able to send you an answer yet. It is still taking shape–I'm in the middle of calculations and sketches–look–But I can make you firm proposals, if you grant me one final extension. Will you do that?

FIRST WORKER: The anxiety–

MILLIONAIRE'S SON: I can well understand. There were dead– I don't dare to think how many victims the disaster claimed. (*With hand encircling his brow.*) And yet I must keep it before my eyes. Then my decision emerges clearly.–Speak.

FIRST WORKER: We are only bringing the same demand we have always made.

MILLIONAIRE'S SON: I know what it is. It keeps running through my mind. I took it as the inspiration of my–(*Curtly.*) I am to dismiss the Engineer?

FIRST WORKER: Today would still be in time.

MILLIONAIRE'S SON: Tomorrow?

FIRST WORKER: Tomorrow we should refuse to work for twenty weeks.

MILLIONAIRE'S SON: Leave the wreckage lying?

FIRST WORKER: Otherwise the plant can be working again in twenty weeks.

SECOND WORKER: The world supply of gas won't last longer than twenty weeks.

THIRD WORKER: The work of the world will come to a halt.

MILLIONAIRE'S SON:—Then why am I to dismiss the Engineer? (As the WORKERS remain silent.) In what way was he negligent? Did the security arrangements break down? At least partially?—Did the alarm not work? I must be fair to him as well, if I make concessions to you. That is only fair.

THIRD WORKER: The gas exploded.

MILLIONAIRE'S SON: Through his fault? No. The formula is correct. Even now.

FIRST WORKER: The explosion happened.

MILLIONAIRE'S SON: According to its own laws. Not according to his.

SECOND WORKER: He worked out the formula.

MILLIONAIRE'S SON: No-one will produce a better one!

(The THREE WORKERS silent.)

FIRST WORKER: The Engineer must go!

SECOND WORKER: He must go today!

THIRD WORKER: His dismissal must be announced now!

FIRST WORKER: We can only return with this declaration!

MILLIONAIRE'S SON: Do you want him as a sacrifice? Is that it? Do you think that way you can silence the dead who are screaming within you? Suffocate this howling that is convulsing your blood? Will you cover up the carnage with the corpses of the newly-killed? Are you still caught in the snare of this vile lust for revenge after the spectacle of all the horror that has happened? Is this to be the fruit of the burning tree that rained down fire and brimstone upon us?

FIRST WORKER:—But the fact is: we can no longer vouch for the attitude of the workers.

SECOND WORKER: There is growing unrest.

THIRD WORKER: The outburst is bound to come.

MILLIONAIRE'S SON: Then tell them–all, all of them!–for surely they have ears to hear and minds to think: it surpassed human capacity. The Engineer's brain carried his calculations to the limit. Beyond surge forces beyond control. The flaw is decreed from the beyond. Undetectable from here. The formula is correct–and the gas explodes!–Don't you understand?

FIRST WORKER: We have our instructions.

MILLIONAIRE'S SON: Will you accept the responsibility, too?

FIRST WORKER: For what?

MILLIONAIRE'S SON: I meet your demand–the Engineer goes–and you return to work.

FIRST WORKER: We can guarantee that.

MILLIONAIRE'S SON: And produce gas?

SECOND *and* THIRD WORKERS: Gas!

MILLIONAIRE'S SON: The formula is valid?

FIRST WORKER: If it is correct–(*hesitant.*)

MILLIONAIRE'S SON: Irrefutably!

(*The* THREE WORKERS *remain silent.*)

MILLIONAIRE'S SON:—Won't the Engineer have to stay now?

(*The* THREE WORKERS *stand staring in front of them.*)

MILLIONAIRE'S SON: Isn't my refusal a protection against the terror? Am I not guarding the gates behind which hell smoulders? Which leave open no way to heaven? Which is a blazing blind-alley? Who is such a fool that he–batters his head against the end wall and says: I have arrived? He has arrived– but at destruction!—Turn back–turn back–the warning echoed–blasted the air apart and crashed thundering down on us!–Turn back–turn back!!

FIRST WORKER: (*straightening up.*) We must work!

SECOND WORKER: It is our work!

THIRD WORKER: We are workers!

MILLIONAIRE'S SON: Tirelessly. Swept on to supreme efforts. Goaded on beyond all bounds by this. (*Pointing to the wall-charts.*) There is the rat-race in tabular form. Your work–all

206

the profits go into the hollow of your hands. That's your inspiration—it spurs you on beyond the gain—work is done for the sake of work. Fever flares up and clouds the senses: work—work—a wedge that drives itself deeper and drills because it drills. Where does it lead? I drill because I drill—I was a driller—I am a driller—and a driller I remain!—— Aren't you horrified? At the mutilation you are inflicting on yourselves? You who are marvellous beings—multifarious—men?!

FIRST WORKER:—We have to take back a definite answer.

MILLIONAIRE'S SON: And I gave you one. But you still don't understand it. It is still new to me—and I am groping towards it with the greatest caution!

SECOND WORKER: Is the Engineer to go?

MILLIONAIRE'S SON: He is to go!

THIRD WORKER: Today?

MILLIONAIRE'S SON: He is to stay!

FIRST WORKER: That is not a straight answer!

MILLIONAIRE'S SON: He goes—and stays: that is how irrevelant the Engineer is going to be to us!

SECOND WORKER: What does that mean?

MILLIONAIRE'S SON: My little secret as yet. Later I'll explain everything and keep nothing back. The plans—look at them! —I haven't completed them yet—my assistant, without whom I can't finish them, is not here yet—and he is the man who is your enemy—and is not your enemy!

FIRST WORKER: Can we give them a firm undertaking?

MILLIONAIRE'S SON: As you will. I'll fulfil everything—and a great deal that no word of yours can promise them!—That must make you go away happy.

(The THREE WORKERS exeunt. MILLIONAIRE'S SON at the drawing-table—bends over the plans.)

CLERK: (getting up from his chair—rapidly.) I—am leaving!

(MILLIONAIRE'S SON straightens up.)

CLERK: There is—no work for me!

MILLIONAIRE'S SON: For the moment.

CLERK: Is that—to continue?

MILLIONAIRE'S SON: More visions? But aren't their outlines brighter this time? Not fata morgana with a green-shaded oasis rising out of the desert?–Go on, make your predictions–you young prophet. You possess the strangest gift. I am curious to hear your prophecies!

CLERK: I can find–nothing more to write!

MILLIONAIRE'S SON: Isn't it tempting? Doesn't health excite you? To use both your hands instead of this single one that writes?–You with your crippled left hand?

CLERK: I–am going!

MILLIONAIRE'S SON: Where?

CLERK: To the others!

MILLIONAIRE'S SON: Assemble–grumble outside the gates. The wheel is still spinning within you–the impulses die away slowly. It takes time to come to a stand-still. Then I will let you in!

(CLERK *goes hurriedly, exits right.* MILLIONAIRE'S SON *once more at the drawing table.* ENGINEER *enters from the left.*)

MILLIONAIRE'S SON: (*turns round to him.*) Unscathed and unharmed?

(ENGINEER *gives him a questioning look.*)

MILLIONAIRE'S SON: Aren't you the scapegoat, into whose body *they* want to drive their own horns? Haven't they attacked you yet?

ENGINEER: I heard cat-calls.

MILLIONAIRE'S SON: That's how the sacrificial offering is singled out today–tomorrow comes the ceremonial slaughter.

ENGINEER: I know that I am free from negligence–or incompetence.

MILLIONAIRE'S SON: But they are after your blood!

ENGINEER: The people should have it proved to them–

MILLIONAIRE'S SON: –that a proof is correct and yet not correct!

ENGINEER:–I cannot leave–I should be accepting it as if it were my fault–!

MILLIONAIRE'S SON: Can't I dismiss you?

ENGINEER: No! If so, you brand me with the mark that makes me an outcast!

MILLIONAIRE'S SON: One must suffer for many.

ENGINEER: (*animated.*) If you are to act for the common good, agreed! But where does it lie here? If you replace me by some one else–the formula remains valid–must remain valid. He will calculate with human intelligence–and human intelligence cannot make the calculation different!–Or else you must revert to a weaker formula!

MILLIONAIRE'S SON: Do you believe in that?

ENGINEER: The world's machines would have to be modified.

MILLIONAIRE'S SON: That wouldn't be insuperable.

ENGINEER: Faced with the necessity for an inferior fuel–

MILLIONAIRE'S SON: Machines could be kept waiting–people cannot!

ENGINEER: When they have realized the danger?

MILLIONAIRE'S SON: If they were blown up ten times–they would get the danger zone working for the eleventh time!

ENGINEER: An explosion like that–

MILLIONAIRE'S SON: Brings them to their senses? Does it reduce the delirium of their fever? Already they are out there knocking on the door: hand the Engineer over to us–then we'll rush onwards–from explosion to explosion!

ENGINEER: And that makes nonsense of my dismissal.

MILLIONAIRE'S SON: (*with a sly smile.*) Unparalleled nonsense! They would come running back in here–into the witches' cauldron–the rascals. The gates must be barred–and for that I am making use of your person. Now I am powerful, while I keep you with me!

ENGINEER: (*passes a hand across his brow.*) Then do you intend—

MILLIONAIRE'S SON: Come over here. (*He leads him to the drawing-table.*) See that?–Plans–in rough outline.–The first crystallization of a project.–In fact, only the beginnings of something of significance.–Preliminary sketches.

ENGINEER: What is all this?

MILLIONAIRE'S SON: Isn't the terrain familiar to you?

ENGINEER: The–works.

209

MILLIONAIRE'S SON: Razed to the ground.

ENGINEER: Are these–the new sheds?

MILLIONAIRE'S SON: With those ridiculous dimensions?

ENGINEER: Are these–yards?

MILLIONAIRE'S SON: The coloured rings?

ENGINEER: Are they–railway-lines?

MILLIONAIRE'S SON: The green lines? (*Engineer stares at the plans.*) Can't you guess? Haven't you any suspicions? And you such a clever chap, a mathematical genius?–Is the puzzle giving you something to think about, with all its bright colours? You are blind, all of you–colour-blind from your eternal daily round–right up until today! Now the new day is beginning to dawn for you, like another spring. Ranging with eyes wide across the countryside: and here the bright earth is all about you!–(*Sketching it in on the plan.*) Green lines–streets lined with trees. Red, yellow, blue rings–lawns luxuriant with plants blooming out of the smooth turf. Squares –houses set down with their little piece of private ground to shelter them!–Great roads outwards–penetrating victoriously into other regions–trodden by pilgrims sent out by us–who preach the simplest message:–us!! (*His gesture is sweeping.*)

ENGINEER: (*perplexed.*) Are you–rebuilding the plant in a different place?

MILLIONAIRE'S SON: It buried itself. At its peak–it collapsed. Therefore we are discharged. You–and I–and everyone!– with a clear conscience. We followed the path fearlessly to the end–now we turn aside. We have the right–every right!

ENGINEER: The rebuilding–is in doubt?

MILLIONAIRE'S SON: (*tapping the plans.*) Here is the decision against it!

ENGINEER: The gas–that can only be produced here?

MILLIONAIRE'S SON:–exploded!

ENGINEER:—The workers??

MILLIONAIRE'S SON: Settlers on the green earth!

ENGINEER: That–is impossible!

MILLIONAIRE'S SON: Are you worried about my plans? I told you they were incomplete. I have been reckoning on your help in carrying them out. Yes, I'm really counting on you. You are better able than anyone else to see a big project through. I have the greatest confidence in you!–Shall we get on with the work? (*He pulls a chair up to the drawing-table and sits down.*)

ENGINEER: (*backing away.*) I am an engineer.

MILLIONAIRE'S SON: You'll be able to make use of your knowledge again here!

ENGINEER: That is not–my line!

MILLIONAIRE'S SON: Here all your abilities will have free play!

ENGINEER: I won't take on–such a job!

MILLIONAIRE'S SON: It is too difficult for you?

ENGINEER: Too–trivial!

MILLIONAIRE'S SON: (*rises.*) What is that you are saying? This is trifling?–to your mind, that can count? Are you in the thrall of your last calculation?–Are you bolted into the beams–of your own making? Have you surrendered arms and legs–and blood and senses–to the clasp of the clamps you yourself forced home? Are you a hollow frame covered over with skin? (*He reaches out to touch him.*) Where are you? With your warmth–your pulsebeat–and your sense of shame?!

ENGINEER: If there is no work for me–in my own line—

MILLIONAIRE'S SON: Don't your hands strike out at your mouth –that is crying murder?

ENGINEER:—I must ask for my discharge!

MILLIONAIRE'S SON: (*supports himself against the table.*) No! –that will bring the others back.–The way will lie open– they will come rushing in–and build up their hell again–and the fever will ravage them once more!–Help me–stay with me —work with me here, where I am working!!

ENGINEER: I am discharged!

(MILLIONAIRE'S SON *looks at him speechless.* ENGINEER *exits left.*)

MILLIONAIRE'S SON: (*his strength at last recovered.*) Then I must force you all!

ACT III

Oval room. The doors—two at the back, one left—are set invisibly into very light panelling. In the centre a round table of small proportions with a green cloth—six chairs standing close together around it.

The Officer enters from the left—in a greatcoat. Scarcely controlled agitation. He looks for the doors—knocks on parts of the panelling. MILLIONAIRE'S SON *steps out, back left.*

OFFICER: (*turns towards him and goes over to him.*) Am I disturbing you?

MILLIONAIRE'S SON: (*surprised.*) Are you both here?

OFFICER: No, I am here by myself.

MILLIONAIRE'S SON: Why without your wife?

OFFICER: She—was unable to accompany me.

MILLIONAIRE'S SON: Is my daughter ill?

OFFICER: She—knows nothing about my trip!

MILLIONAIRE'S SON: (*nodding.*) Certainly not a very comforting sight—her father's works a heap of rubble. Do you want to have a look round?

OFFICER: (*casually.*) The disaster must really have been terrible. Rebuilding progressing vigorously?

MILLIONAIRE'S SON: Have you noticed anything along those lines?

OFFICER: It's only natural that you are feverishly busy.

MILLIONAIRE'S SON: (*shakes his head.*) My time—

OFFICER: You are busy. The work is getting too much for you. (*Indicating the table.*) You are in conference. My arrival is about as inconvenient as could be. (*Almost brusquely.*) But I must ask to talk to you at once!

MILLIONAIRE'S SON: Everything is equally important to me.

OFFICER: Thank you for your readiness to listen to me. It is a question of—saving me!

MILLIONAIRE'S SON: From what?

OFFICER: From being discharged—with ignominy!

MILLIONAIRE'S SON: What?

OFFICER: I have contracted gambling debts–and must settle them by midday tomorrow!

MILLIONAIRE'S SON: Can't you do it?

OFFICER: No!

MILLIONAIRE'S SON: If necessary, fall back on your fortune.

OFFICER: That–no longer exists!

MILLIONAIRE'S SON: It is all spent?

OFFICER: (*flustered.*) I gambled and lost. I tried to recover the losses and speculated. The speculations failed and swallowed up even more. I raised the stakes, so as to win back everything, beyond my means–and my pistol awaits me if I don't pay up!

MILLIONAIRE'S SON: (*after a pause.*) And on your last journey you come to me?

OFFICER: How hard it is for me to come to the man who gave me his trust which I have disappointed!–But despair drives me here. Yet I have deserved your reproaches–any reproof from you will sting me justly. I won't dare to offer you a single word in excuse!

MILLIONAIRE'S SON: I am not–reproaching you.

OFFICER: (*grasps his hand.*) Your forgiving kindness makes my shame burn more intensely. I can only swear to you that, once I have escaped this danger unharmed, I shall–

MILLIONAIRE'S SON: I want no undertaking from you–

OFFICER: I give you my word!

MILLIONAIRE'S SON:–because I can render you no service in return!

OFFICER: (*stares at him.*) Are you saying—

MILLIONAIRE'S SON: If I wished to help you–I can't. I told you at the time that you were marrying the daughter of a worker. That is what I am. I never sought to suggest otherwise. It was made quite clear to you.

OFFICER: Everywhere you have means ready to hand!

MILLIONAIRE'S SON: No.

OFFICER: One word–and banks obey you!

MILLIONAIRE'S SON: Not any more.

OFFICER: The plant that will be working again within weeks–

MILLIONAIRE'S SON: That is shut down!

OFFICER: Shut—??

MILLIONAIRE'S SON: Yes, I have reached a different decision. Will you help me? I need help at every turn. The tower of errors does not sway at the power of one man's push–a thousand hands must shake it!

OFFICER: (*puzzled.*) You won't do anything—

MILLIONAIRE'S SON: I am in need myself. A happy chance brings you here. You have incurred debts–as I have incurred blame. Yet we are both innocent. Now our mouths open– and out flows the accusation against us all!

OFFICER: (*his hands clasped to his head.*) I–cannot–think—

MILLIONAIRE'S SON: Strip your fine uniform from your body and lay aside your sword. You are a splendid fellow unspoilt at heart–my daughter became your wife!–What has clouded this? What tarnishes and obscures it? Whence the temptation to extravagance?

OFFICER: You want me–an officer–to give up—??

MILLIONAIRE'S SON: Confess your guilt–and prove your innocence. Draw every eye to yourself–and let your voice thunder: I remained unfulfilled. So long as I was tricked out for life in this coat–a terrible diversion of the welling powers within me into a single channel–full of deeds undone, because one deed still threatens whose execution brings destruction– directed only to a single end it thrusts forward and runs right to ruin!

OFFICER: (*with a suppressed cry.*) Can you–help me?

MILLIONAIRE'S SON: Yes.

OFFICER: Then give me—!

MILLIONAIRE'S SON: What you are giving me I could not pay for!

OFFICER: My time is running out–!

MILLIONAIRE'S SON: It will last for ever!

OFFICER: Money!

MILLIONAIRE'S SON: Am I to cheat you with money–out of yourself?

OFFICER: (*in the greatest confusion.*) I shall have to leave the army–I shall be drummed out of the regiment–I—

MILLIONAIRE'S SON: (*arm round shoulder, leads him to the*

door.) Yes, it'll make a stir when I let you down. My son-in-law—and I could have drawn upon wealth with both hands. But I didn't. That will catch their attention—that will make them listen. They are the ones I need—and you are bringing them to me. That will be the service you render—and it will be to your credit without any recognition from me. My acknowledgement will be to take it all as a matter of course! (OFFICER exits.)

(MILLIONAIRE'S SON *goes over to the table—runs a hand over the green cloth—nods—exits back left. From the left the* FIRST GENTLEMAN IN BLACK: *above the tightly-buttoned black coat a massive head, grey hair cropped en brosse. The* SECOND GENTLEMAN IN BLACK *enters—identical in dress with the* FIRST GENTLEMAN IN BLACK, *just as are all those who follow—bareheaded.*)

SECOND GENTLEMAN IN BLACK: How are things with you?
FIRST GENTLEMAN IN BLACK: Not a hand's turn being done.
SECOND GENTLEMAN IN BLACK: Same with me.
THE THIRD GENTLEMAN IN BLACK: (*comes in—yellow pointed beard—to the first.*) How are things with you?
FIRST GENTLEMAN IN BLACK: Not a hand's turn being done.
THIRD GENTLEMAN IN BLACK: (*to the second.*) With you?

(SECOND GENTLEMAN IN BLACK *shakes his head.*)

THIRD GENTLEMAN IN BLACK: Same with me.

(The FOURTH AND FIFTH GENTLEMEN IN BLACK *come in—brothers, very alike, thirty years old.*)

FOURTH GENTLEMAN IN BLACK: (*to the* FIRST.) How are things with you?
FIFTH GENTLEMAN IN BLACK: (*to the* SECOND.) How are things with you?
THIRD GENTLEMAN IN BLACK: (*to the two of them.*) And with you?
FOURTH AND FIFTH GENTLEMEN IN BLACK: Not a hand's turn being done!
FIRST GENTLEMAN IN BLACK: Same with us!

SECOND GENTLEMAN IN BLACK: It's the most colossal work-stoppage I've ever known.

FIFTH GENTLEMAN IN BLACK: And the cause of it?

THIRD GENTLEMAN IN BLACK: Our workers are striking in sympathy with them here.

FIFTH GENTLEMAN IN BLACK: Why are they striking?

SECOND GENTLEMAN IN BLACK: Because the Engineer hasn't been dismissed.

FIFTH GENTLEMAN IN BLACK: Why is he being kept on?

SECOND GENTLEMAN IN BLACK: Why?

FOURTH GENTLEMAN IN BLACK: On account of some crazy notion!

THIRD GENTLEMAN IN BLACK: That's right!

FIRST GENTLEMAN IN BLACK: There may be another reason. It is significant as a matter of principle. The dismissal of the Engineer is being demanded—that constitutes the difficulty. If any one of us is faced with demands from the workers—he has to resist unconditionally. That's what has happened here—and in consequence the Engineer remains at his post!

THIRD GENTLEMAN IN BLACK: You are forgetting that he is not one of us.

FOURTH GENTLEMAN IN BLACK: It'll be some crazy notion, like his other one.

SECOND GENTLEMAN IN BLACK: Just as dangerous as his other one. You'll see!

FIFTH GENTLEMAN IN BLACK: If it doesn't prove more dangerous!

THIRD GENTLEMAN IN BLACK: I don't see how it *can* get worse!

SECOND GENTLEMAN IN BLACK: And that one is causing us enough trouble!

FOURTH GENTLEMAN IN BLACK: The whole labour force is looking over its shoulder at this set-up!

FIFTH GENTLEMAN IN BLACK: This profit-sharing for all and sundry is a source of perpetual unrest in every concern!

SECOND GENTLEMAN IN BLACK: The plague-spot we intend to smoke out!

THIRD GENTLEMAN IN BLACK: With fire and brimstone!

FIRST GENTLEMAN IN BLACK: Don't overlook the results brought about on the basis of this arrangement. From shared profits peak out-put–from peak out-put, the ultimate product: gas!

SECOND GENTLEMAN IN BLACK: Yes–gas.

THIRD GENTLEMAN IN BLACK: Gas!

FIFTH GENTLEMAN IN BLACK: Whatever happens, we need gas.

FOURTH GENTLEMAN IN BLACK: In any case.

THIRD GENTLEMAN IN BLACK: We present our demand: dismissal of the Engineer!

SECOND GENTLEMAN IN BLACK: Quite independently of the workers!

FIFTH GENTLEMAN IN BLACK: Quite independently of the workers!

FOURTH GENTLEMAN IN BLACK: That secures our position!

THIRD GENTLEMAN IN BLACK: Have you got the agenda?

FOURTH GENTLEMAN IN BLACK: (at the table.) There's nothing set out here!

FIRST GENTLEMAN IN BLACK: There is only this one point! Are we agreed? (The other GENTLEMAN IN BLACK shake him by the hand.)

(Enter MILLIONAIRE'S SON, left back. He indicates the chairs, on which the GENTLEMEN IN BLACK quickly seat themselves. The MILLIONAIRE'S SON is the last to take his seat between the FOURTH and FIFTH GENTLEMEN IN BLACK.)

FIFTH GENTLEMAN IN BLACK: Who will keep the minutes?

MILLIONAIRE'S SON: No–no, nothing in writing!

THIRD GENTLEMAN IN BLACK: A meeting without–

MILLIONAIRE'S SON: Yes, yes we'll all be able to speak freely!

FIRST GENTLEMAN IN BLACK: In view of the importance of the subject I consider it a matter of urgent necessity–so that in any eventuality, our independence of a similar demand by the workers–

SECOND GENTLEMAN IN BLACK: I move that the minutes of the meeting be made public!

THIRD GENTLEMAN IN BLACK: We'll vote on it!

FIRST GENTLEMAN IN BLACK: Those in favour–

(The GENTLEMEN IN BLACK shoot up their arms in a forceful gesture.)

MILLIONAIRE'S SON: (*pushes down those of the* FOURTH *and* FIFTH GENTLEMAN IN BLACK *beside him.*) Not all against one–that makes me too strong. I shall be putting pressure on you–and I only want to persuade you.

FIRST GENTLEMAN IN BLACK: If our negotiations–

MILLIONAIRE'S SON Are you proposing to negotiate with me? Are you the workers? Aren't you the masters?

THIRD GENTLEMAN IN BLACK: You invited us here without an agenda. We conclude from this that you are leaving its composition to us. That is a justifiable assumption. We have agreed on one single item.

SECOND GENTLEMAN IN BLACK: I think the discussion will be short, and we shall return to our own plants.

FOURTH GENTLEMAN IN BLACK: It is high time we got them started up again.

FIFTH GENTLEMAN IN BLACK: The first night-shift must report for work this evening.

THIRD GENTLEMAN IN BLACK: There are already irreparable losses.

MILLIONAIRE'S SON: You have had losses? In what way have you suffered?

THE GENTLEMEN IN BLACK: (*all talking at once.*) Work has stopped–the plant is completely idle–the workers have come out!

MILLIONAIRE'S SON: (*raising his hand.*) I know: they are mourning the dead. Is that not a worthy reason? Were not thousands burnt?

FIRST GENTLEMAN IN BLACK: The strike has a quite different cause.

MILLIONAIRE'S SON: No, no! You must not heed their talk. It is senseless. When I tell you they are demanding the dismissal of the Engineer!–Isn't that the measure of their confusion? No, out there they don't know what they are doing.

(*The* GENTLEMAN IN BLACK *gape at him incomprehendingly.*)

MILLIONAIRE'S SON: Is the Engineer guilty of anything that his departure can make good? Was his formula wrong? It stood the test–and still does. For what failing can I dismiss him?

SECOND GENTLEMAN IN BLACK: (*nodding.*) The formula has been tested–

THIRD GENTLEMAN IN BLACK: (*likewise.*) Its validity has been proved–

FOURTH GENTLEMAN IN BLACK: (*likewise.*) It is the formula–

FIFTH GENTLEMAN IN BLACK: For gas!

MILLIONAIRE'S SON: You realize that?

FIRST GENTLEMAN IN BLACK: And so any engineer can use it!

SECOND GENTLEMAN IN BLACK: This one or any other!

FOURTH GENTLEMAN IN BLACK: Then the Engineer doesn't matter at all!

FIFTH GENTLEMAN IN BLACK: A new engineer–and the same formula!

THIRD GENTLEMAN IN BLACK: That'll put an end to the strike!

FIRST GENTLEMAN IN BLACK: We are met round the table with this demand: the dismissal of the Engineer!

MILLIONAIRE'S SON: (*staring.*)—Have you forgotten—have you grown deaf—is the crash no longer thundering in your ears— are you no longer swaying on your chairs—have you lost your faculties? ?

SECOND GENTLEMAN IN BLACK: The disaster is a dark episode–

FOURTH GENTLEMAN IN BLACK: We book it–

FIFTH GENTLEMAN IN BLACK:–and turn the page!

MILLIONAIRE'S SON:—The same formula—? ?

FIRST GENTLEMAN IN BLACK: We hope–

SECOND GENTLEMAN IN BLACK: Of course!

MILLIONAIRE'S SON:—The same formula—? ?

THIRD GENTLEMAN IN BLACK: Perhaps there will be longer periods between–

FOURTH GENTLEMAN IN BLACK: We must learn by experience!

MILLIONAIRE'S SON: Twice—three times—? ?

FIFTH GENTLEMAN IN BLACK: Then we shall know the cycle!

SECOND GENTLEMAN IN BLACK: At any rate we shan't live to see it!

MILLIONAIRE'S SON:—I am to let them back in—expose them–?

FIRST GENTLEMAN IN BLACK: But the world's technology cannot remain idle!

THIRD GENTLEMAN IN BLACK: And it depends on gas!

MILLIONAIRE'S SON: Does it?–Am I the force that drives it?–
Is that my power? (*The* GENTLEMEN IN BLACK *look at him in wonderment.*) My voice has power–over horror and joy? My words the power of life and death? My lips' yes or no determine existence or destruction? (*Raising his hands.*) I say:—no!—no!—no! A man–a human being can decide only:—no!—no!—no!

(THE GENTLEMEN IN BLACK *exchange glances.*)

FOURTH GENTLEMAN IN BLACK: Why–
FIFTH GENTLEMAN IN BLACK:–this–
THIRD GENTLEMAN IN BLACK:–is–
SECOND GENTLEMAN IN BLACK: What is this?
MILLIONAIRE'S SON:—The rubble remains—and over rubble fresh soil—layer on layer—the earth growing a new crust—eternal law of growth.
FIRST GENTLEMAN IN BLACK: What's this?
MILLIONAIRE'S SON: No more chimneys smoking here ever again! No clattering machines! Never again shall the inevitable explosion hiss among the howls and shrieks of its victims.
SECOND GENTLEMAN IN BLACK: The works–
THIRD GENTLEMAN IN BLACK: The rebuilding–
FIRST GENTLEMAN IN BLACK: Gas? ?
MILLIONAIRE'S SON: No rebuilding–no works–no gas! I cannot take the responsibility–no-one can take it upon himself!
FIRST GENTLEMAN IN BLACK:—Are we—
THIRD GENTLEMAN IN BLACK:—to do without—
FIFTH GENTLEMAN IN BLACK:—gas—?
MILLIONAIRE'S SON: Without–human sacrifice!
SECOND GENTLEMAN IN BLACK: Our plant is designed–
THE OTHER GENTLEMEN IN BLACK:–to run on gas!
MILLIONAIRE'S SON: Invent something better–or make do with worse!
FIRST GENTLEMAN IN BLACK: This is preposterous. We oppose the suggestion with all the force at our command it means altering all our plant–!
FOURTH GENTLEMAN IN BLACK: The cost would ruin us!
THIRD GENTLEMAN IN BLACK: It does not hinge on whether the

cost would damage one or another of us. I ask: is world production to be reduced?

FIFTH GENTLEMAN IN BLACK: So you must produce gas. It is your duty. If we had never had your gas–!

SECOND GENTLEMAN IN BLACK: You have brought about the highest development of technology. Now you must provide the gas!

FIRST GENTLEMAN IN BLACK: With your dreadful method that gives the workers a share in the profits you have achieved a terrific result–gas. And so we have tolerated this method–now we demand gas!

MILLIONAIRE'S SON: It is dreadful, I've learnt that. But I have only run more quickly ahead of you along the path that you will all have to take: all profits in all pockets!

FIFTH GENTLEMAN IN BLACK: This formula ought never to have been invented–if the supply of gas was ever to be cut off!

MILLIONAIRE'S SON: The invention had to be made: the frenzy of work was unleashed. It raged blindly on, pushing forward to the limit!

FIRST GENTLEMAN IN BLACK: A reduction in the pace that we are accustomed to would be impossible to introduce!

MILLIONAIRE'S SON: No–not a reversion to a weaker grade of movement, I'm not advising that. We must go forward–behind us what is completed, or else we are not worthy. No cowardice must cling to us. We are people–creatures of the utmost courage. Haven't we shown it yet again? Have we not pressed forward to the furthest limits–and only when we left the dead lying in their thousands did we set out for fresh fields!–Have we not tested our powers in parts–strained them to the point of injury –to learn what each is capable of, to see if they could embrace the totality: man?–Is not man the goal of our long pilgrimage– from age to age–one closing today while the next one dawns, the last?

SECOND GENTLEMAN IN BLACK:—Are you proposing to cut off production completely?

MILLIONAIRE'S SON: It is measured against man, who preserves man!

THIRD GENTLEMAN IN BLACK: We have different needs!

MILLIONAIRE'S SON: As long as we wear him down in some other way!

FOURTH GENTLEMAN IN BLACK: Are you trying to talk us round?

FIFTH GENTLEMAN IN BLACK: With pamphlets?

MILLIONAIRE'S SON: I am setting an example on my own land: beside green avenues little plots for all!

FIRST GENTLEMAN IN BLACK:—You are parcelling out the most valuable land in the world for these purposes?

MILLIONAIRE'S SON: For this purpose–which is man!

THIRD GENTLEMAN IN BLACK: You would need to have funds–for the world still counts in cash!

MILLIONAIRE'S SON: Past profits will last us all for such time as our influence takes to extend.

FOURTH GENTLEMAN IN BLACK: You would wait too long for imitators!

MILLIONAIRE'S SON: If you are without the gas?

(The GENTLEMEN IN BLACK are silent.)

MILLIONAIRE'S SON: I could compel you–as you see!–but I don't want to. It would upset you–and I need your help. Six of us are sitting round the table–six stand up and go out: then the words of the six swell to thunder that makes itself heard. The force of the message will penetrate the deafest ear when it is spoken sixfold. You are the great ones of the earth–the black lords over labour–rise and come with me: we will tell of the end of this age that is fulfilled–and say it again and again to those who do not understand because the turmoil that raged in them but yesterday still runs in their blood. Arise and go! !

FIRST GENTLEMAN IN BLACK: (after a pause, looking round the table and meeting answering glances.) Are we agreed? (The GENTLEMEN IN BLACK throw up their arms.) We give you until–this evening: if we have not been informed of the dismissal of the engineer by then–we shall call on the government!–We are leaving! (The GENTLEMEN IN BLACK exeunt.)

MILLIONAIRE'S SON: (sits at the table–runs his hand slowly across the green cloth–and mutters.) No—no—no—no—no—

(ENTER *the* OFFICER–*in the greatest agitation–from the left.* *He takes off his sword and is about to lay it on the table. But* *he snatches it up and buckles it on again.*)

OFFICER: I—cannot—do it! (*He stands by the wall at the back* *and shoots himself in the chest.*)

MILLIONAIRE'S SON: (*looks across–rises.*) Let others–set the world to rights!

ACT IV

Concrete hall; circular, haze-high. From the dome the incandes- *cence of arc-lamps. A narrow iron platform rises steeply in the* *centre. Workers' meeting; many women. Silence. Voices with* *rapidly increasing volume. 'Who?' A GIRL mounts the platform.*

GIRL: (*arms raised.*) I!

(*Silence.*)

GIRL: Of my brother I say this!–I did not know I had a brother. A person left the house in the morning and returned in the evening–and slept. Or he left in the evening and was back in the morning–and slept!–One hand was big–the other small. The big hand didn't sleep. It jerked back and forth in a single movement–day and night. It battened on him and waxed on his whole strength. This hand was the man!–What became of my brother? Who used to play beside me–and built sandcastles with both his hands?–He was swallowed up in his work. It needed only one of his hands–that raised and lowered the lever–minute by minute up and down–reckoned to the second! –He never failed to lift it–at the right moment the lever engaged, as he stood before it like a dead man operating it. He never made a mistake–never erred in the counting. His hand counted out of his head and it came to obey his hand alone! That's what remained of my brother!—Remained? One midday it struck. The sea of fire poured out of every crack and cranny. And the explosion consumed his hand as well. So my brother made the final sacrifice!—Is that too little?–Had my brother haggled over the price, when his hand was needed for the lever? Did he not willingly discard the role of brother and shrivel up into the counting hand?–Did he not end up by paying with the hand itself?–Is the payment too paltry—to claim the Engineer?—It is my brother's voice—: no more work until the Engineer has left the plant!–No more work–it is the voice of my brother! !

GIRL: (*pressing forward below.*) It is my brother! ! (*The* GIRL *goes down to them.*)

(*Silence. Voices rising again. 'Who?'* MOTHER *mounts the platform.*)

MOTHER: I!

(*Silence.*)

MOTHER: The explosion crushed a mother's son. What is that? What did the fire destroy? My son?–I no longer knew him–I buried him the morning he first went off to the works!–Are two eyes, glazed with the staring at the gauge, a son? Where was my child–that I had borne–with a mouth for laughter–with limbs to swing? My child–who put his arms round my neck and kissed me in his happiness? My child?–I am a mother and I know that what is born in pain is lost in sorrow. I am a mother–and make no complaint. I shall not release the cry caught in my throat. I am a mother–without protest or accusation—Not I–here it is my child that speaks. With his birth he left my womb–in death he flows back into me–from mother to mother! My son is with me again. Doesn't he rage in my blood? Doesn't he tear at my tongue and shake loose the cry:–Mother!–where have you been all this time?–Mother–you were not with me!–Mother–you left me alone so soon–Mother–you did not smash the gauge–and it no bigger than a finger and thin as a fly's wing!—Why didn't he snap it himself between his feeble fingers?–Why did he make this sacrifice, when he has a mother?–Why was his body crippled–to channel all its strength into the staring eyes? Why did the flames put them out? Why? ! Why? ! Is he to give his all–and ask nothing? Is he great despite his loss? Here: a mother–and there the Engineer! !

(WOMEN crowd close below.)

WOMEN: It is my son! !

MOTHER: You, mother and you and you–your sons clamour within you–do not drown their cry: stay away from the works –stay away from the works—the Engineer is there! !

WOMEN: Stay away from the works! !

(MOTHER leaves the platform and mingles with the women. Silence. Voices loud. 'Who?')

WOMAN: (on to the platform.) I!

(Silence.)

WOMAN: There was a wedding one day. Piano music at midday. Everyone dancing through the rooms. A whole day–morning–noon–and night. My tall husband was with me for one day. One day from morning till night. One day was his life!–Is that too much? Because a day has its morning–afternoon–and evening? And then the night? Is that too long for a lifetime? It's wonderfully long–twenty-four hours–and a wedding –and the piano–and dancing: that's a life. What more does a man ask! To live for two days? What an age that is! It stretches out to eternity! The sun would grow tired with shining on him! A wedding comes once–and the trolley is always moving. Forwards–and backwards–backwards–forwards–the man moves with it. The man moves with it–because the foot is attached to him. Only his foot matters–pushing the gear-pedal –for stop and start–then pushing and pushing and pushing without the man who moves with it. If only the foot were not so firmly fixed to the man! The man could live–but his foot keeps him on the trolley that moves backwards and forwards–day in, day out, with the man fixed to the foot!–Wasn't there an explosion? Why was my husband burnt? Why the whole man? Not the foot alone, which was all that mattered? Why my husband's limbs and body for the sake of one foot?–Because foot and body and limbs are my husband–and his foot

225

won't work the pedal without the man. His foot doesn't work the pedal by itself–it needs my husband!—Isn't the plant like my husband–who lived on one wedding-day–and was dead all his life?–Aren't parts exchanged for new parts–and the plant functions as before? Isn't each one a part, to be interchanged with every other–and the plant keeps on running?—Do not replace the man at the lever—do not replace the man at the gauge—do not replace the man on the trolley—: the Engineer is barring your way—the Engineer is barring your way! !

WOMEN: (*surrounding the platform.*) Do not replace my husband! !

GIRLS: Nor my brother! !

MOTHERS: Nor my son! !

(WOMAN *leaves the platform.*)

WORKER: (*mounts the platform.*) Girl–I am your brother! My oath makes me your brother. My oath caused me to be burnt. I lie under the rubble until you send me to the lever–in place of your brother, who was blown up!—Here is my hand–broad and firm enough to make the *one* movement of the clicking lever!—The hand had its pay–it was heaped in its hollow–and it bore it eagerly home. But it didn't count it!–there it lay in the drawer–filling the box!–And it was worthless!–What does a hand buy itself–the hand that was the death of your brother?–What sort of wants does a hand have? One single hand–and all the earnings in the box?–The hand gets its pay–not your brother! He was burnt and he is alive again—he is here, shouting to be paid–: hand over the Engineer–hand over the Engineer! ! (WORKERS *surrounding the platform.*) I am a brother! !

(WORKER *goes down among them.*)

WORKER: (*has already gone up.*) Mother–I am your son!–His body grew again–around the eyes–fixed on the gauge. Your son is pulse and voice once more!–Mother–I sacrificed myself for a gauge no bigger than a finger!–Mother–I delivered myself up for my eyes on a gauge!–Mother– my whole body died and I shrank into my two eyes!—I rolled the money across the table to you--you didn't catch it in your apron--it rattled onto the floor!--you no longer bend down for it now--don't gather it up--and pile it in columns--these bear no beams your son lives under:--he is bounded by the gauge--narrow and venomous!—Read the charts to find the price of a mother!-- Of my blood and my mother's blood--that the eyes on the gauge drank—Calculate the quotas for dividing the profits--and add them all together: do they pay for a mother and a mother's son? ! ! The eyes on the gauge had their profit--the mother's son went away empty!—Can he not summon heaven and earth for his debt? ?—Is he not prepared to accept the smallest compensation in payment of the debt? ?—What is it worth for his sacrifice:—the Engineer? ! !—Just the Engineer--and my eyes will look past my mother and stare into the gauge!— Just the Engineer—just the Engineer!

WORKER: (*down beside the platform.*) I am a son!

(WORKER *down from the platform among them.*)

WORKER: (*mounts the platform.*) Wife--you shall have your wedding again! The day--with morning, noon and night shall be yours again! One day--and every day thereafter is no day for you!--Your husband travels on the trolley again--backwards and forwards--a man on the foot that shifts the gears! Aren't you laughing--*one* day is your life!—Wife and husband with one whole day--isn't time wasted while the trolley tears along? --Doesn't the foot feel for the pedal in the middle of the dance?--Does the piano drown the clatter of the wheels on the track?—No day is for you--for you and your husband!--No day has morning, noon and night--not an hour for wife and husband!--The trolley runs--and the foot keeps the rhythm--and the rhythm keeps the man captive!--Will a drop from a bucket grow into a river--a thousand days into a single day's living? Don't deceive yourselves--life is not contained in *one* day! --Don't be deceived by the profit--no profit is spent in *one* day! --You have the profit--and have no life!--What use to you are the profits that the foot makes--when they make a man's life poor?-- You have lost time—and with time, life--you have lost every-thing—time and life—and spit on the profit that is valueless—

227

beside this loss!–Shout out your loss—and fill your mouths with anger and accusation—shout: time and life lost—shout! !—shout! !—Shout out your demand—shout out your will—shout out that you have a will—that you have voices—shout out that you can shout:—the Engineer! !

WORKERS: (*throughout the hall.*) We are shouting! ! ! !

(WORKER *leaves the platform.*)

WORKER: (*on the platform.*) Girls and girls–we make you this promise!–Women and women–we make you this promise!–Mothers and mothers–we make you this promise–: not one of us rakes over the rubble–not one of us builds up a brick–not one of us rivets the steel! Our resolve remains unshakeable: all work stopped–without a new engineer! !—Crowd this hall each day–brothers and brothers–sons and sons–husbands and husbands–each one sharing the resolve of all–and in the gathering a single unbending will–raise your arms–unloose the vow from your lips—no gas—with this engineer! !

ALL THE MEN AND ALL THE WOMEN: No gas! !—With this engineer! !

(WORKER *leaves the platform.*)

VISITING WORKER: Our resolve strengthens yours–I come to you from our factory–which is idle!–We wait at your side–until you give us the signal to start work again. Count on us–and make your demand!

ALL THE MEN AND ALL THE WOMEN: The Engineer! ! ! !

(VISITING WORKER *leaves the platform. Another* VISITING WORKER *goes up.*)

VISITING WORKER: I am a stranger to you. You do not know me. I come from a factory far away. I bring this message: we have stopped work in our plant because you are not working. We are your allies to the last. Hold out–stand firm–: you must press your demand–you press it for all–you bear the responsibility for all! !

ALL THE MEN AND ALL THE WOMEN: The Engineer! ! ! !

(VISITING WORKER *comes down.*)

WORKER: (*above.*) The hall won't burst with our shouting! ! Though it thunders in the dome and crashes against the concrete–its roar will not burst forth! !—Out of the hall– away to his house–the cry goes up to him–into the ears of the man who is keeping the engineer! !—Throng in a column– over the rubble—go to him—here he won't hear us—here he won't hear us! !

ALL THE MEN AND ALL THE WOMEN: To his house! ! ! ! !— here he won't hear us! ! ! (*Crowding towards exits– growing tumult.*)

VOICE OF MILLIONAIRE'S SON: I hear you here!

(*Dead silence.*)

VOICE OF MILLIONAIRE'S SON: I am in the hall—I have heard you!

(*Muttering as the crowd seeks him.*)

VOICE OF MILLIONAIRE'S SON: I will answer you—here in the hall!

(*Movement grows.*)

VOICE OF MILLIONAIRE'S SON: You shall hear me now!

CLERK: (*passage already opening before him; rushing onto the platform.*) Don't let him speak! !—Don't let him up here! ! —Crowd close—don't make way! !—Run out of the hall! ! —Run to the works! !—Run—and clear the rubble—set up scaffolding—build the works! !—Don't listen to him! !— don't listen to him! !—Run! !—Run! ! —I'll run ahead! !—to my desk!—I'll write!—write! !—write! ! (*Descends.*)

MILLIONAIRE'S SON: (*above.*) I have been in the hall from the start. You couldn't recognize me, because I shouted with you. To you, girl, I was as much a brother as any–to you, woman, I was as much a husband as any–to you, mother, I was as much a son as any. No other cry than yours came from my mouth!–Now you see me here.–Now I am standing here above you–because my mouth is forming the final appeal–that you fail to voice!–You make your demand–and what you demand is but a grain from the mountain of the demands that you must make. You squabble and bicker about what matters least. What is the Engineer? What is the Engineer to you? What is he to you, who come out of fire and falling buildings? To you, who survive the devastation? What is the Engineer to you? ! It is what you shout–a shouted cry that has no sense–only sound!—I know: the Engineer provokes you to it–the sight of him will renew the horror in you, if you see him. The Engineer and the explosion are one–the formula did not keep the gas in check–and this engineer had charge of the formula–which brought the explosion. You will not exorcise the explosion until you drive away the engineer. So the first thing you shout for is the Engineer!—Don't you know the formula is correct? That it was correct and remains correct to the end of all the calculations any engineer can ever make?—You know it–and yet you shout for the Engineer!

VOICES: (*muttering.*) The Engineer!

MILLIONAIRE'S SON: Your cry wells up out of deeper depths:– Your demand claims more and more–I urge you on—demand more—demand more! ! (*Voices remain silent.*) What was so terrible about the explosion? What did it blast or burn? Did it spit and hiss at any one of you–who was not maimed even before the explosion? Girl–your brother: was he unmaimed? –Mother–your son: was he unmaimed?–Wife–your husband: was he unmaimed? Was there one who was not maimed in the works that blew up? What further harm did the explosion cause you? !—You were butchered before everything collapsed–blasted before the blast—: with *one* foot–with *one* hand–with burning eyes in a dead head you were already cripples! —Can the Engineer recompense you for *that?*—Can *one* demand compensate for that?—Demand more—demand more!

GIRLS, WIVES, MOTHERS: (*shrill.*) My brother–! My son–! My husband!

MILLIONAIRE'S SON: Brothers and brothers–sons and sons– husbands and husbands: the cry goes up that penetrates beyond the . hall–over the rubble–over the rubble piled on brother and brothers–on son and sons–on husband and hus-

bands—and flows full circle back to you:—demand yourselves! ! demand yourselves! ! (*Silence.*) Demand—and I will
fulfil—You are human–as son–as brother–as husband! Multi-
plicity flowing from you to all about you. None is part–the
individual perfected in community. The whole is as *one* body–
and the body is whole! Join together out of your separation–
and heal yourselves of your injuries: be human! ! (*Silence.*)
Demand—and I will fulfil!–Brother–you are human. Your hand
on lever maiming you no more!–Son–you are human–your eyes
wander from the gauge into the distance!–Husband–you are
human–your day is a day of the time that is yours for living! !
(*Silence.*) Space is yours–and wholeness in the space that houses
you!–You are human beings in it! Human–familiar with
every miracle–resolved to reach your full potential!–Heaven
seethes within you and the surface surges with the green
grass!–There is glory in the daily round--with new discoveries
in you–who are not new!–You are made perfect–as from this
beginning!–Human beings–the last shift worked–finished with
the task to which you were pledged!–You have worked the
shift to the limit of capacity—The ground is strewn with dead
—you are vindicated! ! (*Silence.*) What you demand–I fulfil:
–tomorrow you are human, in unity and abundance!—Broad
meadows of green are your new province! The settlement
stretches over ruins and rubble left lying. You are released
from drudgery and profits!–Settlers with the least demands–
and the ultimate reward:–human beings! ! (*Silence.*) Come
out of the hall—enter the new territory—measure out the
plots! The labour is little–but what it creates borders on the
immeasurable! !—Come out! ! (*He leaves the platform.
Silence.*)

(*The* ENGINEER *mounts the platform.*)

VOICE: (*shrill.*) The Engineer!
ENGINEER: I am here!–Listen to this: I will bow to your will–
and disappear! I accept the blame with which my brow will be
branded–when I go. I will collect all the curses screamed at
my back–when my departure becomes the confession of my
immense guilt:–I want to take the blame!—I am going—so

231

that you may return to work!–The way lies open—into the works! !

MILLIONAIRE'S SON: (below.) Come out. Leave the workshed—and build the settlement!

ENGINEER: Stand your ground here!—here in the workshed! ! –I am become a great voice–thundering out to you here! !

MILLIONAIRE'S SON: Come out. Leave the workshed!

ENGINEER: Stay in the workshed—and do not betray your work!

(VOICES raised in discontent.)

MILLIONAIRE'S SON: Here words of abuse re-echo–outside they will be blown away!

ENGINEER: I am branded, disgraced by your deceit. I am going–now you must return to work! !

MILLIONAIRE'S SON: Burst open the doors–into the light of day!

ENGINEER: You must return to work!–Do not heap deception on deception—by deceiving yourselves! !—Recognize the break-through–that makes your fame:–gas! !—Your labours create marvels of steel. Power pulses in machines of your driving–gas! !–You propel the speed of trains that thunder your triumph over bridges you rivet!–You launch leviathan liners into the sea–that they cleave in courses set by your compass! –Quivering towers you build sheer into the whistling wind that threatens the aerials the ether-waves speak into!–You raise engines from the ground which howl with rage in the sky at the annihilation of their weight flying along in the clouds!—You–such defenceless creatures–in your weakness the prey of the beast that attacks you–vulnerable in every pore of your skin–you are the conquerors of the whole world! !

(Deep silence.)

MILLIONAIRE'S SON: (at the foot of the platform pointing at the ENGINEER.) He is opening the picture-book for you again–you read it like children–for these are the deeds of your infancy. Now you are growing up into the new age!

ENGINEER: You are heroes–in soot and sweat! Heroes at the lever–in front of the gauge–at the gear-switch!–You endure amid the swish of driving-belts and the thunder of the clattering pistons!–And even the harshest trial causes you no lasting terror:–the explosion!!

MILLIONAIRE'S SON: Come out of the hall!

ENGINEER: Where would you go now?–Out of your kingdom into the sheep-pen? To trot from dawn to dusk within the square of your settlement? To plant tiny seedlings with your hands that raised up mighty towers? Your eager energy–now merely sustaining–and not creating? !

MILLIONAIRE'S SON: Come out of the hall!

ENGINEER: Here you are the rulers–in the work of all-powerful production–you make gas! That is your domain–which you built up in shift upon shift–by day and night–filled with feverish toil!–Will you exchange your power for a blade of grass growing as it pleases?—Here you are the rulers—there you are—: Peasants!!

A VOICE: (shouts.) Peasants!

VOICES: Peasants!!

NEW VOICES: Peasants!!

ALL: (surge of shouting and clenched fists.) Peasants!!!

(ENGINEER stands with sweeping gesture of triumph.)

MILLIONAIRE'S SON: (on the steps of the platform.) Will you heed him—or me?

ALL: The Engineer!!!

ENGINEER: The explosion did not make cowards of you. Who is shaken with fear?

MILLIONAIRE'S SON: Am I trying to frighten you?–Am I not making a greater call on your courage?–Am I not asking you for:–humanity?–How could you be peasants again–after once being workers?–Is not a further advance being demanded of you?–One that has already overtaken the peasant–and is now leaving the worker behind–and has humanity as its goal? !–Are you not mature–after this last experience?–Where can you go now–with the labour of your hands and work-shifts?—Are your rumbling railways and the sweep of your bridges and your flying engines sufficient reward for your fever?–Ridicule such mean reward!—Are you tempted by the

rich profits we share?–You would squander them once again
–just as you would work yourselves to death again!—It is a
fever in you–an insubstantial frenzy of work. It devours you–
it is not you who are building your house!–You are not
the warders–you are behind the bars. There are walls round
you–erected by yourselves. Come out now! !—You are heroes–
there is no trial you shrink from!–Boldly you press on to the
end of the road–no fear makes you falter in your stride!–
The road has ended–*one* road has ended again–exalt your
courage with fresh courage:—humanity is here! ! ! !

ENGINEER: You are peasants with your lazy toil! !

MILLIONAIRE'S SON: Human beings in unity and universal-
ity! !

ENGINEER: Petty needs will make much of your aspirations! !

MILLIONAIRE'S SON: Your every expectation will be fulfilled! !

ENGINEER: Apathy will deaden your day! !

MILLIONAIRE'S SON: Your work will be unbounded by time! !

ENGINEER: No plans will come to fruition! !

MILLIONAIRE'S SON: You are released into your true form–as
human beings! !

ENGINEER: (*revolver high above his head.*) Demand my destruction! !

MILLIONAIRE'S SON: Go beyond destruction into perfection–
become human! !

ENGINEER: Demand my destruction again–and flock back to
work! ! (*Barrel at his temple.*)

(*Silence.*)

ENGINEER: Dare to demand! !

VOICE: (*bursting out.*) The Engineer shall lead us!

VOICES AND VOICES: The Engineer shall lead us! ! !

ALL: The Engineer shall lead us! ! ! !

ENGINEER: Come out of the hall!—into the works! !—from
explosion to explosion! !—Gas! !

ALL: Gas! ! ! !

(ENGINEER *leaves the platform. Both doors open:* WORKERS
pour out.)

MILLIONAIRE'S SON: (*staggering to the platform.*) Do not kill human beings!—Do not make cripples!—Brother, you are more than a hand!! Son, you are more than two eyes!!—Husband, you shall live more than *one* day!!—You are all eternal and perfect from your very beginnings—do not mutilate yourselves beyond time and help!!—Aspire to something greater–aspire to yourselves—yourselves!!!!

(*Empty hall.*)

MILLIONAIRE'S SON: (*firm.*) I have glimpsed humanity—I must save it from itself!

ACT V

Brick wall–partly swept away and blackened by the explosion. In it a wide door–half blown off its hinges. Rubble heap. Outside soldier with fixed bayonet. MILLIONAIRE'S SON–*standing under cover of the wall–bandage round his head.* CAPTAIN *waiting in the centre.*

MILLIONAIRE'S SON: It's a ghastly misunderstanding. I must be allowed to speak–and clear it up.

CAPTAIN: You were received with flying stones.

MILLIONAIRE'S SON: They won't do it a second time, when they see that they have injured me.

CAPTAIN: I can't guarantee that.

MILLIONAIRE'S SON: What provokes them is: the soldier in front of them. But I want to tell them the reason!

CAPTAIN: You asked for protection yourself.

MILLIONAIRE'S SON: Not for myself. I want to bar the way into the works. That can be explained in a word or two.

CAPTAIN: They won't give you a chance to get in the first one.

MILLIONAIRE'S SON: They ought not to attack me, when I'm trying to explain myself.

CAPTAIN: Keep close to the wall!

MILLIONAIRE'S SON: Are you prepared to go out there with me?

CAPTAIN: No.

MILLIONAIRE'S SON: You won't?

CAPTAIN: I might be hit too–and I would be forced to have them fired on.

MILLIONAIRE'S SON: No–no–not that!—Then I must wait till they come to their senses!

(*Outside the soldier is relieved by another. Rising clamour from a thousand voices.*)

MILLIONAIRE'S SON: Why are they shouting now?

CAPTAIN: The guard is changing!

MILLIONAIRE'S SON: The confusion is terrible!–Can't they understand what I'm trying to do? They are my brothers–I am only a little older and more mature–so I must hold a protecting hand over them!

(GOVERNMENT OFFICIAL *enters from the right.*)

GOVERNMENT OFFICIAL: (*at the gate, peering out.*) Looks bad. (*To the* CAPTAIN.) Are you prepared for every eventuality?

CAPTAIN: Machine-guns.

(*Again the tumult outside has grown, and the uproar continues until the* GOVERNMENT OFFICIAL *moves away from the gate.*)

GOVERNMENT OFFICIAL: (*to the* MILLIONAIRE'S SON *briefly raising his top hat–searching in his leather case for documents.*) The unprecedented and dangerous nature of the events at your works has prompted the government to discuss them with you. You will see my instructions from this.

MILLIONAIRE'S SON: (*takes the document–reads–looks up.*) Full powers?

GOVERNMENT OFFICIAL: In certain circumstances.–Are we to talk here?

MILLIONAIRE'S SON: I'm not moving from this place.

CAPTAIN: I most strongly recommend you to stay behind the wall!

GOVERNMENT OFFICIAL: (*puts away the document–takes out another.*) We had better establish correctly the series of events leading up to this disturbance: after the disaster the workers refused to commence the rebuilding of the works until a demand put to you by them concerning the dismissal of the Engineer was complied with.

MILLIONAIRE'S SON: But that would not have prevented future disasters!

GOVERNMENT OFFICIAL: The government can only take cognizance of facts.

MILLIONAIRE'S SON: But the explosion is bound to recur: there is only this formula–or no gas!

GOVERNMENT OFFICIAL: Future possibilities cannot be taken into consideration.–The workers' demand was rejected by you. As a result the workers remained on strike, and this has spread to neighbouring works and further plants are being affected daily!

MILLIONAIRE'S SON: Yes–yes!

GOVERNMENT OFFICIAL: Meanwhile the Engineer has announced his voluntary resignation–to a meeting of the workers. Thereupon a change in their attitude caused the workers to withdraw their demands, after which the retention of the Engineer was requested.

MILLIONAIRE'S SON: Yes!

GOVERNMENT OFFICIAL: Thus the cause of the disturbance was removed and the workers were ready to return to work.

MILLIONAIRE'S SON: They are insisting on being let back in.

GOVERNMENT OFFICIAL: Then you stepped in with your ban on their return. You took the view that you couldn't be responsible for the production of gas.

MILLIONAIRE'S SON: Not for the destruction of humanity!

GOVERNMENT OFFICIAL: The government is by no means unaware of the unusual severity of the unfortunate accident that has occurred.

MILLIONAIRE'S SON: That is contemptible!

GOVERNMENT OFFICIAL: The number of the victims has aroused the deepest sympathy. The government is preparing a declaration to that effect in Parliament. The government is of the opinion that, with this expression of sympathy at the highest level, justice will have been done to you and to the labour force.

MILLIONAIRE'S SON: Yes. More is not in your power. The rest is up to me!

GOVERNMENT OFFICIAL: The government has noted your further intention in connection with the permanent closing-down of the works with the greatest regret.

MILLIONAIRE'S SON: Make no mistake about my strength, I shall carry out my plans!

GOVERNMENT OFFICIAL: (*with yet another document.*) Measures for overcoming the danger have already been under discussion.

MILLIONAIRE'S SON: Provide me with soldiers and make it safe for me to talk to them out there!

GOVERNMENT OFFICIAL: The danger threatening as a result of the suspension of the production of gas has led the government to send you confidential information.

MILLIONAIRE'S SON: (*stares at him.*) You–are asking for–gas? !

GOVERNMENT OFFICIAL: The whole armaments industry is based on gas. The lack of this fuel would jeopardize the manufacture of defence equipment in a most serious manner. We are faced with war. Without the productive energy of gas the armaments programme cannot be carried out. For this overriding reason the government cannot tolerate an interruption in the delivery of gas for any length of time!

MILLIONAIRE'S SON: Am I–not master–of my–own land–here?

GOVERNMENT OFFICIAL: The government is genuinely anxious to reach an understanding with you. It is prepared to assist the reconstruction in every way. To this end four lorryloads of tools will be arriving at any minute. A start can be made at once with clearing the rubble!

MILLIONAIRE'S SON: —Armaments–to destroy people? ! !

GOVERNMENT OFFICIAL: I must ask you to treat these disclosures in the strictest confidence.

MILLIONAIRE'S SON: I shall—shout! !—I shall seek allies everywhere! !

GOVERNMENT OFFICIAL: I can understand that you are upset. Nonetheless the government finds itself faced with the harshest necessity!

MILLIONAIRE'S SON: Do not blaspheme! !—Humanity is the necessity! !—Inflict no new wounds on it.—It will be difficult enough to heal the old ones! ! Let me go out to them all—I must— (*At the gate. Received with a chorus of yells.*)

CAPTAIN: (*pulls him back.*) You'll unleash the storm!

MILLIONAIRE'S SON: (*reels back against the wall.*)—Are we all crazy!

GOVERNMENT OFFICIAL: Now it is important for the government to know if you intend to stand by your refusal to admit the workers!

MILLIONAIRE'S SON: Only now do I see—the duty! !

GOVERNMENT OFFICIAL: You are maintaining your previous rejection?

MILLIONAIRE'S SON: As long as I can breathe and speak! !

GOVERNMENT OFFICIAL: Then I must invoke the powers vested in me. Due to the threat to the country's defences, the government finds itself compelled to deprive you until further notice of the use of your works and to carry on the production of gas under state control. The rebuilding of the plant is to be carried out with the money advanced by the state and will be put in hand immediately. We express the hope that you will make no attempt at resistance. We should regret having to take harsher measures against you!–Captain, open the gate –I will give the workers the necessary directions!

(*At the gate. A roar of noise goes up.*)

CAPTAIN: Get back! !—Stones! !

GOVERNMENT OFFICIAL: (*retreating to the safety of the wall.*) This is beyond belief!

(*The tumult continues.*)

GOVERNMENT OFFICIAL: These people are simply preventing me–
MILLIONAIRE'S SON: I am not afraid! !

(*At the gate. Outside deafening tumult.* MILLIONAIRE'S SON *waving his arms high above his head. Surge of shouting comes nearer.*)

CAPTAIN: (*shouting to the* GOVERNMENT OFFICIAL.) They're coming! !

(*Through the gate–calls an order to the left. Machine-gun*

detachment enters and quickly takes up its position. CAPTAIN,
his sword held high—ready to give the signal. Deep silence.)

GOVERNMENT OFFICIAL: (beside the MILLIONAIRE'S SON.)
Don't you want to prevent bloodshed?

(MILLIONAIRE'S SON stands paralysed.)

GOVERNMENT OFFICIAL: Here—! (He gives him his handkerchief.) The signal will be readily understood. Wave the white
flag!

(MILLIONAIRE'S SON does everything mechanically.)

GOVERNMENT OFFICIAL: You see—it works. They are dropping
the stones! (To the CAPTAIN.) The gate wide open! (Soldiers
open the gate.) Withdraw the cordon! (CAPTAIN and machine-
gun detachment exeunt. To the MILLIONAIRE'S SON.) I'll tell
them out there where the lorries with the tools are arriving. I
shall lead the people there! (Exits through the gate.)

(High-pitched, cheerful sounds outside—rapidly fading in the
distance. Silence. MILLIONAIRE'S SON seats himself on a heap
of rubble. DAUGHTER—in black—enters.)

(DAUGHTER goes to him and puts an arm round his shoulders.)

(MILLIONAIRE'S SON looks up in surprise.)

DAUGHTER: Don't you recognize me?
MILLIONAIRE'S SON: Daughter—in black?
DAUGHTER: My husband is no longer alive.
MILLIONAIRE'S SON: Hurling reproaches?—Stones hurled at me
even from your hands?
DAUGHTER: (shakes her head.)—Are you alone here?
MILLIONAIRE'S SON: Ultimately alone, like all who tried to
become one with all men!
DAUGHTER: (touches the bandage round his brow.) Have they
hit you?
MILLIONAIRE'S SON: I too was hit. I too. There are arrows
that rebound and wound both—marksman and target!
DAUGHTER:—Has the danger passed?
MILLIONAIRE'S SON: Has humanity been born? Of humans—

men who do not shout hideous threats? Did time outrun itself—
and bring man into the light? What picture does he present?

DAUGHTER: Tell me!

MILLIONAIRE'S SON: His picture faded from me. What did he
look like? (*He takes her hands.*) These are hands—and are
organic to the body—(*Grasping her arms.*) These are limbs—
are united with the trunk—parts working as one—and *one*
impulse in each!—

DAUGHTER: Tell me!

MILLIONAIRE'S SON: Does the stream not rush too wildly and
flow over the banks that cannot contain it? Cannot the dam
be built to stem the flood? Must the frenzy go unchecked and
overflow into the fields and run riot in its rank growth over
the expanses of green? Is there no stopping it?!—(*Drawing
his* DAUGHTER *close in front of him.*) Tell me: where is
humanity? When will man make his appearance—and call
himself by name:—man? When will he comprehend himself—
and shake his perception down from the branches? When will
he conquer the curse—and re-new creation that he
corrupted:—humanity?!—Have I not already seen him—did
he not appear to me with every sign of his abundance—mighty
in his great power—quiet in full voice that cries:—humanity?!—
—Was he not close to me—can he die again—must he not
arrive—tomorrow and tomorrow—and in the space of an hour?!
—Am I not a witness to him—and to his origin and advent—
is he not known to me with his strong countenance?!—
Am I still to doubt?!!

DAUGHTER: (*kneels down.*) I will give him birth!

GAS II

Play in Three Acts

Translated by B. J. Kenworthy

MILLIONAIRE-WORKER
CHIEF ENGINEER

FIRST ⎤
SECOND
THIRD
FOURTH ⎬ BLUE Figures
FIFTH
SIXTH
SEVENTH ⎦

FIRST ⎤
SECOND
THIRD
FOURTH ⎬ YELLOW Figures
FIFTH
SIXTH
SEVENTH ⎦

WORKERS (men and women, young, old, and adolescent)

ACT I

Concrete hall. Light cascading from arc-lamps. From the hazy height of the dome a cluster of wires vertically down to the iron platform and thence distributed to small iron tables—three right, three left. The wires coloured red to the left—green to the right. At each table a BLUE FIGURE—*sitting stiffly in uniform staring at a glass panel in the table, which—red left, green right—colours the face as it lights up. Slantwise across the front of the stage a longish iron table with chequered top, in which green and red plugs are being manipulated by the* FIRST BLUE FIGURE. *Silence.*

SECOND BLUE FIGURE: (*before red-glowing panel.*) Report from third battle-sector: enemy concentration growing.

(*Panel-light fades.* FIRST BLUE FIGURE *crossplugs red contact.*)

FIFTH BLUE FIGURE: (*before green-glowing panel.*) Report from third workshop: production one point below quota.

(*Panel-light fades.* FIRST BLUE FIGURE *crossplugs green contact.*)

THIRD BLUE FIGURE: (*before red-glowing panel.*) Report from second battle-sector: enemy concentration growing.

(*Panel-light fades.* FIRST BLUE FIGURE *crossplugs red contact.*)

SIXTH BLUE FIGURE: (*before green-glowing panel.*) Report from second workshop: production one point below quota.

(*Panel-light fades.* FIRST BLUE FIGURE *crossplugs green contact.*)

FOURTH BLUE FIGURE: (*before red-glowing panel.*) Report from first battle-sector: enemy concentration growing.

(*Panel-light fades.* FIRST BLUE FIGURE *crossplugs red contact.*)

SEVENTH BLUE FIGURE: *(before green-glowing panel.)* Report from first workshop production two points below quota.

(Panel-light fades. FIRST BLUE FIGURE *crossplugs green contact. Silence.)*

SECOND BLUE FIGURE: *(before red-glowing panel.)* Report from third battle-sector: enemy attack pushing forward.

(Panel-light fades. FIRST BLUE FIGURE *crossplugs red contact.)*

FIFTH BLUE FIGURE: *(before green-glowing panel.)* Report from third workshop: production three points below quota.

(Panel-light fades. FIRST BLUE FIGURE *crossplugs green contact.)*

THIRD BLUE FIGURE: *(before red-glowing panel.)* Report from second battle-sector: enemy attack pushing forward.

(Panel-light fades. FIRST BLUE FIGURE *crossplugs red contact.)*

SIXTH BLUE FIGURE: *(before green-glowing panel.)* Report from second workshop: production five points below quota.

(Panel-light fades FIRST BLUE FIGURE *crossplugs green contact.)*

FOURTH BLUE FIGURE: *(before red-glowing panel.)* Report from first battle-sector: enemy attack pushing forward.

(Panel-light fades. FIRST BLUE FIGURE *crossplugs red contact.)*

SEVENTH BLUE FIGURE: *(before green-glowing panel.)* Report from first workshop: production eight points below quota.

(Panel-light fades. FIRST BLUE FIGURE *crossplugs green contact. Silence.)*

SECOND BLUE FIGURE: *(before red-glowing panel.)* Report from third battle-sector: enemy break-through spreading.

(Panel-light fades. FIRST BLUE FIGURE *crossplugs red contact.)*

FIFTH BLUE FIGURE: *(before green-glowing panel.)* Report from third workshop: production nine points below quota.

(*Panel-light fades.* FIRST BLUE FIGURE *crossplugs red contact.*)

SIXTH BLUE FIGURE: (*before green-glowing panel.*) Report from second workshop: production eleven points below quota.

(*Panel-light fades.* FIRST BLUE FIGURE *crossplugs green contact.*)

FOURTH BLUE FIGURE: (*before red-glowing panel.*) Report from first battle-sector: enemy break-through spreading.

(*Panel-light fades.* FIRST BLUE FIGURE *crossplugs red contact.*)

SEVENTH BLUE FIGURE: (*before green-glowing panel.*) Report from first workshop: production twelve points below quota.

(*Panel-light fades.*)

FIRST BLUE FIGURE: (*into the telephone in front of him.*) The Chief Engineer!

(CHIEF ENGINEER *enters: aged into the petrifaction of fanatical working-energy; angular profile—crest of white hair; white overall.*)

FIRST BLUE FIGURE: Control-stations registering reduced production of gas. By points performance up to twelve behind target.
CHIEF ENGINEER: Collapse of workers at gauge–gear–pedal–lever.
FIRST BLUE FIGURE: Why no replacement?
CHIEF ENGINEER: Every shift combed–not a spare man or woman.
FIRST BLUE FIGURE: Any epidemic in the works?
CHIEF ENGINEER: No visible signs of it.
FIRST BLUE FIGURE: Is the food-supply failing?
CHIEF ENGINEER: Steady delivery with generous priorities.
FIRST BLUE FIGURE: Are they disappointed by the pay from the share-out of the profits?
CHIEF ENGINEER: Even young lads are amassing vast sums in ready cash.
FIRST BLUE FIGURE: —How do you account for–the reduction?
CHIEF ENGINEER: Movement became autonomous. Excessive duration of the *one* action blunts the goad of the will to

work. Gas is no longer the goal–and becomes lost in trivial tasks, repeating and repeating what ceases to have purpose as a part without the whole. Planlessly the man works at the machine–the work loses its coherence as the man slides deeper and deeper into the unvaried monotony. Wheel whirrs by wheel and no longer engages the hub of counterwheel and counterwheel. Impetus rushes on loadless and without resistance hurtles to the ground.

FIRST BLUE FIGURE: Can you discover no means of ensuring production?

CHIEF ENGINEER: New masses of workers into the plant.

FIRST BLUE FIGURE: There are none, now they have been seven times sifted.

CHIEF ENGINEER: Children are already working the full shift.

FIRST BLUE FIGURE: What is to happen?

CHIEF ENGINEER: A steeply-rising shortage of gas.

FIRST BLUE FIGURE: (pointing to the table.) You see that? Tabulation of attack and defence. How the forces counterpoise.

CHIEF ENGINEER: Red is advancing.

FIRST BLUE FIGURE: Enemy gaining ground.

CHIEF ENGINEER: Green giving way.

FIRST BLUE FIGURE: Gas not supporting defence.

(CHIEF ENGINEER silent.)

FIRST BLUE FIGURE: This table records the calculation. In numbers we are weaker in battle–but in technical equipment superior. That balances the outcome. Provided we don't lag in our equipment!–The work of our factories is powered by gas, produced only by us, beyond the capability of the enemy in his factories. One point less gas production than calculated here—and we lose more quickly our prospect of preservation—than we have forfeited it so far!

CHIEF ENGINEER: (stares.) Crushing of enemy no longer—? ?

FIRST BLUE FIGURE: Today a fantasy!

CHIEF ENGINEER: The end?

FIRST BLUE FIGURE: At best a draw with both parties in check!

(CHIEF ENGINEER supports himself against the table.)

FIRST BLUE FIGURE: That makes the decision easier. It has been reached in the only way it could be. Struggle and destruction. Attack and defence draining each other's blood. Downfall of adversary with adversary. Of peoples a remnant remains that dies off exhausted. Not one person escapes the destruction. (*Firmly to the* CHIEF ENGINEER.) Only we know that!

CHIEF ENGINEER: (*pulls himself together*.) What is to happen?

FIRST BLUE FIGURE: Increased production of gas without regard to man, woman or child. No more shifts–shift merges into shift without remission reckoned in hours. From collapse to collapse each at full stretch. No longer time for rest! Falls the last dead hand from the lever–slips the last dead foot from the gear-pedal–sinks the last dead eye from the gauge—so the sum works out: last enemy effaced from the earth–and the last of our fighters no longer breathing!

CHIEF ENGINEER: (*strong again*.) I will meet the demand!

FIRST BLUE FIGURE: (*holds out his hand to him*.) In we go then, into the tunnel with no way out!

CHIEF ENGINEER: (*hand-shaking*.) Gas! (*Exits*.)

(*Immediately afterwards high, shrill sirens nearby–from the distance new sirens–ebbing–silent*.)

FIRST BLUE FIGURE: (*into telephone*.) The Millionaire-Worker!

(MILLIONAIRE-WORKER *enters: middle-twenties; working clothes-cropped hair–barefoot*.)

FIRST BLUE FIGURE: Is your shift working?

MILLIONAIRE-WORKER: (*shakes his head*.) Relief-shift that has been called out.

FIRST BLUE FIGURE: Prematurely.

MILLIONAIRE-WORKER: The decision must have been forced on you.

FIRST BLUE FIGURE: By what compulsion?

MILLIONAIRE-WORKER: No worker can last through the previous shift any longer.

FIRST BLUE FIGURE: Your advice?

MILLIONAIRE-WORKER: What does my opinion matter here?

FIRST BLUE FIGURE: As you see, I'm asking.

MILLIONAIRE-WORKER: You can enquire of any worker in the factory.

FIRST BLUE FIGURE: I'm not asking any worker–I want to know from the boss.

MILLIONAIRE-WORKER: Who is boss?

FIRST BLUE FIGURE: (*looks hard at him.*) Before me–the boss.

MILLIONAIRE-WORKER: —Are you stepping down?

FIRST BLUE FIGURE: The new task demands doubled forces:– the boss and we will achieve it in united effort.

MILLIONAIRE-WORKER: What is required?

FIRST BLUE FIGURE: Gas with tenfold powers!

MILLIONAIRE-WORKER: (*shoulder-shrugging.*) You decide the output.

FIRST BLUE FIGURE: It is not sufficient. The workers are flagging. Orders would seep away in their spent brains without spurring them on.

MILLIONAIRE WORKER: Impose more stringent punishments.

FIRST BLUE FIGURE: That deprives us of workers.

MILLIONAIRE-WORKER: Have all become indispensable?

FIRST BLUE FIGURE: For the supreme effort!–Annihilation on both sides–annihilation!

MILLIONAIRE-WORKER: (*flinches–collects himself.*) What do you want of me?

FIRST BLUE FIGURE: To send the current through the works that will sweep everyone along with it. What must be done: infuse them with fanaticism for their own destruction. Fever of hate and pride will warm the coldest vein in each–night becomes day in the service of the final goal, that swells into a blood-red beacon!

MILLIONAIRE-WORKER: That is the goal?

FIRST BLUE FIGURE: Announced by your lips! Stand in the sheds–mingle your voice with the crash of the pistons and the swish of the driving-belts–outshout the clatter with your clarion call, showing the way and proclaiming the purpose:– hands hard again on the lever–feet firm on the gear-pedal–eyes

clear at the gauge. Work flows through flood-gates flung wide–
and gas becomes force to balance superior forces!

MILLIONAIRE-WORKER: (*very calm.*) I shall be punished if I
miss the shift.

FIRST BLUE FIGURE: You are a worker no longer.

MILLIONAIRE-WORKER: You cannot discharge me, because I
am a worker in the factory.

FIRST BLUE FIGURE: I'm sending you into the works on a special
assignment.

MILLIONAIRE-WORKER: I am not accepting it.

FIRST BLUE FIGURE:—Are you making conditions?

MILLIONAIRE-WORKER: I repeat the one and only condition,
the one that was the demand of my mother and my mother's
father: derequisition the works.

FIRST BLUE FIGURE: (*vehement.*) Your grandfather and your
mother protested against the production of gas. That necessit-
ated the compulsory administration of the works. Otherwise
our rearmament was condemned to stagnation!

MILLIONAIRE-WORKER: That was demonstrated by their unshakeable refusal.

FIRST BLUE FIGURE: We are engaged in a struggle such as no
party was ever involved in.

MILLIONAIRE-WORKER: I have obeyed every order in silence.

FIRST BLUE FIGURE: Now your speech is necessary.

MILLIONAIRE WORKER: Against myself and against my mother?

FIRST BLUE FIGURE: For the workers, who want gas to be made!
They returned after the explosion–they built up the works–
they remained in the sheds despite the danger hourly threatening them–they willingly bowed to the master that was
named gas—and whose name today is destruction, if a voice
commanding attention should proclaim it! Yours is the voice
that will penetrate–with your agreement the surf of the
yes upon yes of the masses will swell into a crushing tidal wave.
Your turning to us will revive the half-dead at their work!

MILLIONAIRE-WORKER: I am protecting my grandfather's
legacy.

FIRST BLUE FIGURE: The workers laughed at his plans!

MILLIONAIRE-WORKER: The shape of humanity will reveal itself.

FIRST BLUE FIGURE: To others, who survive. We have no future.

MILLIONAIRE-WORKER: A way out always remains.

FIRST BLUE FIGURE: Will you seek it without us?

MILLIONAIRE-WORKER: With you and within you!

FIRST BLUE FIGURE: (after a moment's thought.)–We will achieve the production-target with punishments! (Gesture of dismissal.)

(MILLIONAIRE-WORKER exits. Silence.)

SECOND BLUE FIGURE: (before red-glowing panel.) Report from third battle-sector: limitless enemy pressure unceasing.

(Panel-light fades. FIRST BLUE FIGURE crossplugs red contact.)

THIRD BLUE FIGURE: (before red-glowing panel.) Report from second battle-sector: limitless enemy pressure unceasing.

(Panel-light fades. FIRST BLUE FIGURE crossplugs red contact.)

FOURTH BLUE FIGURE: (before red-glowing panel.) Report from first battle-sector: limitless enemy pressure unceasing.

(Panel-light fades.)

FIRST BLUE FIGURE: (jumps up.) No report from the factory? !

CHIEF ENGINEER: (hurries in.) The whole works disrupted! Shift-change standstill! Relief not dovetailing with work-shift! For the first time a gap gapes in the impetus of year on year! The pendulum hardly swinging! Automaton whirring to a stop!

FIRST BLUE FIGURE: Your instructions?

CHIEF ENGINEER: Announced with sirens! Answered by shift with work-stoppage–by relief with refusal!

FIRST BLUE FIGURE: Is anyone inciting resistance?

CHIEF ENGINEER: No ring-leaders! The automaton is running wild–and running down because sudden change alters the mechanism! New time-schedules break the rhythm and slow the speed by seconds–time enough for the thought that leads to rethinking! Lightning flashes in their brains and illuminates the course that through repetitive years has whipped on their frenzied tempo! The delirium took on a face–and its fearful grimace grins into their terror-chilled minds!

FIRST BLUE FIGURE: Now—a strike?

CHIEF ENGINEER: What is strike?

FIRST BLUE FIGURE: Leaving lever and gear-pedal and gauge?

CHIEF ENGINEER: Already a thing of the past! Standstill turned into movement!

FIRST BLUE FIGURE: Revolt?

CHIEF ENGINEER: Flaring up through the sheds! No voice– no shouting–no flood of words!—icy silence–only staring before them–and at the same time peering at the next man– and he past him to his workmate and to workmates beyond! Out of eyes is arising–something to shatter us:—the tempest!

FIRST BLUE FIGURE: Cordon round the sheds and any leaving stopped at the gates! !

CHIEF ENGINEER: Have we time! !

FIFTH BLUE FIGURE: (before green–glowing panel.) Report from third workshop:—

CHIEF ENGINEER: (across–reading.) Work at standstill–workers leaving the sheds! !

FIRST BLUE FIGURE: Lock up the other workshops!

SIXTH BLUE FIGURE: (before green–glowing panel.) Report from second workshop:—

CHIEF ENGINEER: (across.) Work at standstill—

SEVENTH BLUE FIGURE: (before green–glowing panel.) Report from first workshop:—

CHIEF ENGINEER: (across.) Workers leaving the sheds! !

FIRST BLUE FIGURE: Alarm throughout works area! !

CHIEF ENGINEER: Too late! We are crushed under the pressure of the weight of numbers! The wave is towering more terribly –provoked by us, who will be here when they come! !

FIRST BLUE FIGURE: Are they forcing their way in? !

CHIEF ENGINEER: Marching this way without willing it! Impelled back to the centre from which our goad drove them on! That is where the hurricane will gather force! Its release will hit us–if we are still here to be hit!

FIRST BLUE FIGURE: (with a quick movement reduces the plugs

at the switchboards to a confused tangle.) The equation did not balance–there was a remainder! (*Exits with* CHIEF ENGINEER *and* BLUE FIGURES. *Empty hall.*)

(*From the hazegrey periphery the crowd slowly swells to form a ring:* WORKERS–*men: old, young, and adolescent in grey garb, haircropped, barefoot; women* WORKERS–*old and young–in like garb, barefoot, with kerchiefs bound tight round their hair. At a little distance from the tables the dead-silent advance halts. Then in a surging outburst–yet wordless –quickly: the tables are pushed over and passed overhead from hand to hand into the shadowed depths of the concrete hall–the wires from the platform to the tables–from the dome to the platform–are torn down. Then total silence. The women snatch the kerchiefs from their heads and start to shake loose their hair.*)

ALL : (*having exchanged looks–with a great cry.*) No gas! ! !

ACT II

Concrete hall. Arc-lamp light diminished. Full hall.

VOICES : (*muttering–rising–loud.*) What of us? !

GIRL : (*on to the platform–shaking out her hair.*) Morning for us with day that remains dawn so full of joy and brightness to halt the passing of its hours. Sunbeams dart in the morning's beginning–as no morning yet began for us. The eye opens shyly and blinks in confusion, hesitant to extend the vision that plunges into the vortex of white and of bright colours–soon the miracle becomes accustomed and is contained in the viewing :–morning for me brings me my beloved !

YOUNG WORKER : (*up onto the platform to the* GIRL.) Morning for you and for me that fuses into our fulfilment. The living and longing made up of day after day is empty without the existence of you and me until this morning, splendid and radiant.–Now the torrent breaks through the flood-gates, spilling out over the banks that gain a new mean-ing !–islet abundant with colour and sounds of a wedding !

254

GIRL: (*throwing her arms round the* YOUNG WORKER.) Morning for you!

YOUNG WORKER: (*holding the* GIRL.) Morning for you!

GIRLS AND YOUNG WORKERS: (*thronging round the platform—embracing each other.*) Morning for us ! !

(GIRL *and* YOUNG WORKER *leave the platform.*)

VOICES: (*of the others.*) More for us!

WOMAN: (*onto the platform.*) Noon for us. Never yet have I followed the curve that soars to the heights–it crawled flat on the floor. Between man and wife there was nothing beyond the morning–an empty husk crackled, that riveted but never united. Now a rain of resplendence scatters its sparkling arch over me. Shot through with gold, the pride-puffed clouds dissolving above and on every side shower down beneficent drops, that warm and soak lavishly, on the fallow-dead crust: –granules loosen and give access again–from this beginning the advance into fullness lies opened wide–: noon becomes the hour of our union of woman and man with the last breath of the one to the other, when what is the one and what the other blend in loss of identity:–no asking is left without answer– whose eager ring resounds with the brightness of noontide, because noonday blue is above us!

MAN: (*to the* WOMAN *on the platform.*) Noonday for you with a host of blue-edged clouds dancing. Noon drawn over me like a canopy of constancy–firm ground, where I am destined for you. No way out that leads astray, where nothing is rewarded –no will that defies, where nothing signifies:–on the mere breath of a syllable hangs understanding that is binding on both. Desire grew bold and unstinted–body committed to body: no excesses affronting the union–out of doubling of being and being without deduction our law arises that neither forbids nor permits:–the one knowing no constraint or resist- ance–an indivisible whole of man and woman in their noontide!

WOMAN: (*holding out her hands to him.*) Noontide for you!

MAN: (*grasping them.*) Noontide for you!

WOMEN AND MEN: (*round the platform–seeking each other with their hands.*) Noontide for us! !

(WOMAN *and* MAN *and leave the platform.*)

VOICES : (*of the others.*) More for us!

OLD WOMAN : (*onto the platform.*) Evening for us. For once the daily round at peace and the ankle at rest over the shoe. What remained under the husk of my morning and noon? I did not see the difference between noon and morning. It was one dull round with no sign of change to the other. It slid like a muddy stream over humps in the river-bottom, to whose bed we cannot see. Such was life of morning and noon.–Was I alone? Was no one with me at the outset and later? Was I so much alone? Did I sink by myself and merely grasp at my one hand with my other to save myself from sinking? Have I already died a lonely death?–The evening gives a whole life and gathers every hour misspent to hour upon hour yet to come. Time is allotted in new measure–I cup my hand and grasp no longer–riches pour into it–I blink at the profusion:–and then is revealed the one who vanished at morning and noon and appeared again only at evening!

OLD MAN : (*to the* OLD WOMAN *on the platform.*) For us the evening. Aimless trot comes to rest beneath shade-hung tree. Where is the clatter of noise? Where is the rush? Tired bird in the branches points the stillness–dying wind rustles. Day ebbs away smoothly. What if it is late? Morning is pressing of hand in hand without end. Where is the chasm of our loss? The curve of a lip gives lavishly. You suffered no privation– and I denied myself nothing:–our evening reveals inexhaustible abundance. (*He leads the* OLD WOMAN *down from the platform.*)

OLD WOMEN AND MEN : (*approach each other–support each other.*) Evening for us! !

VOICES : (*of the others.*) More for us!

A VOICE : (*high.*) What of us!

VOICES : (*Scattered.*) More for us! !

VOICES : (*answering.*) What of us?

VOICES : (*surging.*) More for us! ! !

VOICES : (*surging back.*) What of us? ! !

VOICES AND VOICES: (*intermingling.*) More for us! ! ! What of us? (*Break-off at height of shouting.*)

(*Silence.*)

A VOICE: The Millionaire-Worker!
ALL VOICES: (*swelling–uniting–acclaiming.*) The Millionaire-Worker! ! !

(*Silence.*)

MILLIONAIRE WORKER (*mounts the platform.*) I am of my own will before and above you only by virtue of the steps I am climbing! (*Above.*) No mind thinks more–no mouth speaks more eloquently to you: you call out morning and noon and evening–and name the expressible in words eternally valid.– For you, Girl, morning is that time of your life when you set forth from your starting–and for your sisters beside you and your sisters after you. So it was ordained from the outset!– Youth, in your blood and pulse the ardour of morning awakens after a first embrace–as in your brothers beside you and your brothers after you. So it was ordained from the outset! For you, Woman, day is great in its noontide, that brings you the fruit of every fulfilment–and for all women beside you and all the women after you. So it was ordained from the outset! –Man, the field of your forehead burns brown from the high sun and brands you with the strong stamp of noonday–and all men beside you and all the men after you. So it was ordained from the outset!–Old Woman and old Man, over your shoulders and loins evening descends from the shade and the stillness–you are tranquil before nightfall, when your sleep comes with no shouting or terror. So it was ordained from the outset!–(*Stronger.*) Once more day surrounds you–a whole day with morning and noon and evening:–the distorted law shines out from a tablet made new!–You are yourselves again– enforced drudgery left behind–you undertake your last task!
VOICES: What of us? !
MILLIONAIRE-WORKER: Outcry from you, seeking yourselves in your own invention!–You, who were flung to the ground by a force of the utmost severity–impressed and impounded

257

like beasts to the slaughter–you have proved yourselves worthy! Your experience affirms with oath and seal:–it is no cheating trick. Your cry carries the day–avouched with all truths–in each breath a full affirmation!!

VOICES AND VOICES: What of us?

MILLIONAIRE-WORKER: Yourselves telling who you are in your unfolding!–Your discovery becomes wickedness if what you have found is kept secret. To stay silent is to be terribly blackened with shame. Where you dwell the air will grow foul around you if you shutter the windows and do not let the light shine into the street. Not a curse will be slow to fall on you and damn you!!

ALL VOICES: What of us?!

MILLIONAIRE-WORKER: Proclaim yourselves to the others!! Send your cry out of the hall through the air to them all. Spare no effort, it will be your last–give up the wealth you can never spend but only invest at tenfold interest—: roll the dome clear!!

(Silence.)

VOICES AND VOICES: Roll the dome clear!!

ALL VOICES: Roll the dome clear!!!

MILLIONAIRE-WORKER: Rig the antenna!

VOICES AND VOICES: Rig the antenna!!

ALL VOICES: Rig the antenna!!!

MILLIONAIRE-WORKER: Send out to the fighters on both sides the signal that fighting has ceased!!

VOICE: Send out the signal!

VOICES AND VOICES: Send out the signal!!

ALL VOICES: Send out the signal!!!

YOUNG WORKER: (by the platform–arms pointing at the dome.) By us–the dome rolled clear! (Exits.)

(Silence.)

VOICE: (overhead.) We–in the dome now!

VOICES: (below.) Roll the dome clear!

VOICE: (overhead.) Rust clogging the rails!

VOICES: (below.) Loosen rivets!

258

VOICE: (*overhead.*) Pressure is enormous!

VOICES: (*below.*) Set off a charge under the dome!

VOICE: (*overhead.*) Plates loosened already!

VOICES: (*below.*) Enlarge the gap!

VOICE: (*overhead.*) Dome sliding!

ALL VOICES: (*below.*) Roll the dome clear! ! ! !

(*A broad shaft of light shoots down out of the dome and stands like a lambent pillar from the floor of the hall. Dazzled silence–all faces upturned.*)

MILLIONAIRE-WORKER: (*calling aloft.*) Press on with the work without pausing!

VOICE: (*overhead.*) Wire rigged sheer!

MILLIONAIRE-WORKER: Make haste to completion!

VOICE: (*overhead.*) Transmission signal strong!

MILLIONAIRE-WORKER: Operate as I tell you!

VOICE: (*overhead.*) Transmitter ready!

MILLIONAIRE-WORKER: Send out the watch-word: Hands are loosed from their labours–hands are released from labour for mutual destruction–hands are free to grasp the hands of all others in ours that are working no more:–no gas!

VOICE: (*overheard, repeating.*) Hands are loosed from their labours–hands are released from labour for mutual destruction–hands are free to grasp the hands of all others in ours that are working no more:–no gas!

ALL VOICES: (*below.*) No gas! ! ! !

MILLIONAIRE-WORKER: Listen well for the answer!

VOICES: (*below.*) Tell us the answer!

MILLIONAIRE-WORKER: Don't miss the answer!

(*Silence.*)

VOICE: (*overhead.*) No answer given!

(*Silence.*)

MILLIONAIRE-WORKER: Send out the call: delirium evaporated out of the blood–fever gave way to coolness–sight opens eyes towards you, who greet us–workshift dissolved into lasting life:–no gas! !

259

VOICE: (*overhead, repeating.*) Delirium evaporated out of the blood–fever gave way to coolness–sight opens eyes towards you, who greet us–workshift dissolved into lasting life:–no gas! !

ALL VOICES: (*below.*) No gas! ! ! !

MILLIONAIRE-WORKER: Be alert for the answer!

VOICES AND VOICES: (*below.*) Call out the answer! !

MILLIONAIRE-WORKER: Pay good heed to the answer!

(*Silence.*)

VOICE: (*overhead.*) No answer given!

MILLIONAIRE-WORKER: Press for response: Country conjoined with country–frontier dispersed into space–even the farthest away become neighbours–gathered unto ourselves we are yet a part of you and are one whole:–no gas! ! !

VOICE: (*overhead, repeating.*) Country conjoined with country–frontier dispersed into space–even the farthest away are neighbours–gathered unto ourselves we are yet a part of you and are one whole:–no gas! ! !

ALL VOICES: (*below.*) No gas! ! ! !

MILLIONAIRE-WORKER: Listen well for the answer!

ALL VOICES: (*below.*) Shout us the answer!

MILLIONAIRE-WORKER: Do not confuse syllable with syllable of the answer! !

VOICE: (*overhead.*) No answer given!

(*Dead silence.*)

VOICE: (*from the extreme edge of the hall.*) Strangers approaching!

VOICES AND VOICES: Yellows approaching!

ALL VOICES: Enemy approaching! ! !

(*Passage opens before* SEVEN YELLOW FIGURES *who advance to the centre.* MILLIONAIRE-WORKER *staggers from the platform.*)

FIRST YELLOW FIGURE: The equation left a remainder. An unknown has come into play. Your side played the cards. We trumped. Book your loss to our credit.

(*Silence.*)

FIRST YELLOW FIGURE: The energy of the gas produced by you will serve our requirements. Your output will offset your debt to us, that remains unpaid. Gas will power our industry.

(*Silence.*)

FIRST YELLOW FIGURE: The works cease to be for your use and fall under our control. The schedules guaranteeing profit-sharing are cancelled. The profits shall no longer pour into the hands of all–payment according to amounts required to keep you alive will be law.

(*Silence.*)

FIRST YELLOW FIGURE: The factory makes gas again from this moment. Shift goes on duty straight from the hall here–shift working after shift. Demand for gas determined by us–the Chief Engineer to be responsible for production.

(*Enter* CHIEF ENGINEER.)

FIRST YELLOW FIGURE: The Chief Engineer has power to give orders and punishments.

(*Silence.*)

FIRST YELLOW FIGURE: (*to the* CHIEF ENGINEER.) Get the hall ready.

CHIEF ENGINEER: (*upwards.*) Close the dome!

(*Slowly the sunlight diminishes–disappears.*)

CHIEF ENGINEER: Set up the tables!

(*With noiseless activity the tables are passed overhead to the centre–set in place.*)

CHIEF ENGINEER: Rig the wires!

(*With apathetic industry the wires lowered from the dome are pulled to the platform–drawn taut to the tables.*)

CHIEF ENGINEER: Switch on the arc-lamps!

(*Cascade of light.*)

CHIEF ENGINEER: Back to the works!

(*Retreat to the sides of the hall–crowd disappears.* SIX YELLOW FIGURES *seat themselves at the tables.* FIRST YELLOW FIGURE *arranges the plugs in the chequered table-top.* CHIEF ENGINEER *waits.*)

FIRST YELLOW FIGURE: (*to the* CHIEF ENGINEER.) Gas!

(CHIEF ENGINEER *exits.*)

ACT III

Concrete hall. Light cascades from arc-lamps. At the tables SEVEN YELLOW FIGURES. *Silence.*

SECOND YELLOW FIGURE: (*before red-glowing panel.*) Report from supply-depot: allocation for third district up two units.

(*Panel-light fades.* FIRST YELLOW FIGURE *crossplugs red contact.*)

FIFTH YELLOW FIGURE: (*before green-glowing panel.*) Report from third workshop: production one unit below quota.

(*Panel-light fades.* FIRST YELLOW FIGURE *crossplugs green contact.*)

THIRD YELLOW FIGURE: (*before red-glowing panel.*) Report from supply-depot: allocation for second district up two units.

(*Panel-light fades.* FIRST YELLOW FIGURE *crossplugs red contact.*)

SIXTH YELLOW FIGURE: (*before green-glowing panel.*) Report from second workshop: production one unit below quota.

(*Panel-light fades.* FIRST YELLOW FIGURE *crossplugs green contact.*)

FOURTH YELLOW FIGURE: (*before red-glowing panel.*) Report

from supply-depot: allocation for first district up four units.

(*Panel-light fades.* FIRST YELLOW FIGURE *crossplugs red contact.*)

SEVENTH YELLOW FIGURE: (*before green-glowing panel.*) Report from first workshop: production two points below quota.

(*Panel-light fades.* FIRST YELLOW FIGURE *crossplugs green contact. Silence.*)

SECOND YELLOW FIGURE: (*before green-glowing panel.*) Report from supply-depot: allocation for third district up five units.

(*Panel-light fades.* FIRST YELLOW FIGURE *crossplugs red contact.*)

FIFTH YELLOW FIGURE: (*before green-glowing panel.*) Report from third workshop: production six points below quota.

(*Panel-light fades.* FIRST YELLOW FIGURE *crossplugs green contact.*)

THIRD YELLOW FIGURE: (*before red-glowing panel.*) Report from supply-depot: allocation for second district up eight units.

(*Panel-light fades.* FIRST YELLOW FIGURE *crossplugs red contact.*)

SIXTH YELLOW FIGURE: (*before green-glowing panel.*) Report from second workshop: production ten points below quota.

(*Panel-light fades.* FIRST YELLOW FIGURE *crossplugs green contact.*)

FOURTH YELLOW FIGURE: (*before red-glowing panel.*) Report from supply-depot: allocation for first district up eleven units.

(*Panel-light fades.* FIRST YELLOW FIGURE *crossplugs red contact.*)

SEVENTH YELLOW FIGURE: (*before green-glowing panel.*) Report from first workshop: production TWELVE points below quota.

(*Panel-light fades.*)

FIRST YELLOW FIGURE: (*jumps up–into the telephone.*) The Chief Engineer!

(CHIEF ENGINEER *enters–unhurried.*)

FIRST YELLOW FIGURE: Control-stations registering reduced output of gas. By points performance up to twelve behind target.

CHIEF ENGINEER: (*calm.*) Does that surprise you?

FIRST YELLOW FIGURE: Is there any question of a personal opinion?

CHIEF ENGINEER: (*shoulder-shrugging.*) If you can deny your own nature.

FIRST YELLOW FIGURE: Automaton like everyone else in the works.

CHIEF ENGINEER: In the workshops the automatons are running with strange noises.

FIRST YELLOW FIGURE: —What are they whispering?

CHIEF ENGINEER: Not for me.

FIRST YELLOW FIGURE: Meaning?

CHIEF ENGINEER: Not for me: this hand lifting the lever. Not for me: this foot's thrust on the gear-pedal. Not for me: this eye's gaze at the gauge. My labours create–not for me My sweat stings–not for me. My drudgery brings profit–not for me.

FIRST YELLOW FIGURE: Do you know your responsibility?

CHIEF ENGINEER: For gas.

FIRST YELLOW FIGURE: You will answer for every minus point in output.

CHIEF ENGINEER: (*in a peculiar tone.*) I am prepared–for the reckoning.

FIRST YELLOW FIGURE: Have you made use of your powers?

CHIEF ENGINEER: (*as before.*) Not yet.

FIRST YELLOW FIGURE: Have you imposed punishments?

CHIEF ENGINEER: On whom?

FIRST YELLOW FIGURE: On anyone who jerks at the lever–who allows his foot to slip on the gear-pedal–who falters at the gauge.

CHIEF ENGINEER: Then the shift would be without man or woman or child.

FIRST YELLOW FIGURE: Are all resisting?

CHIEF ENGINEER: Shift grows slacker with each shift.

FIRST YELLOW FIGURE: What is still being produced?

CHIEF ENGINEER: (*loud.*) Gas!

FIRST YELLOW FIGURE:—Why did you not flog the first defaulter?

CHIEF ENGINEER: I–did not flog him.

FIRST YELLOW FIGURE: Did you doubt that seeing the fate of the one would drive on the others?

CHIEF ENGINEER: I–had no doubt.

FIRST YELLOW FIGURE: Why did you hide what is happening?

CHIEF ENGINEER: I–kept it quiet.

FIRST YELLOW FIGURE:—Are you encouraging the revolt?

CHIEF ENGINEER: With all my powers!

FIFTH YELLOW FIGURE: (*before green-glowing panel.*) Report from third workshop: work—

CHIEF ENGINEER: –at a stand-still!!

SIXTH YELLOW FIGURE: (*before green-glowing panel.*) Report from second workshop: work—

CHIEF ENGINEER:–at a stand-still!!

SEVENTH YELLOW FIGURE: (*before green-glowing panel.*) Report from first workshop: work—

CHIEF ENGINEER:–at a stand-still!!

(*The* THREE YELLOW FIGURES *leave their tables.*)

FIRST YELLOW FIGURE: Who–??

CHIEF ENGINEER: I gave the order! As I left to come here. With the powers that you invested me with. Obedience followed my bidding. No longer the jerk of hand on lever for others–no longer the thrust of foot on gear-pedal for others–no eye peering at gauge for others. Hand sinks and clenches fist against you–foot falls away and makes to run at you–eye turns aside and darts its glance at you. Gas for us—and gas against you!!

FIRST YELLOW FIGURE:—You realize the consequences?

CHIEF ENGINEER: No consequences for us!

FIRST YELLOW FIGURE: The works are encircled by gun-emplacements.

CHIEF ENGINEER: In a three-fold circle.

FIRST YELLOW FIGURE: Ready to fire at the first sign of revolt.

CHIEF ENGINEER: Revolt is seething!

FIRST YELLOW FIGURE: The works and every living soul reduced to rubble by a single salvo.

CHIEF ENGINEER: Are you sure?

FIRST YELLOW FIGURE: We'll allow you the briefest respite and expect the resumption of work with your report! (*He beckons to the* YELLOW FIGURES–*to depart.*)

CHIEF ENGINEER: (*at the table in front–into the telephone.*) Out of the works and into the hall–to the assembly!

(*Hesitant arrival–pushing and crowding to the centre–full hall.*)

VOICE: (*at last–shrill, frightened.*) Who has dismissed us?

CHIEF ENGINEER: (*onto the platform.*) Whoever fills the hall, squeezing against the surrounding wall. Whoever left his bench and abandoned lever and gear-pedal and gauge. Whoever finds his voice out of the silence of slave-labour!

VOICES AND VOICES: Who has dismissed us?

CHIEF ENGINEER: Whoever clenches his fist in defiance. Whoever lifts his foot to charge and attack. Whoever measures with his eye the size of the slave-driver!

ALL VOICES: Who is releasing us?!!

CHIEF ENGINEER: Your command sways your own fate. Your words shower their own law over you. Yesterday work-slaves producing tenfold profit–today you are the masters!!

(*Silence.*)

VOICE: What of us?!

CHIEF ENGINEER: For you remission of guilt and of the blame of guilt. Lightening of the burden of atonement! Release from the strangling vicegrip!

ALL VOICES: What of us?!

CHIEF ENGINEER: Rising erect from your knees for you. Growth from weakness to strength for you. Forward from fear to the fray with you!

ALL VOICES: What of us? ! !

CHIEF ENGINEER: Unleash the undirected anger within you. Unleash the hate that stagnated within you. Unleash the poison oozing inside you. The vengeance is yours! !

VOICE: Have we power?

CHIEF ENGINEER: You are thrown into the light from the shadows. From poverty clad in the purple. Out of nothing exalted in plenty!

VOICES AND VOICES: Have we power?

CHIEF ENGINEER: In such measure as it was never before given. No gun firing as you all aim your blow. No shell crashing home as you expire. You are victors even as you march to battle!

ALL VOICES: Have we power? ! !

CHIEF ENGINEER: Without the loss of a finger-tip you will survive the fight. Without the duration of half a day you will finish the fight. You are terrible with your weapon of conquest:—poison-gas! !

CHIEF ENGINEER: (takes a red sphere from his overall.) I invented it for you. Among you I was consumed by shame that degrades us like beasts of burden. Not for a second did I lose sight of the goal that sweeps aside the tyrant—hate and shame formed the formula that finally resulted in the means of freedom. Now there is triumph in a new thin glass membrane that blasts out and at once eats away the flesh, leaving bleached, brittle bones!

(Silence.)

CHIEF ENGINEER: Horror crazes fearfully whoever witnesses the force of annihilation. Paralysing madness enters the brain of the beholder, seeing men alive a moment before now bleached bones. Resistance shouts itself down out of the mouth of the first inquisitive man who comes running up and screams the end of the world!

(Silence.)

CHIEF ENGINEER: You are victorious from this hour, whose decision is eternal. Do the sum that easily solves all calculations. Throw this capsule from the crest of the dome–aim for the line of besiegers—forestall their attack–throw the capsule! !

VOICE: Poison-gas!

CHIEF ENGINEER: Be revenged!

VOICES AND VOICES: Poison-gas! !

CHIEF ENGINEER: Be fighters! !

ALL VOICES: Poison-gas! ! !

CHIEF ENGINEER: Be victors! ! !

(YOUNG WORKERS *jostle up the steps of the platform–hands outstretched for the capsule.* MILLIONAIRE-WORKER *squeezes between them–pushes aside the upraised arms.*)

MILLIONAIRE-WORKER: Do not clutch at the capsule. Resist the temptation. Do not destroy your power with the throw!

VOICE: The Millionaire-Worker.

MILLIONAIRE-WORKER: Do not heed his promptings. Do not aim into the darkness. Do not pay the huckster your tribute!

VOICES AND VOICES: The Millionaire-Worker! !

MILLIONAIRE-WORKER: Preserve what exalts you and makes you elect. Know the means by which you conquer. Build the house that stands steadfast on foundations of rock!

ALL VOICES: The Millionaire-Worker! ! !

(The YOUNG-WORKERS *have retreated from the steps.*)

MILLIONAIRE-WORKER (*goes higher up the steps.*) Widen your vision for the new that intermingles with the primal. At last, the beginning–a genuine one, out of the store of truth already proclaimed. Tides of greatness flood into your time and repeat themselves. You are not wearied with the work of invention– your fulfilment withdraws behind testing and proving. Your lot is drawn from the wheel that was turning millennially –your mission emerges pure after sifting and sifting! (*Silence.*) No way with its winding and winding points like your path that leads you to perfection. All profits were accounted to you–your tables overflowed with abundance. Around you possessions piled up, placed there by hands–: you were given over to owning and it consumed you! (*Silence.*) That vanished as sand is sent flying by a child playing. The rising wind never hesitates to shatter what the day's toil raised–you will not seal the springs that are black from the birth of the hurricane which never leaves the earth quiet. You were struck down by the discharge with a violence that hurled you flat on the ground. The force of your fall went deep. The tower of your eminence buried you! (*Silence.*) Once you were counted great—now you become something more:—martyrs! ! (*Silence.*) The never ending sickness fell from you:–daily work! You were possessed by something other, that without name satisfies without limit. Transform what was held true when its time has run out–undermine values that yield no further profit:—be martyrs at your work—released to be yourselves! ! (*Silence.*) Build the kingdom! ! No burden weighs on you with fresh discovery–nor distance deters: new dawn approaches out of a promise that was never niggardly– collection of law upon law was complete long ago–preparation out of time and time overdue–use your existence, to which all things are added:—build the kingdom that you are within you with final fortification! (*Silence. He continues up on the platform.*) Now success is yours in the venture through generations and generations. Over meadows of green you were lured by one before me–you rightly rejected him. Nothing around you fosters what is worthwhile within you–there can be no cooping-up in the four walls of settlements:—THE KINGDOM IS NOT OF THIS WORLD! ! ! ! (*Silence.*) Slave for the foreigner–pay the paymaster interest–leave him the wage–pour out profits for him–suffer the demands made of you–give the lie to the goad that draws its own blood against you:—be the kingdom! !

(*Breathing silence.*)

CHIEF ENGINEER: (*a few steps down.*) Have you no outcry to make at the betrayal spat in your faces? Does your censure fall silent at a suggestion that means your murder? Have you forgotten the cheers that carried your pledge to me? !

MILLIONAIRE-WORKER: Keep faith with the selves that you are –freed to be yourselves!

CHIEF ENGINEER: Be mindful of what you remain–stripped of your rights. Backs for the driving whiplash–workshift for sneering abasement–cattle yoked and mishandled. Toil dragging on without end–a treadmill whose turning lulls you into languor and stupor. Till your very joints crack torment will rack you. Such is your serfdom!

MILLIONAIRE-WORKER: Set up the kingdom whose rule is omnipotent in you!

CHIEF ENGINEER: Calculate the power that will be your prize. Works and profits will be yours–without a single finger's lifting. Gas will work for you as if by magic–your serfs will be held fast at the lever–the gear-pedal–before the gauge. You will use your victory after the example set by yesterday's victors!

MILLIONAIRE-WORKER: Liberate yourselves in suffering from slavery that touches nothing within you!

CHIEF ENGINEER: Add up the tribute that will fall to you. No zone of earth that does not pay its toll at your bidding. No ship's hold but is bounden to you with its cargo. No bridge's span that does not arch over with supplies for you. No pulsing wire but is charged with your orders. Your will's decision is all-commanding dominion!

MILLIONAIRE-WORKER: Hear him who rehearses what has happened already:–again the glitter that entices and blinds is being shown off among you!

CHIEF ENGINEER: Proclaim your intent with a cry that binds you irrevocably!

MILLIONAIRE-WORKER: Outbid this petty resolve which commends itself cheaply!

CHIEF ENGINEER: Bargain with the time still left you–before the bombardment! !

MILLIONAIRE-WORKER: (*a few steps down.*) Return to work and perform the task that is trivial to you!

CHIEF ENGINEER: (*up on the platform.*) Aim the capsule that decides in your favour with a single use of the poison!

MILLIONAIRE-WORKER: Return to work! !

CHIEF ENGINEER: (*the red sphere held high.*) Establish your dominion! !

MILLIONAIRE-WORKER: Set up the kingdom! !
CHIEF ENGINEER: Set off the poison-gas! ! !

(Silence.)

MILLIONAIRE-WORKER: Fall silent and hear how heaven and earth hold their breath while you make your decision that seals the world's fate! !

(Silence.)

VOICE: Poison-gas! !
VOICES AND VOICES: Poison-gas! ! ! !
ALL VOICES: Poison-gas! ! ! !
CHIEF ENGINEER: (triumphant.) Power is ours! Ours the world! ! Aim the capsule—be quick with the throw—forestall the bombardment! ! !—Who?

(YOUNG WORKERS surge up round the platform.)

YOUNG WORKERS: I! !
CHIEF ENGINEER: Take care of the dangerous sphere!
MILLIONAIRE-WORKER: (holding back the YOUNG WORKERS—turning to the CHIEF ENGINEER.) I am the chosen one! I have rights before others!
ALL VOICES: The Millionaire-Worker! ! ! !

(CHIEF ENGINEER gives him the capsule–leaves the platform.)

MILLIONAIRE-WORKER: (up on the platform–the capsule in raised hand.) The blood of my blood beat for our reformation! My ardour burnt with the ardour of mother and mother's father! ! Our voice could have awakened the desert —humanity could not hear it! ! I am vindicated! ! I can finish the work! ! (He throws the sphere above his head–it falls back and breaks with a slight tinkle.–Silence.)
CHIEF ENGINEER: Poison-gas! ! !
ALL VOICES: Poison-gas! ! ! !

(Stunned silence. With a huge crash the bombardment sets in from outside. Immediate darkness–and the rumbling collapse of walls. Silence.)

271

(Gradual illumination: the hall is a rubble-field of concrete slabs jumbled one on top of the other like ripped-up gravestones—jutting up, blanched already, the skeletons of the people in the hall. YELLOW FIGURE—steel helmet, headphone, unrolling wire behind him—comes running over the heaped debris.)

YELLOW FIGURE : *(checks—crazed glance wanders—shouts into the telephone.)* Reporting effect of bombardment:—turn the guns against yourselves and annihilate yourselves—the dead are thronging from their graves—judgment day—dies irae— solvet—in favil—*(He shoots the rest in his mouth.)*

(In the haze-grey distance clusters of fireballs hurtle against each other—clearly in self-destruction.)